AF352625

BEYOND ROMANTICISM

*Tuckerman's
Life and Poetry*

BEYOND ROMANTICISM

Tuckerman's Life and Poetry

EUGENE ENGLAND

BRIGHAM
YOUNG
UNIVERSITY

Library of Congress Cataloging-in-Publication Data

England, Eugene.
    Beyond romanticism: Tuckerman's life and poetry / Eugene England.
      p. 270 cm.
    Includes bibliographical references and index.
    ISBN 0-7914-0791-8
    1. Tuckerman, Frederick Goddard, 1821–1873. 2. Poets, American—19th century—
Biography. 3. Romanticism—United States.
I. Title.
PS3104.T5Z64   1990
811'.3—dc20
[B]   90-24401
                                             CIP

All quotations from the Houghton Library manuscripts are used by permission of
    Houghton Library, Harvard University.
All quotations from family papers in possession of Hugh Clark, Amherst,
    Massachusetts, used by permission of Hugh Clark.
All quotations from manuscript materials by Emily Tennyson and Alfred, Lord
    Tennyson, used by permission of their heir, the present Lord Tennyson of
    Paris, France.
Parts of chapter 3 were published in "Tennyson and Tuckerman: 'Two Friends . . . on
    Either Side the Atlantic,' " *New England Quarterly* 57 (June 1984).
An earlier version of chapter 4 appeared as "Tuckerman's Sonnet I: 10: The First
    Post-Symbolist Poem," *Southern Review*, n.s., 12 (Spring 1976).
Parts of chapter 5 were published in "The Forms of Loss in Tuckerman's Elegy,"
    Encyclia 59 (1982).
All are used by permission.

Brigham Young University, Provo, Utah 84602

© 1991 by Eugene England. All rights reserved.
Printed in the United States of America.

Distributed by State University of New York Press, State University Plaza, Albany, New
York 12446–0001

Contents

For
Dora Rose Hartvigsen England,
who gave me life and poetry.

Frederick Goddard Tuckerman (1821–1873).
Used by permission of Hugh Clark,
Amherst, Massachusetts.

I

PERSPECTIVES

He is isolated in an intense integrity toward nature, toward his own mind, and toward the unknown God.

Witter Bynner (1931)[1]

TUCKERMAN'S isolation and his intense involvement with nature, as well as with his own mind and with God, were not unusual in the America of the middle years of the nineteenth century. But his integrity, which proved to be especially costly and moving as it revealed itself in his ability to develop and maintain clear distinctions between Nature, Self, and God, was unusual. It demanded an inner struggle unique

---

[1] Witter Bynner, the young poet and critic who was most responsible for rescuing Tuckerman from oblivion, also gave us, in the few words used for this chapter's epigraph, perhaps the best short description of Tuckerman and his work and of the reasons for his unique and important contribution. They are from the "Introduction" to *The Sonnets of Frederick Goddard Tuckerman,* ed. Witter Bynner (New York: Alfred A. Knopf, 1931), 34. Bynner became interested when he came across an essay written by Walter Prichard Eaton on Tuckerman and his poems in the January 1909 issue of *Forum.* Eaton had seen two of Tuckerman's sonnets in the manuscript of an anthology of American poems that had been compiled by Louis How but had never been published. Eaton then, with some difficulty, found a copy of Tuckerman's one volume of *Poems,* last published in 1869, and wrote the essay published in *Forum.* Bynner was so impressed by the poetry Eaton liberally quoted that he, with Eaton's help, contacted Tuckerman's descendants in Amherst, Massachusetts. He discovered in their keeping the unpublished poems and in 1931 included in his edition all five series of the sonnets, only two of which were in the *Poems,* with an appreciative but discriminating introduction that gave good reasons for his ranking Tuckerman's sonnets among "the noblest in the language . . . not bettered in their kind by anyone of his time or since."

I

among the writers and thinkers of his time, and that struggle informed a remarkable body of poetry.

Though still largely unknown by many teachers and students of literature (neglected, I believe, partly because of the precociousness, historically, of his technique and the unexpectedness of his particular kind of achievement), Tuckerman's poetry stands as a challenging resolution to basic aesthetic and epistemological dilemmas posed by Romanticism and still haunting modern thought and experience. It is also a first-rate artistic achievement in its own right.

Tuckerman's isolation was not unlike that of Hawthorne or Melville or Dickinson: a conscious leave-taking, a way of insulation from certain aspects of popular American culture and values, a Romantic withdrawal into self, even a form of the moral alienation Hawthorne feared. It was a choice made by all four of these writers (who could usefully be grouped as the American "anti-Romantics") and made quite deliberately—after some experience with the shallow, sterile alternatives. Tuckerman's isolation was unusual in that for a time he shared it in an intensely profound relationship with his wife and children and in full and effective relationships with a few close friends and one famous poet, Tennyson. That isolation was also unusual, as Bynner says, in its "intense integrity" toward both nature and his own mind—to external and internal resources. He was able to take special advantage of the impulses and sensitivities the Romantic movement was bringing to America. He could also turn his precise, even scientific, apprehension of details in nature into a unique tool, both for self-understanding and for realization of some of the possibilities of meaning in the external world.

My purpose is to explore carefully Tuckerman's unusually fruitful isolation and integrity and their results in his poetry. This will require explication and also evaluation. Rather than survey all the poetry, I focus on a few of the characteristic and, I think, most brilliant achievements of thought and artistry. These achievements were ignored or misunderstood by many of Tuckerman's contemporaries, whose vision was obscured by various Romantic, Transcendentalist, and Sentimentalist assumptions, and therefore he was left out of the canon of his time, the "Schoolroom Poets" and the "Genteel Tradition." The achievements have also been rejected or neglected by many twentieth-century readers and critics (even some who have appreciated certain of his strengths) because Tuckerman's work does not fit neatly into Modernist or anti-Modernist expectations—and thus he has been left out of the new canon that was formed in the 1930s and 1940s. Right now, when the canon is being reconsidered and expanded—and when much of the necessary work of editing and basic critical discussion has been done—it is time to consider carefully why he should be fully included.

I look first at certain crucial Romantic quests and commitments and then describe responses to those quests and commitments in Tuckerman's work, particularly the responses that reveal the continuing relevance of his poetry to the Romantic concerns which are, I am convinced, the great human ones. This process unavoidably requires some attention to Tuckerman's biography, but not because Samuel Golden is correct in his view that for Tuckerman "the biography and the work are inseparable."[2] A certain amount of biographical information and inference, much of it the fruit of my own research, is useful in explaining the major influences on the development of Tuckerman's thought and poetry. But the work reveals the mind and life more than the life the work.

---

[2] Samuel A. Golden, *Frederick Goddard Tuckerman* (New York: Twayne, 1966), 8. Golden's book, the only one previous to this to appear on Tuckerman, though valuable for the overview it provides of the life and work, is marred, I think, by his stretching of the poetry to fit what understanding of Tuckerman's life he was able to gain at that time from other sources. I am indebted to Golden for his pioneering work (starting in 1948) with such direct biographical sources, but even with my additional related discoveries those sources remain particularly sparse in Tuckerman's case, and I am convinced that the more inferential work I have done to describe the influences on Tuckerman and the shape of his apprenticeship is more crucial than biographical "facts" to an understanding of the poetry.

Before looking directly at Tuckerman's poetry, I try to define some special perspectives for understanding that poetry, for seeing its importance. This requires that I first reexamine the philosophical, moral, and aesthetic principles that were Tuckerman's most immediate intellectual and emotional background, and then consider carefully an unusual way in which those principles can relate to the writing of great poetry.

TUCKERMAN was a Romantic. He was influenced by and participated in that major shift in Western culture, the implications of which we are still living out. He shared the high Romantic courage, which struggled with the possibility that the Ultimate is organic, living, related to man's mind and sensibility in the most fundamental way. He shared in the temptation and the attempt to deify nature and to naturalize deity, as well as to reduce everything to a two-term system—the ego and the nonego. He also yearned to bridge that ultimate void by an educative journey of the self back to a higher form of the primal unity with the divine essence from which the self had emanated.[3]

Tuckerman was also an anti-Romantic. He shared the high Romantic vision and hope; but a combination of his own qualities, his training, and his opportunities enabled him to avoid and in some cases resolve crucial Romantic dilemmas. He shared, for instance, the Romantic distrust of abstraction and of cognitive reasoning and the Romantic hope for spontaneous, divine insight; but his poetic practice avoided the

---

[3] This view of the Romantic movement, comprehensively explored by M. H. Abrams in *Natural Supernaturalism: Tradition and Revolution in Romantic Literature* (New York: Norton, 1971), seems to me accurate and also enormously useful in stimulating thinking about Romanticism, but Abrams's essentially descriptive approach does not incline him to look analytically at the inherent *problems* in Romantic thought and artistic practice. I examine certain of those problems from time to time in this volume, as part of my argument, because of their particular relevance to Tuckerman's struggle and achievement.

Romantic tendency to discard proven resources of the human mind, particularly those associated with language, when new ones were discovered. He learned to use his rational capabilities, as well as his highly developed perceptiveness, to create imagery that is informed with moral and intellectual themes adequate to carry the weight of his direct feelings and illuminations. He early developed the Romantic sensitivity to nature, but more than most Romantic poets he carefully cultivated the ability to see with precision and honesty the details and contradictions of nature. He retained the clear vision and skill of allegorical thinking, which enabled him to understand his experience and to use images from nature to help express that understanding—but in combination with the other resources, not as a sufficient equivalent. In finding this particular combination of the hard-won gains from the whole tradition of English poetry he was almost by himself.

Certainly Emerson was of little help. He served effectively as an awakener and energizer for the young men of Tuckerman's generation and was the major transmitter of the Romantic "spirit of the age" into American literary culture. However, Emerson and some of his more ardent disciples down to the present have been guilty of perverting the hopes of the Romantic movement by heightening them (as in the expectation of complete merging with a "perfect" nature or of creating "pure" poetry) beyond what human nature and language could possibly fulfill. The pursuit of those goals by those of a more violent integrity to his ideas than Emerson himself possessed has been damaging, even destructive, to language, sensibility, and perhaps—in cases like that of Hart Crane—to life.

I have just expressed, of course, Yvor Winters's assessment of Emersonian Romanticism.[4] Time has, I think, proved to be on Winters's side. Despite the hostility with which his analyses

---

[4] See Yvor Winters, *In Defense of Reason* (Denver: Alan Swallow, 1947), particularly the essays "Jones Very and R. W. Emerson" and "The Significance of *The Bridge* by Hart Crane."

and judgments were greeted in the mid-1930s, much supportive work by others has been forthcoming. However, there has
been little explicit recognition of Winters's influential perception of the continuing fundamental Romanticism of modern
poetry, despite its contrary disclaimers, and his pioneering
analysis of the inconsistencies and dangerous implications in
Emerson's particular Romantic platform. Other critics of Romanticism have been more polite about their judgments, but
they have been sufficiently influential that there have actually
been some self-consciously revisionist attempts to rehabilitate
Emerson.[5]

Winters took literature too seriously, and its effects too personally in a moral sense, to be polite, and he overstated his
case, I think. His fidelity to good poetry and sensible ideas
made it difficult for him to give sufficient credit to Emerson
merely as a fertile sensibility and a motivating force or to see
charitably the changes in thinking Emerson made later in his
life. In addition, the isolation Winters felt in the American literary community and the harrowing nature of what was for
him the almost physical seductiveness of Romanticism, which
haunted him and gave lasting power to his best poetry and his
only fiction, gave his criticism an offensive edge.[6]

------

[5] See, for instance, F. O. Matthiessen in his *American Renaissance: Art and
Expression in the Age of Emerson and Whitman* (1941; reprint, New York: Oxford
Univ. Press, 1968), and Perry Miller in various essays in his *Nature's Nation*
(Cambridge, Mass.: Harvard Univ. Press, 1967), where the sharpness of the
implicit criticism—which does much to counter popular assumptions about
the value of the poetry and the quality of the thought in Emerson and his
disciple Whitman—is masked by the descriptive format. Especially Matthiessen's work on Emerson and Whitman participates in the too-common
critical tendency to let mere bulk of explication imply substance and value.
Hyatt H. Waggoner, in *American Poets from the Puritans to the Present*, rev. ed.
(Boston: Houghton Mifflin, 1968), claims that Emerson's reputation had so
much declined by 1968 that a major reconstruction effort was necessary to
put him back at what Waggoner feels is his rightful place at the center of
American poetry.

[6] See particularly the impatient, almost arrogant, tone in Winters's chapter on "The Sentimental-Romantic Decadence of the Eighteenth and Nine-

Tuckerman provides a strong vindication of Winters's basic position. The poems I examine in this volume demonstrate that Romantic idealism did not need to issue in the bland vagueness or the imprecise, mainly ornamental imagery and mechanical meters of much of Emerson's poetry. Tuckerman knew and appreciated Emerson and his work (and was helped by Emerson to publish his own poetry and get criticism of it), but Tuckerman also knew his Coleridge and Wordsworth, his Keats and Shelley—firsthand, not in Emerson's idealistic interpretation. In addition, Tuckerman achieved a knowledge of the details of nature and of language that Emerson, in his pantheistic concern for the large picture, never approached.

Tuckerman would not have agreed with Emerson that "the age is Swedenborg's." Tuckerman's experience and analysis made it impossible for him to surrender to the Swedenborgian notion of "correspondence"—that not only words but things are directly symbolic. His experience was that nature has its own independent reality, which is diverse, even contradictory—not merely "a metaphor of the human mind."[7] Tuckerman did not, like Emerson, claim too much for the poets ("liberating gods") nor for their alleged power to make anything on which their eyes might rest "obey the impulses of [their] moral nature."[8] Paradoxically, he was freed by such humility to use the powers of mind and language to form symbols that used the actual resources of nature as tools. He thereby developed a dependable, though limited, means of

------

teenth Centuries" (and the dismissal of *any* discussion of Emerson, Thoreau, or Whitman) in his last and summary critical work, *Forms of Discovery: Critical and Historical Essays on the Forms of the Short Poem in English* (Denver: Alan Swallow, 1967). For a chilling evidence of his horrified fascination with the Romantic dangers, see his only piece of published fiction, "The Brink of Darkness," originally in *Hound and Horn* 5 (1932): 547–61, with a revised version in *The Collected Poems of Yvor Winters,* ed. Donald Davie (Manchester, England: Carcanet New Press, 1978), 213–24.

7 "Nature," in Ralph Waldo Emerson, *Emerson: Selected Prose and Poetry,* ed. Reginald Cook (New York: Holt, Rinehart, and Winston, 1950), 19.

8 "The Poet," in ibid., 332, 336.

genuine connection between the mind and that which is outside it. Tuckerman saw what Swedenborg and Emerson did not, that the poet's precise vision and mastery of language are not simple givens but can be developed if encouraged and taught. The Transcendentalists' yearning for ultimate unity, and their hope that the poet would have unique power to reattach dispersed nature and the human soul, led them to ignore the process and the limitations attendant on such an ideal.

Emerson, for instance, seems not to have had anything like Tuckerman's understanding of the significance of the tension between meter and rhythm in affecting the quality of feeling in a poem (though a few of Emerson's poems, notably "Days," make intuitive use of that tension). Emerson seldom, if ever, saw with accuracy the details of nature or brought those perceptions into language in the actual, feasible process of relating the human to the nonhuman. Tuckerman often did.

THE ATTEMPT to bridge the gulf between what is self and what is outside self, between the fact out there and the idea in here, has been a perennial challenge to the human consciousness, particularly for the artist. That was the great Romantic cause, and, as Perry Miller has asked concerning Thoreau's commitment to it, "For what more sublime a cause, even if it be a questionable thesis, can a man expend himself?"[9] It is particularly in his intense integrity to that cause, which in fact is what led him to isolate himself, that Tuckerman is a Romantic.

Because Emerson saw the universe as merely an externalization of the soul, which made nature "a symbol in the whole and every part," he helped give poets access to all of nature and all of experience as a source for symbol-making. But his Neoplatonic emphasis on the Whole, on an undifferentiated Oversoul, kept him from being able to give adequate attention to the distinctions in nature and to the means necessary to

---

[9] Miller, *Nature's Nation*, 183.

bridge fact and idea. Thus, he never quite found the artistic form he needed. Thoreau was able to find his form—in prose—because he was, though also moved by Transcendentalist impulses, an expert in natural history and was able to give some detailed content to the Transcendentalist claim that the universe, as he expressed it, "constantly and obediently answers to our conceptions."[10] In this faith and the skill that supported it, Thoreau was like Tuckerman. Their achievement is connected in that both of them gave close attention to natural detail and each isolated himself from pernicious contemporary influences sufficiently long to create individual forms of language adequate to his ideals.

Thoreau made some flippant statements about his preference for packing boxes and newspapers over Europe's architectural and literary legacy, but those exaggerations must be seen in the context of his attention to detail in language and landscape and his clearly knowledgeable appreciation of our cultural past everywhere revealed in his work. They must also be recognized as an expression of Thoreau's central impulse toward simplicity, toward optimistic appreciation of American potential, toward rejecting the elitist pretensions and uncritically inherited forms of European culture. I think Matthiessen is right that Thoreau had the necessary integrity to resist being swamped by European forms (as Tuckerman had also, after his early work) or the use of form as mere decoration.[11] Thoreau, *more* than Emerson, successfully expressed the great Romantic impulse toward organic creation. He worked diligently with the possible forms of writing and, through close attention to language, gave that impulse shape as his work developed—from the journals to the final revisions of *Walden*.

Emerson was (as even Van Wyck Brooks could write, though he did not see the consequences) "a lover of nature who, as a

---

[10] Quoted in ibid.

[11] Matthiessen, *American Renaissance*, 174.

matter of fact, scarcely knew a robin from a crow."[12] Thoreau did not have this handicap, nor was he indolent as a writer or self-indulgent as a thinker—not at least until after *Walden* was written. That careful attention to detail is crucial, and it protected Thoreau, as well as Tuckerman, from the "green wine" (Matthiessen's phrase) of Emerson. In their best work, at least, they did not violate nature by treating it as a mere extension of themselves, personifying it, pretending that it obeyed their impulses. They looked at it attentively and honored it as reality exterior to themselves. Nature was capable of being a source of understanding and feeling, but only as it was recreated through the symbol-making powers of human language. In the case of Tuckerman this involved a conscious refusal of the Romantic temptation, a refusal worked out in the poetry at first rather didactically but finally in powerfully integrated and moving symbolic forms that I examine later.

Tuckerman knew what it was to strive with all his awareness for meaning, to "tease the sunbreak and the cloud / For import," following those (a specific jab at Emerson?) "that go before the throng, / Reasoning from stone to star, and easily / Exampling this existence" (Sonnet I: 9, p. 7).[13] But, even from his youth, when he already "knew each bleached alder root" he had also stood

> In utter solitudes, where the cricket's cry
> Appals the heart, and fear takes visible shapes;
> And on Long Island's void and isolate capes
> Heard the sea break like iron bars. . . .
>
> (Sonnet II: 30, p. 33)

---

[12] Van Wyck Brooks, *The Flowering of New England: 1815–1865,* rev. ed. (New York: E. P. Dutton, 1937), 291.

[13] All quotations of Tuckerman's poetry are, unless otherwise indicated, from N. Scott Momaday, ed., *The Complete Poems of Frederick Goddard Tuckerman* (New York: Oxford Univ. Press, 1965); hereafter I merely indicate the title and page number in parentheses.

He knew he had thus "a deeper lesson learnt": The details of nature, clearly seen and taken in themselves, reveal no infallible good, no ultimate, divine Unity, such as an Oversoul. If we surrender to such a seductive possibility, "chasing false fire, we fare from bad to worse" ("As sometimes in a grove," p. 144). In mere landscape is not to be found our salvation: "Wind cometh and goeth, / But sorrows abide" ("When the dim day," p. 165). Emerson was simply mistaken in believing that "Nature never wears a mean appearance."[14] He was wrong in his feeling that the stars infallibly "awaken a certain reverence"[15] (Dickinson's "The Moon upon her fluent Route" and Tuckerman's ironically titled "Inspiration" show how they can be a source of overwhelming doubt, even despair). Emerson believed that "ethical character so penetrates the bone and marrow of nature, as to seem the end for which it was made" and that in that teaching, elevating capacity "all the endless variety of things make an identical impression."[16] Thoreau creates, though he seems only partially to understand, a refutation of this in reporting in *Walden* his visit to the hut of John Field, the Irish immigrant who learns absolutely nothing from that nature which is supposedly tutoring Thoreau. Emerson on the one hand was arrogant in finding the whole of nature merely an analogy for the human mind. On the other hand he demeaned the mind's capacities by exalting above them that supposedly primal phase of language in which there is simple one-to-one correspondence of words with things and events.

Emerson was wrong in a great cause. Responding to a yearning felt by many in Western culture, he seized upon and sometimes, especially at first, exaggerated or misinterpreted attractive notions and assertions of the early Romantics, particularly Coleridge. During the Enlightenment, faith was lost in the old three-storied universe, in which humans were at home in the center and were guaranteed, by their creaturely status as chil-

---

14 "Nature," in *Emerson: Selected Prose and Poetry*, 5.
15 Ibid.
16 Ibid., 24.

dren of God, the possibility of genuine relation to the created universe around them. The failure of the French Revolution brought complete loss of hope in achieving a literal earthly paradise through political means; and young idealists all over Europe, and later America, focused their dreams on a spiritual millennium, a renewal of meaning for mankind through a union of mind and nature.[17]

Thoreau described one version of this new hope that is particularly relevant to an understanding of Tuckerman. He expected that he could find meaning by affirming the divinely created connections of the mind with what is outside itself and then by realizing and developing those connections in conscious art:

> The eyes were not made for such groveling uses as they are now put to and worn out by, but to behold beauty now invisible. May we not *see* God? Are we to be put off and amused in this life, as it were with a mere allegory? Is not Nature, rightly read, that of which she is commonly taken to be the symbol merely? When the common man looks into the sky, which he has not so much profaned, he thinks it less gross than the earth, and with reverence speaks of "the Heavens," but the seer will in the same sense speak of "the Earths," and his Father who is in them. "Did not he that made that which is *within* make that which is *without* also?" What is it, then, to educate but to develop these divine germs called the senses? For individuals and states to deal magnanimously with the rising generation, leading it not into temptation,—not teach the eye to squint, nor attune the ear to profanity. But where is the instructed teacher? Where are the *normal* schools?[18]

The desire for such a natural *connection* is common, but it is expressed here with uncommon force. In this sample, in a minor way, we see the beginning of that attention in Thoreau's work to *language*—its sources, potential, connections with the

---

[17] Abrams, *Natural Supernaturalism*, 65.

[18] Henry David Thoreau, *A Week on the Concord and Merrimack Rivers* (Boston: Houghton Mifflin, 1893), 504.

world through the mind, and effects—that would eventually make of *Walden* one of the finest realizations of the hope Thoreau had expressed in this earlier passage. Twenty years after *Walden* Tuckerman would, in "The Cricket," express and realize the hope for connection even more powerfully—and also movingly define some of the limits of that hope.

Thoreau was one of the first Americans to comprehend (and to feel the yearning to solve) the basic Romantic problem, defined by Perry Miller as that "of striking and maintaining the delicate balance between object and reflection, of fact and truth, of minute observation and generalized concept."[19] As Miller notes, Thoreau from the first had an insight that perennially escaped Emerson. Rather than positing a universal Oneness which would turn the poet into a mere "transparent eyeball,"[20] Thoreau conceived of a genuine relationship between two realities:

> [The Poet] must be something more than natural—even supernatural. Nature will not speak through but along with him. His voice will not proceed from her midst, but, breathing on her, will make her the expression of his thought. He then poetizes when he takes a fact out of nature into spirit. He speaks without reference to time or place. His thought is one world, hers another. He is another Nature,—Nature's brother. Kindly offices do they perform for one another. Each publishes the other's truth.[21]

With this precariously maintained stance, Thoreau was able in *Walden* to combine minute observation with generalized concept—to use precise observations, expressed in language fully informed by his knowledge of all its powers, both to particularize and to generalize. Thus he made his experience both moving and intelligible. Unlike Tuckerman, he did not persist

---

[19] Miller, *Nature's Nation*, 177.

[20] "Nature," in *Emerson: Selected Prose and Poetry*, 6.

[21] From an entry on "The Poet," in Thoreau's journal, March 3, 1839; quoted in Miller, *Nature's Nation*, 177.

in that stance and late in life turned in almost the opposite direction. But he was able to shape the experience of his stay at Walden Pond into a structure of language with a particular kind of confidence that many of us who follow him have lost: "The universe constantly and obediently answers to our conceptions." The operative word is *answers,* not the Emersonian *corresponds.*

Unlike Emerson, Thoreau did not believe that such responsive "answering" from nature came easily or automatically, but only through a great effort that in fact finally became desperate for him. He began with the same simple assumption as Emerson and all the Romantics: between the moral law and the natural law there are analogies; natural facts, selected and expressed through human agency, can be made to flower into human truths (though with much more emphasis than Emerson on *made*). Thoreau thus transcended the Romantic fear of the pathetic fallacy: the Romantics had profound anxiety (despite the *claims* in their poetry and essays) that the feeling that their experience was typified in nature was only a delusion and that there was really no ontological connection between the mind and the world.

Apparently the source of Thoreau's faith in that connection, which was strong enough to move him to create examples and not just anxious claims, was his early conviction that the God of Christianity is not mere allegory, but a moral, personal, related being who had created man in his image and formed nature after the images in his mind—a mind to which man's mind is related.[22] At any rate, such a faith is a major source of Tuckerman's similar resolution of the Romantic dilemmas. That achievement, made at the personal conceptual level and

---

[22] Miller quotes the following from Thoreau's journal: "When I walk in the woods, I am reminded that a wise purveyor has been there before me; my most delicate experience is typified there." Miller then comments, "If at one and the same time nature is closely inspected in microscopic detail and yet through the ancient system of typology makes experience intelligible, then Thoreau will have solved the Romantic riddle, have mastered the destructive Romantic irony" (*Nature's Nation*, 177).

realized powerfully in his finest poems, recommends him to us, both in our attempt to understand some of the great and enduring human concerns and in our need to be sustained by the achievement of poetry.

IN 1953 M. H. Abrams documented most effectively the central elements in that great sea change in human culture we call the Romantic movement. *The Mirror and the Lamp: Romantic Theory and the Critical Tradition* describes the shift in the eighteenth century away from seeing art as a mirror—an *imitation* of external nature to be judged by its effectiveness with an audience and its fidelity to a rational universe, including the work of art's own rationally defined nature. By the early nineteenth century there was, in theory and practice, nearly complete emphasis on art as *expression* of the artist, with his divine (or divinely given) power to illumine, even to transform, external nature. Art was to be judged by its passion, its intensity, its evidence of intuitive expression, of overflow unimpeded by rational control—or not even to be judged at all, because the artist, endowed by nature or God, is thus a hero, and his work stands in judgment on *us*.

In 1971, in *Natural Supernaturalism: Tradition and Revolution in Romantic Literature,* Abrams documented the central impulse and myth of this movement. He shows that the early Romantics, in their desire to retain a sense of belonging and possible meaning in a universe that was being mechanized and divested of indwelling spirit and had lost the potential of a solution through social changes, turned their hopes to the powers inherent in human consciousness. They developed means to explore and express the possibility of a "circuitous journey" for the self (if not the world) back to its original unity. Through the journey the self could be transformed to a higher state by an organic process of growth that would allow it to reclaim its relation to the external world from which it was originally alienated. This was not the mere emanation and return of Neoplatonism, or the falling into sin and being reclaimed by God of traditional Christianity. For the Romantics the original fall is fortunate: It makes possible a return to a higher state and a secularized redemption by means of progressive self-education based on perception and experience in *this* world.

In a review of Abrams's later book, Charles Rosen suggests that the myth of the circuitous journey is easily identified in much eighteenth- and nineteenth-century literature precisely because it is *not* uniquely Romantic.[23] But Abrams is convincing in his catalog of the special forms the myth took in the Romantic period that were responsive to, first, the new ways of thinking and feeling and viewing the world that developed then, and second, to the particular crises of that time. The view of the world as a mechanism had gained in power, and with it came a growing sense that man was essentially alien and disconnected from the universe. The early Romantics felt and developed the intuition that intrinsically, or because of the nature of its Creator (himself a living, imagining, even, according to Schelling, *changing* being), the universe itself is still evolving according to organic laws, not merely *functioning* through mechanical ones.

A central early Romantic thinker and poet was Coleridge, who, as I show later, shared Tuckerman's Anglican religious tradition and influenced him both indirectly through the Transcendentalists and directly through the American publication of his *Aids to Reflection.* Coleridge became (at least for English-speakers) the crucial figure in changing the metaphor for the universe from a dead machine to a growing plant, a change that had enormous effect both in philosophy and in the theory, practice, and criticism of art. He found the Cartesian ''Mechanico-corpuscular Philosophy'' useful as a fiction of science but deadening to life and art when taken as a supposed fact. After a careful review he decided that the eighteenth-century ''association'' theory of poetic invention, though also useful, could not account for the vital *process* of creation in the

---

[23] Charles Rosen, "Isn't It Romantic?" *New York Review of Books* 20, no. 10 (June 14, 1973): 12–18.

mind. He extended the organic analog so that, in his view, the universe is an ongoing, developing creation, expressing the organic nature of its Author (who is definitely not the Deists' watchmaker). The Creator's mind is imaged in man's, in both its perceptive and its recreative powers.[24]

For Romantics, then, the world is related, and amenable, to the human mind. Both the mind and the world have a fundamentally similar nature, which undergirds artistic creation by human beings. The distinctive Romantic emphasis was thus on becoming, not being; on celebration of life and growth; on organic forms in nature and looking to them to find images for both the form and the content of art. This, of course, led to that other distinctive Romantic quest, to bridge the gulf between our sense of the *reality* of external facts, including both nature and our sense experience, and our sense of their *meaning*. Such a desire then produced the concern to overcome the alienating power of analytic self-consciousness, which is the very source of our sense of that gulf between experience and understanding.

The concern was magnificent, and it and various forms of the Romantic wrestling with such angels remain with us as perhaps the major force in our literary experience, certainly since the ascendancy of post-structuralism.[25] Tuckerman felt that concern deeply and participated along with his contem-

---

[24] See M. H. Abrams, *The Mirror and the Lamp: Romantic Theory and the Critical Tradition* (1953; reprint, New York: Norton, 1958), 168–72, 280–83.

[25] René Wellek, "Romanticism Re-examined," in Northrop Frye, ed., *Romanticism Reconsidered* (New York: Columbia Univ. Press, 1963), 107–33, provides additional documentation of the distinctive Romantic themes that emerged and reinforced each other throughout Western culture at the beginning of the nineteenth century, particularly the great Romantic ambition to reconcile art and nature, language and reality, subject and object. Robert Pinsky, in the first chapter of *The Situation of Poetry: Contemporary Poetry and Its Tradition* (Princeton, N.J.: Princeton Univ. Press, 1976), has most powerfully demonstrated the persistence of these ambitions and the resultant anxieties as well as their consequences for style in modern poetry, arguing persuasively that the best poets continue to be those who recognize their own modernist nominalism and use language carefully "to fence back the blind silence as little as possible" (p. 96). Joseph G. Kronick, in *American Poetics of*

poraries in many varieties of the struggle—particularly, of course, through the developing techniques and perspectives in his poetry, but he did so in ways that allowed him to create unique responses, in his life and art, to the dilemmas involved.

Tuckerman had the particular emotional sensibility that Wordsworth recommended in *The Prelude*. As Perry Miller points out, though *The Prelude* did not become available in America until 1850 and only then made explicit Wordsworth's great "Idea" that Emerson had been recommending, the essence of that idea was already abroad in the land: It was the disposition to let experience come to oneself, through the "feminine" trait of receptivity, rather than going out to conquer it like those in the eighteenth century did with their formal gardens and quest for the picturesque.[26] But Coleridge and other early Romantics saw the danger of such receptivity: The eye could enslave the mind to mere outward impressions.

To prevent such impressionism Wordsworth distinguished "nature" from that surface of the world we see with the unaided eye. He felt there must be an interplay, a balance in perception, "an ennobling interchange of action from within and from without," between the equal powers of the mind and outward sense.[27] Tuckerman was capable of standing nearly alone, in the intellectual climate of his time and place in America, for this kind of balance and genuine interchange. He found ways to use quite traditional but enlivened poetic conventions and rationally disciplined but impassioned language to share with us his finest perceptions and expressions. Thus he made available to us an unusual human sensibility, one fully responsive to intuition and passion yet able to give pow-

---

History: From Emerson to the Moderns (Baton Rouge: Louisiana State Univ. Press, 1984), reveals the disastrous results of completely giving in to the Romantic temptation toward pure nominalism in its modern form of poststructuralism. He concludes that "the poet is no longer the namer of nature, man, and spirit; instead, he is a reader of texts, at once the assembler and the dissembler of fragments."

[26] Miller, *Nature's Nation*, 176–79.

[27] Abrams, *Natural Supernaturalism*, 369.

erfully structured form to the nonrational gestures of his body and mind as they responded to a reality outside his mind.

TUCKERMAN suffered from those special Romantic maladies, melancholia and hypersensitivity to sensual experience. He recognized them as in some sense endemic to his situation, his experience, his yearnings. In an early poem he imagined someone *not* like him and thus "Guiltless of grief, or high romantic love / Of natural beauty . . . " ("The Stranger," p. 120). But, on the evidence of his poetry, he continued to walk disconsolately forth to confront nature at all seasons of the year and hours of the day and night. His search was to know its "import," the ways it might help him work out the meaning of his own life and deal with its most profoundly influential event, the death of his young wife. At times he is one "unto whose feverish sense / The stars tick audibly, and the wind's low surge / In the pine, attended, tolls and throngs and grows / On the dread ear, a thunder too profound / For bearing, a Niagara of sound!" (Sonnet I: 17, p. 11). Sometimes his work approaches the preternatural sensitivity (like that of a convalescent from illness) that we associate with the French Symbolists—when, for instance, "as in a sick man's happy trance,"

> He rides at rest; while from the distant dam,
> Dim and far off as in a dream, he hears
> The pulsing hammer play, or the vague wind
> Rising and falling in the wayside willow,
> Or the faint rustling of the watch beneath his pillow.
> (Sonnet II: 28, p. 32)

The quest for "import" was, of course, a concern shared by many besides the Romantics; it was a perennial Platonic and Christian obsession, which was intensified even more in the New England Calvinists' spiritual life by their search for evidence of election and of God's providence. Tuckerman shared in this inheritance too. Like Hawthorne's, his resistance to the

Transcendentalist idealism that ignored the contradictions, even outright destructiveness, in nature, did not injure his art but rather gave variety, scope, and continuing authenticity to his created symbols. Emerson, in slipping toward pantheism, had to posit universal good and therefore resisted seeing the alien elements in nature; he thus missed its varieties, its details. Tuckerman was more in tune with the European Romantic anguish to create an adequate theodicy in the face of real pain and evil in the world; he needed to justify God's ways to man in forms appropriate to post-Miltonic beliefs.

It has seemed strange that Wordsworth and Coleridge (and other Romantics) wrote much about *dejection,* while celebrating *joy* as the precondition and end of art. However, that occurred precisely because the temptation to hopelessness, in the face of natural destructiveness and human evil and suffering, was a profoundly experienced challenge to their joy and creativity and had to be honestly faced in their art. Tuckerman's series of sonnets, as he finally shaped them, constitutes his own melancholy theodicy, an honest quest to justify his wife's death and to cope with his own pain and anguish. His poetry is both the means and the result of his facing up to the terror he experienced in nature and the life unaccountably given him to live. In this he stood with Melville.

The early Romantics naturalized the old Christian faith that there is a supernatural resolution to human suffering achieved through God's salvation of his elect. They sought a justification *within* human experience, and they found their answer in the qualified hope that individual growth could result from a self-educative journey through life's joy and pain. Tuckerman's sonnets and long ode ''The Cricket'' constitute such a journey, conducted with the same hope and qualified by full attentiveness to the genuine losses that come with experience, even with growth. He successfully worked his way through the dark night of his soul, a grief that obsessed him for years and brought him close to madness and suicide, and reached a position that can be both understood and felt in the poetry.

Tuckerman's theodicy was not a simple reconciliation either

to the traditional Christian God or to Romantic Nature. He earned a complex emotional and intellectual acceptance of the life and world he knew and developed a faith refined and tested in thought and experience. Thus he ultimately was able to fully affirm a creator God. However, that God is one sufficiently related in mind and feelings to himself, and sufficiently expressed in our organic, changing universe (a universe that embodies the possibility of growth as well as the reality of loss), to be understood, at least in part, and to be trusted.

THE ROMANTIC yearning for a return to wholeness and unity, to some imagined primal integrity, sometimes took the form—particularly as pushed to an extreme in some varieties of Transcendentalism—of a temptation to merge completely with nature. Many wished to surrender consciousness in order to escape its reminders of disintegration and loss of innocence. Tuckerman worked his way through to a position much closer to that of Wordsworth and Coleridge and the philosopher Hegel than to that of Emerson, Poe, or Whitman. For instance, "The Cricket" is written in the form of an afternoon's self-educating journey of the poet's mind that symbolizes the long struggle of Tuckerman's life and thought and art. It evokes as powerfully as any British or American Romantic poetry the seductiveness of the temptation to merge with nature. But more impressively than any Transcendentalist work (and most Romantic ones) it conveys the decision to preserve individuality and retain consciousness.

Geoffrey Hartmann has provided evidence that a central Romantic concern was how to remedy the "strong disease" of analytic thought and the alienating self-consciousness that comes over the child as it grows to maturity.[28] Many European Romantics sought "to draw the antidote to self-consciousness

---

[28] "Romanticism and 'Anti-self-consciousness,' " *Centennial Review of Arts and Sciences* 6 (1962): 553–65.

from consciousness itself." The greater German and English Romantics did not wish to escape from or limit knowledge in a primitivistic return to nature but rather to convert knowledge "into an energy finer than intellectual." Consciousness should remain separate from nature "so that it can finally transcend not only nature but also its own lesser forms."[29] Abrams is weak on this matter, since he does not face the unavoidable contradictions implicit in the Romantic search for a solution to the pains of self-consciousness. Charles Rosen's critique of Abrams is helpful here:

> This division of the self is, indeed, a fall from grace; the act of reflection is the knowledge of good and evil. But Abrams does not carry it far enough. For Fichte, the ego (the self) does not *exist* except as the act of self-alienation, and comes into being only at the moment of the act. I can be myself only in so far as I am aware of myself as something distinct from the totally subjective, only as my own mind takes a part of itself as an object; otherwise there is no "I." The Fall from grace continuously re-enacted at every moment is the condition of life. Alienation, for Fichte and for Coleridge, is synonymous with existence.[30]

If this is true, then "the impulse to heal the division, to integrate the ego with itself and with nature, is threatened. . . . This is the ambiguity at the heart of the 'circuitous journey'; the lost paradise regained is death." Success in the quest for identification of the self with nature can have only one result: in the words of Hartmann, "Nothing is lost by this sublimation except all."[31]

No matter what *form* the Romantic myth of salvation took, at its *end* lay some form of identity-destroying unity, a kind of death that doomed the very values and meaning and means of

---

[29] Ibid., 554–56.

[30] Rosen, "Isn't It Romantic?" 16.

[31] Ibid., quoted from "Reflections on the Evening Star," in Geoffrey Hartmann, ed., *New Perspectives on Coleridge and Wordsworth* (New York: Columbia Univ. Press, 1972).

the journey. Growth, education, higher consciousness, language, poetry—all are lost. Poe accepted the consequences of his insatiable yearning for primal unity with a kind of obsessed horror, giving himself over to images of incest and mutual self-destructiveness; Whitman's pantheistic yearning to sanctify and merge with all things led him to remove all value distinctions in poems like "When lilacs last in the dooryard bloom'd," a supposed elegy that tends to subvert any purpose for elegy in its praise of death. But Tuckerman came to accept as primary the journey itself—the process, not the end. He accepted self-consciousness and perception and language, despite their pains and limitations, as necessary accoutrements of the journey—as sources of joy and growth and meaning.

Meaning as a quest and question was (and continues) a source of special anxiety to Romantics, at least those with the integrity to understand or at least feel their essential nominalism. They retained a strong element of philosophical realism in their concern for connection to nature, their hope to elicit educative understanding from their experience with external reality, their faith in the "truth" of their conceptions and the effectiveness of language. But they also felt intensely the growing conviction, in the world of the "new science," of the absolute separation of mind and matter—a deep nominalistic skepticism. If we trace the effects on poetic style of this nominalist anxiety about a terrible void between writers and their subject matter, it turns out that almost all of the Romantics and their heirs are caught between the hopelessness of nominalism and unwillingness to give it up. Such a dilemma is crucial for a poet because nominalism challenges the meaning and value of language itself, questions the essential reality of linguistic concepts. The poet with a nominalist world view must either despair, doubt the reality of language completely, and retreat into silence, or he must make compromises. These compromises will in large measure constitute his style.

Tuckerman appears, on the basis of the anxieties revealed in his poetry, to be much more of a nominalist than Emerson, who talks easily of correspondences and is insensitive to particulars. On the other hand, Tuckerman's mature style quite surpasses Emerson's in achieving, and I think vindicating, a kind of philosophical realism—faith in the reality and connecting power of language based on an understanding of its *resources* as well as its limitations.

T H E "First Series," the first of the five sonnet sequences that constitute Tuckerman's major work, was begun, I believe, not long after his extremely important visit with Tennyson in January 1855. It later developed and was finally shaped (before publication in 1860) as an effort to come to terms with his wife's death in May 1857. This first sonnet sequence reveals a mature command of the particular form that Tuckerman apparently needed for his unique genius to flower, and it speaks with a mature voice distinct from that in his earlier poetry. The series as a whole gives, in unusually personal terms, a journey of the mind from general skepticism and self-doubt, through overwhelming grief, to a measure of peace. The sonnets are interconnected and cannot be adequately considered in isolation; but, for purposes of our discussion at this point, some summary and quotation can be useful.

The first sonnet questions the validity of the poetic enterprise itself:

> Sometimes, when winding slow by brook and bower,
> Beating the idle grass,—of what avail,
> I ask, are these dim fancies, cares and fears?
> What though from every bank I drew a flower,—
> Bloodroot, king orchis, or the pearlwort pale,—
> And set it in my verse with thoughtful tears?
> What would it count though I should sing my death
> And muse and mourn with as poetic breath
> As in damp garden walks the autumn gale
> Sighs o'er the fallen floriage? What avail
> Is the swan's voice if all the hearers fail?

> Or his great flight that no eye gathereth
> In the blending blue? And yet depending so,
> God were not God, whom knowledge cannot know.
>
> (Sonnet I: 1, p. 3)

Tuckerman has begun with a credo: Even though it may seem to no avail to put natural objects into his verse, even though the limits of language as a bridge from the objects of experience to the mind leave potentially meaningless such things as the flight and voice of the swan, "if all the hearers fail," yet, in this human condition, the possibility of God remains for Tuckerman an antidote to despair. God would not be the rational, Christian divinity that it is possible to believe in if knowledge (language, perception) were of no avail to know him. Thus, the very existence, in any meaningful sense, of God—as well as the poet—depends on language.

The next two sonnets show that for Tuckerman the possibility of such knowledge through language surely remains, vindicated in part by the achievement of great poetry itself (though that, too, as competition and standard, can contribute to his personal insecurity). He attacks, with this belief, the "dark doubt" that the poetic vocation is useless but is goaded into further despair by himself, by "a weapon of my weakness made," when he compares his "proudest thoughts" to the achievements of others before him and considers his own presumption:

> What have thy dreams, a vague prospective worth?
> An import imminent? or dost thou deem
> Thy life so fair that thou wouldst set it forth
> Before the day? or art thou wise in grief,
> Has fruitful sorrow swept thee with her wing?
>
> (Sonnet I: 3, p. 4)

He responds with a startling vignette of his own grief and then goes on, with the following poems of the five series of sonnets, to *show* the fruitfulness of his sorrow.

In the fifth series, written probably ten years later, after Tuckerman had published part of his work (and been re-assured that at least a few hearers could hear) and had thought and felt his way through successive layers of doubt and faith in dealing with the implications of his wife's death, he was able to create a brilliant image of the resolution toward which he had continually, patiently worked. Nature's function is described in the first sonnet of that last series as crucial but limited. She "feeds the world / And so fulfills her births and offices." But "Causal or consequential cares not she":

> . . . her desire
> Is but to serve, and her necessity.
> The invention and authority are His,
> In the whole past or what remains to be.
> (Sonnet V: 1, p. 59)

The second sonnet in the Final Series continues:

> Nor, though she seem to cast with backward hand
> Strange measure, sunny cold or cloudy heat,
> Or break with stamping rain the farmer's wheat,
> Yet in such waste no waste the soul descries,
> Intent to glean by barrenest sea and land.
> For whoso waiteth, long and patiently,
> Will see a movement stirring at his feet—
> If he but wait nor think himself much wise.
> Nay, from the mind itself a glimpse will rest
> Upon the dark; summoning from vacancy
> Dim shapes about his intellectual lamp,
> Calling these in and causing him to see;
> As the night-heron waking in the swamp
> Lights up the pools with her phosphoric breast.
> (Sonnet V: 2, p. 59)

That last image provides a powerful solution to the dilemma of the mirror and lamp and the anguish of the temptation to solipsism. Tuckerman bridges the Romantic revolution with a symbol of the mind *interacting* with a reality *external* to, but also *related* to, itself. The mind is neither all mirror nor all lamp—neither an essentially passive reflector nor a merely self-sufficient creator of an external world. It can, given sufficient patience and humility, combine the resources gleaned—won—from observation of "barrenest sea and land" with those developed by its own powers. The poet's "intellectual lamp" can thus produce a means by which to reach out into the dark, the meaningless world of immediate experience, "summoning from vacancy dim shapes" that are neither independently meaningful nor mere imaginations. They are in fact those creations of language that make possible meaning and understanding and allow a measure of connection across the subject-object void. The phosphoric mind can attract and illumine, can summon into meaning, from vacancy, the elusive but not merely imagined fact.

II

INFLUENCES

Her beauty came to his distrustful heart
As comes a bud to flower in bracing air;
For its perception had been dulled to sleep
By disappointment, doubt, and worldly wear,
The fear of wrong, and coldness everywhere.

"Elidore"

THE passage above, from an early poem, conveys Tuckerman's sense of what his life and education, his cultural milieu in Boston and his response to it, had brought him to in 1847. It also conveys the effect on him, that year, of meeting and marrying Hannah Jones and removing permanently to her hometown of Greenfield in western Massachusetts. Edward Tuckerman, the poet's father, came from a wealthy and noted English line whose progenitors immigrated to the Plymouth Colony in 1649. He was one of the upper-class merchants who built the energetic but insensitive Boston society of the early nineteenth century (about which Emerson said "things" were in the saddle). However, he also went through a period of religious reflection as a young man, leading to a deep recommitment to Episcopalianism, and shared in the philanthropic efforts of his more famous brother, Joseph, a Unitarian minister who became known for promoting "ministries at large" to seamen and the urban poor in Boston and London. Frederick's mother, Sophia May (Edward's second wife), was descended from John May, an officer in the Revolutionary War who also became part of the

Boston merchant class, and from Oliver Wolcott, a signer of the Declaration of Independence.[1]

Tuckerman was born February 4, 1821, grew up in the substantial home still standing at 33 Beacon Street across from the Common (later used as the residence for Boston's mayors), attended an Episcopal boarding school and the Boston Latin School, an excellent preparatory school, and entered Harvard in 1837, just after Emerson's address on "The American Scholar." Emerson later described the break in generations that made him in that address a liberator to the young and an infidel to the old:

> The former generations acted under the belief that a shining social prosperity was the beatitude of man, and sacrificed uniformly the citizen to the State. The modern mind believed that the nation existed for the individual, for the guardianship and education of the every man . . . ; the individual is the world.[2]

In a retrospective survey Emerson emphasized the characteristic "modern" youth's rebelliousness, his inclination to solitude—"to find all his resources, hopes, rewards, society and deity within himself"—and to criticism: "The young men were

---

[1] E. Douglas Branch, in his entertaining and useful study of the broad range of American culture in this period, *The Sentimental Years: 1836–1865* (1934; reprint, New York: Hill and Wang, 1962), makes the following generalizations, which seem to accord well with the sense Tuckerman and others, as well as Emerson, had of the life in Boston: "Altruisms and evasions, the pebbles of fact and the cement of illusion: so was builded an American tradition of being socially comfortable, practically successful, spiritually progressive, and privately warmed with self-esteem" (11). I am indebted to Samuel Golden for his genealogical work on the Tuckerman family and also to Anna M. M. Reid, whose more recent research has uncovered additional material, especially concerning Edward and his scientific work that greatly influenced Frederick. See "Edward Tuckerman (1817–1886), Pioneer American Lichenologist: The Early Years," *Mycotaxon* 26 (July–September 1986): 3–16.

[2] Ralph Waldo Emerson, "Life and Letters in New England," in *The Complete Writings of Ralph Waldo Emerson,* ed. Edward Waldo Emerson (New York: W. H. Wise and Co., 1929), 1043.

born with knives in their brain, a tendency to introversion, self-dissection, anatomizing of motives."[3]

Tuckerman certainly developed many of the traits of his generation, and his father had many of those of the "former generations." For instance, Van Wyck Brooks gives examples of how Boston's patrician elders valued art for its capacity to commemorate them and glorify their city. Though not themselves poetic, they respected poetry and raised their sons to make verses.[4] Tuckerman was thus named for a kinsman, F. W. Goddard, who was accidentally drowned in Switzerland just after traveling with Wordsworth in 1820 and was memorialized by the English poet in some "Elegaic Stanzas" that (with a prose introduction) make up number 32 of his "Memorials of a Tour on the Continent." By the age of ten Tuckerman himself was writing occasional verse.[5] The next year, in a letter to his oldest brother, Edward, Jr., from Bishop Hopkins's Episcopal School in Burlington, Vermont, he reported he was getting into Caesar and "doing well in drawing and in music."[6] Music became the field of his other older brother, Samuel Parkman Tuckerman, but Frederick's continuing skill in drawing is

---

[3] Ibid., 1044.

[4] Van Wyck Brooks, *The Flowering of New England: 1815–1865,* rev. ed. (New York: E. P. Dutton, 1937), 130.

[5]   *On New Years Day*
>   The old year is past and is gone,
>   From us it forever has fled,
>   But a beautiful New one has come,
>   And the beautiful old one is dead.

This example is among the pitifully small number of personal papers that have survived as a resource for reconstructing biography and the growth of Tuckerman's mind and talent. It is in the keeping of the only heir, his great-grandson, Hugh Clark, of Amherst, Massachusetts. The letters and other materials at the Clark home are hereafter referred to as Tuckerman Papers, Hugh Clark, Amherst, while the other such materials, which are all at Harvard's Houghton Library, given by the poet's granddaughter, Margaret Tuckerman (Mrs. Orton Loring) Clark, are referred to by the appropriate manuscript number, followed by the abbreviated name Houghton, or, if letters, as Houghton Autograph File.

[6] Houghton Autograph File, dated April 29, 1833.

apparent in a few sketches preserved from his youth and drawings he made in books read when he was mature. The early
training of his eye for detail may have helped give his poetry
its precision of observation.

In 1835 Edward gave Frederick *The Beauties of Washington
Irving,* and in the front the following is inscribed in Tuckerman's elegant youthful handwriting (he was then fourteen):

> My brother gave this book
> When he from college came,
> And I the present took
> And in it wrote my name.
>
> And now I've read it through
> I much should like another
> Although I can't expect
> Two presents from my brother.
>
> Although I like to write
> I like to read much better
> So wish that he'd indite
> To me a good long letter.

Something of Tuckerman's precocity, his early concern with a
reputable *American* literary culture, and a rather unusual sense
of humor are revealed in a note inside the back cover of this
same volume (apparently written the next year when Tuckerman was fifteen):

> Literary Club
> [undecipherable] Court
> 29th August, 1836
>
> a poor collection printed in a most slovenly manner—
> There are some sentences not intelligible, and others—
> in Europe—would tell *ill* of the scholarship and ortho-
> graphy of the American press—
>
> ———

> The ghosts of Johnson, Gibbon, Burke, Reynolds, Beau-
> clerk, Langton, Hawkins, Boswell, Murphy, etc.—in the
> special council convened upon the Present State of Liter-
> ature have determined and decreed
>
> That by the equal Laws of a National Criticism the Book
> entitled "Beauties of Washington Irving" is unworthy of
> the award of satisfaction by the Literary Club.
>
> Bozz.   Fiat   Sam. Johnson
> Sec.   Pres.

It was perhaps only the backwardness of New England literary culture—but it could well have been positive good taste on the young Tuckerman's part—that made him choose as arbiters the pre-Romantic circles around Johnson.

Except for two letters to members of his family and an incomplete assignment from law school, nothing else has been preserved of the writing Tuckerman "liked" to do during this period of his late teens and early twenties. However, his law professor, Joseph Story, was to refer, in a letter of recommendation in 1844, to his "literary attainments." Of the *reading*, which he liked "much better," we fortunately know a great deal. The volume of Irving is one of about forty books preserved from Tuckerman's library. Because of their numerous and unusual notes and markings, those books are an excellent indication of the quality and growth of Tuckerman's mind; they not only show directly what and how carefully he read, but through Tuckerman's noting of allusions they indicate a much broader range of literature with which he was astonishingly familiar.[7]

The volumes that give direct evidence of Tuckerman's reading during this early period before his marriage include John Gay's poetry (notations include the comment "I think there is

-----

[7] The books, except for four of the seven Tennyson volumes (which are in the Houghton Library at Harvard), are in the keeping of Hugh Clark and are referred to as part of Tuckerman Papers in Amherst. (See Appendix I for a complete listing of the books preserved and of references Tuckerman made to his other reading.)

little if any poetry in Gay" and call attention correctly to a case of "false metre" and to "alliteration extraordinary"). There is also Robert Southey's *Thalaba the Destroyer,* Samuel Singer's ten-volume edition of Shakespeare, Chaucer's *Works,* W. E. Channing's *Poems,* J. Lempriere's *Classical Dictionary,* John C. Lavater's *Moral Teachings,* and Coleridge's *Aids to Reflection in the Formation of a Manly Character* (the 1829 edition by James Marsh, President of the University of Vermont, the volume through which Coleridge's Christian Romanticism became influential in America). I demonstrate in detail in the next chapter that the notes in works Tuckerman read later prove that in this early period he had studied with great care (and what seems nearly total recall) almost every British and American author of any reputation, both of his own day and of the past.

Apparently such independent reading in the library (along with the English essays or "forensics" that had taken the place of Latin disputations and were of such great benefit to Thoreau) was the only recourse then for underclassmen at Harvard who wanted a liberal education. Samuel Eliot Morison tells us that this period was Harvard's "Augustan Age" in its development, under Josiah Quincy, of the material side of the college and acquisition of staff. But he says it failed during the same period to accomplish the reforms in the lecture system that George Ticknor, the young professor of modern languages fresh from his experience with European methods, began to fight for in 1823. Worse, Quincy thought of the ideal course as "thorough drilling" and added to the already detested system of recitations a daily marking and ranking procedure that further poisoned relations between students and instructors.[8] Nevertheless, there were fine teachers despite the system: Ticknor, John Farrar in natural sciences, and particularly E. T. Channing in English. Channing invited students into his home for readings and discussion and provided extremely disciplined instruction in rhetoric and writing that

---

[8] Samuel Eliot Morison, *Three Centuries of Harvard: 1636–1936* (Cambridge, Mass.: Harvard Univ. Press, 1946), 260.

was gratefully remembered by those he taught, including Thoreau.[9]

Jones Very, the Calvinist mystic who flirted with Transcendentalism and whose poems were edited in 1839 by Emerson, was Tuckerman's Greek tutor in the recitations inflicted on freshmen. During this period Very was writing his own best poetry, almost all sonnets and expressed in the haunted voice of mystical assurance that was lost in his later writing after he became a good, steady clergyman. At this time he was trying (with a sincerity that chilled those around him and led to his voluntarily and pleasantly spending a short time at the McLean Asylum) to practice a perfect surrender to God, and he was able to consider his own speech and writing as God's. He was capable of announcing to a class in Greek (which might well have included the young Tuckerman), "Flee to the mountains, for the end of all things is at hand." And he once, Emerson himself reports, told Emerson that his "spirit was not quite right." The Concord Sage felt that "it was as if a vein of colder air blew across me."[10]

Very's extreme integrity to his sense of mystical experience and the surrender of his will to a personal, immanent God and to the absolutes communicated by the Spirit were probably a continuing influence on Tuckerman. It seems evident from the letter Very wrote, responding to Tuckerman's request for permission to send him a copy of his recently published *Poems* in 1861, that Tuckerman had not only remembered Very through the years but had continued to read Very's poetry (Very writes, "I am glad that any words of mine should have been the means, meanwhile, of continuing our friendship").[11]

---

[9] Brooks, *Flowering of New England,* 43–44; Samuel Osgood, *Student Life: Letters and Recollections for a Young Friend* (New York: James Miller, 1861), 27.

[10] All the quotations of Emerson on Very are from Emerson's Journals, quoted in the memorial by William P. Andrews, in his edition of Very's poems, published at Boston by Houghton Mifflin in 1883; they are quoted from that source in Yvor Winters's "Jones Very and R. W. Emerson: Aspects of New England Mysticism," *In Defense of Reason* (Denver: Alan Swallow, 1947), 262–73.

[11] Houghton Autograph File, dated at Salem, March 25, 1861.

From the evidence of Tuckerman's own poetry it is clear that Very's exactly traditional use of the sonnet form did not influence him but that what Nathan Lyons has called the "grave, spare, uncompromising voice" possibly did.[12] The two unusual poets share an honest, plain, often homely diction, a passionate and thoughtful search for spiritual significance, and a serious, precise, even sophisticated use both of natural details and of conceptual distinctions to explore profoundly moral personal experience.

After a year at Harvard, Tuckerman dropped out of school for a year. The reason was not, as his classmate Thomas W. Higginson later conjectured, "from such family obstacles as his older brother met" but, as Dr. Frederick Tuckerman, the poet's son, indicated in a letter to Eaton, because of serious trouble with his eyes.[13] As Dr. Tuckerman admits, his grandfather sent the oldest son Edward to Union College "so that he should not be too early exposed to the religious influences

---

[12] Nathan Lyons, ed., *Jones Very: Selected Poems* (New Brunswick, N.J.: Rutgers Univ. Press, 1967), 4. For a thorough comparison of both the similarities and differences between the sonnets of Tuckerman and Very, see David Seed, "Alone with God and Nature: The Poetry of Jones Very and Frederick Goddard Tuckerman," in *Nineteenth-Century American Poetry*, ed. A. Robert Lee (London: Vision Press, 1985), 166–93.

[13] Higginson's opinion is in a letter to Walter Prichard Eaton, who was gathering information on the poet for his essay "A Forgotten American Poet," in *Forum* 41 (January 1909): 63. There is a copy of the son's letter in the Tuckerman Papers, Hugh Clark, Amherst; it is reprinted in Witter Bynner, ed., *The Sonnets of Frederick Goddard Tuckerman* (New York: Alfred A. Knopf, 1931), 24–25. In one of the sonnets Tuckerman indicates that he used his eye problem to escape the drudgery of school and to indulge his early desire to be alone in the natural landscape:

> How oft in schoolboy-days, from the school's sway
> Have I run forth to Nature as to a friend,
> With some pretext of o'erwrought sight, to spend
> My schooltime in green meadows far away! (Sonnet II: 29, p. 33)

But that the problem was real enough is indicated in a letter from school to his brother Edward when he was twelve: "My eyes do not trouble me much except when I write or study very steadily and then they pain me a good deal" (Houghton Autograph File, dated at Salem, March 25, 1861).

and tendencies at Cambridge, which my grandfather regarded either with disfavor or suspicion." However, by the mid-1830s Harvard's catholicity and openness to tolerant religious discussion were well established under Quincy. If it is true, as Morison says, that "Unitarianism had sealed Harvard with its spirit,"[14] this was found so little of a threat that Edward did go to Harvard (for an LL. B.) in 1839 and later returned for a B.A. and M.A. in 1847 and a degree from the Divinity School in 1852.[15] Calvinists had more to fear than Episcopalians from the "fortress of the liberal outlook and faith" that Harvard had become. The essentially Anglican Tuckermans were no doubt better prepared than most of their contemporaries for a place where, as Morison says, "after [the students'] stern upbringing in the expectation of a hard struggle to escape eternal damnation . . . hell was not mentioned, and venerable preachers treated the students, not as limbs of Satan, but as younger brothers of their Lord and Savior."[16]

The senior Edward Tuckerman, the poet's father, left the Anglican faith of his parents as a young man, in 1793. The Revolution had severely damaged the largely Loyalist Episcopalian church; but by the end of the century a gradual recovery had begun, which was then stimulated greatly by the work of the Evangelical Movement within the church. By 1811 a turning point was reached, particularly because of the appointment of energetic bishops like Viets Griswold in New England.[17] Two

---

[14] Morison, *Three Centuries of Harvard*, 244.

[15] The Tuckerman Papers, Hugh Clark, Amherst, include a letter from Josiah Quincy to Tuckerman's father giving permission for the son to attend Episcopal services with his family—a practice, according to Morison, that Quincy had inaugurated his first year, in 1829.

[16] Morison, *Three Centuries of Harvard*, 244–45. In the following analysis of the effect on Tuckerman's poetic development of his religious faith, "Episcopalian" refers to the specific church he and his parents belonged to, "Anglican" to the general philosophical and religious tradition from the sixteenth century.

[17] There is a good summary of these changes in Sydney E. Ahlstrom, *A Religious History of the American People* (New Haven, Conn.: Yale Univ. Press, 1972), 623–25.

years later Tuckerman's father rejoined the Episcopal church and became one of its aristocratic stalwarts in Boston (even though his brother Joseph became a noted Unitarian preacher and he himself continued to maintain close ties with the Unitarian elite, including Quincy and the Channings).

The children grew up under strong and lasting Episcopalian influence, which included the characteristic Anglican openness. The poet's brother Edward, in addition to his extraordinary contributions to botany, continued to write on Episcopalian theology and church matters throughout his life. Samuel Parkman Tuckerman, the second eldest, became an important figure in Episcopalian music, the influence of his organ and choir compositions and lectures extending to England and Rome. After receiving his doctorate from the Archbishop of Canterbury and performing and studying for eight years more in England, he became the organist at Trinity Church, New York.

Direct evidence of Frederick's own involvement with Anglicanism can be found in his attendance at boarding schools directed by John Henry Hopkins (both while Hopkins was assistant minister of Trinity Church in Boston in 1831 and then later in Burlington when he became the first Protestant Episcopal bishop of Vermont the next year). There is also a letter to his father when Frederick was home alone in the summer of 1840,[18] which mentions the new course of sermons at church and the inquiries of the ministers after the welfare of the members of the family away traveling. Most significant, there is Frederick's participation with his wife and children in the Episcopal parish at Greenfield. The poetry itself clearly confirms that it is Tuckerman's Anglicanism that best accounts for his differences from Emerson and the Transcendentalists and for his unique response to Romantic influences. We will better see this when we understand how those influences were transmitted to Tuckerman through his fellow Anglicans,

---

[18] July 16, 1840, Tuckerman Papers, Hugh Clark, Amherst.

Coleridge and Tennyson, whose own particular versions of Romanticism he was thus particularly well prepared to comprehend accurately.

T H E "Anglican tradition," going back to Richard Hooker and his development of a theological method distinct from that of seventeenth-century Calvinists, remained alive for Tuckerman and thus distinguished him from the other poets in New England, who were in one way or another primarily heirs of the Calvinists. I will briefly review some of the main elements of this tradition to help identify precisely how its influence on Tuckerman was a powerful antidote to certain dangerous tendencies in the Calvinist tradition that influenced those other American Romantics.

Hooker's answer to the question of a source of authority for an "ecclesiastical polity" was "Law," as opposed to the Puritan "will of God." His development of that idea gave to Anglican theology a "rationalistic" (rather than "voluntaristic") cast that it never lost. That emphasis was also important to the other major influence upon Tuckerman, which we shall look at shortly, because it predisposed Anglicans, in the words of the excellent summary by H. R. McAdoo, "to accept and to assimilate the work of the scientists and naturalists."[19]

Law, according to Hooker, though originating with God, does not consist of arbitrary promulgations, subject to God's arbitrary will, but is "that order which God before all ages hath set down with himself, for himself to do all things by."[20] It is a living linkage of rational causation in the created universe, devised to direct God's creatures—rationally, because

---

[19] H. R. McAdoo, *The Spirit of Anglicanism: A Survey of Anglican Theological Method in the Seventeenth Century* (New York: Charles Scribner's Sons, 1965), 5; this book gives a good overview both of the theology and of the history of Anglicanism.

[20] Richard Hooker, *Of the Laws of Ecclesiastical Polity,* 2 vols. (1907; reprint, London: J. M. Dent and Sons, 1954), 1:154 (1st bk., sec. 2, part 6); other quotes from Hooker are from Book 1 in Volume 1 of this same source.

their own minds can respond rationally—toward their own perfection. As McAdoo writes:

> The key to Hooker's thought is to be found in the idea that law is an implanted directive, that it is reason, inherent, governing the universe, an inner principle expressing itself by the fulfillment of proper ends.[21]

Man is so created as to be responsive to laws, they being, according to Hooker, "that which God himself hath set down as expedient to be kept by all his creatures, according to the several conditions where with he hath endued them" (sec. 3). One of those conditions for man is reason, and law takes the form of natural law amenable to reason: "The natural measure whereby to judge our doings is the sentence of reason" (sec. 8). The scriptures retain authority as the source of "laws of duties supernatural" but do not have the absolute, undiscriminated authority they have for Calvinists; they are understood to *include* natural law, to be themselves responsive to reason and its ability to distinguish between the necessary and the less important and between different levels of truth and morality.

Hooker was also aware of the limitations of individual human reason. He grounded the Anglican theological method in a conservative deference to the sense of a continuing invisible church in history, particularly the "undivided Church" of the first five centuries but also the continuing authority of "the sentences of wise and expert men." He saw that "nature is no sufficient teacher of what we should do that we may attain unto life everlasting" and that we might well defer to qualified authority since "in defect of proof infallible, the mind doth rather follow probable persuasions. . . . Such as the evidence is . . . such is the heart's assent thereunto."

In contrast, for Calvinism, in McAdoo's words, "the stress was on a transcendent authority working on the human situation from without, as against an implanted directive expressing itself as and through reason within a situation in which

---

[21] McAdoo, *Spirit of Anglicanism*, 6.

freedom was real and grace not irresistible."[22] Despite its heretical trappings, Emerson's Transcendentalism derived directly from the Calvinist tradition. His "self-reliance," because of the implicit pantheism, was really God-reliance, ultimately a surrender to impulse as divine authority; it was capable of taking a determined practitioner with fewer conditioned habits of intentional thought and action than Emerson to sheer automatism, complete loss of freedom. For Anglicans, authority for thought and action was not transcendent; it included a directive within each human that expressed itself through reason, not impulse. Calvinistic moral determinism and irresistible grace, carried over into Emerson, take the form of his exaltation (uneasy though he was when he considered Napoleon) of the winners and doers, of the heroes who venture beyond rational constraint—the ones who were to become the very destroyers of Emerson's culture. Those Calvinist doctrines also encouraged his early blindness to moral as well as other kinds of distinctions, his cheerful insensitivity to evil itself, as he expressed it in "Compensation": "An eternal, beneficent necessity is always bringing things right."

In contrast, the Anglican tradition kept Tuckerman in touch, from the first, with the Roman Catholic tradition of ethical scholarship, which took seriously and tried to understand and evaluate the subtle details of moral experience.

The strength and attractiveness of Calvinism was that it opposed a comprehensive *system* of creedal claims to the mere *method* of the Anglicans. The latter, rather than a secure set of doctrines, offered merely a *way* of seeking truth and salvation that kept in balance the equal authority of human reason, the traditions of human experience in history, and God's revelations. However, Calvinism's uncompromising formulations and inexorable syllogistic logic *within* its system led it increasingly into obscurantism, a focus on pure transcendent metaphysics rather than awareness of the tangible world. For

---

[22] Ibid., 9.

instance, its purely functional reason took it to the soul-destroying extreme of the doctrine of predestination but was unable to open it to realities beyond its own presuppositions. As might be expected, "the decline of Calvinism coincided with the rise of the Royal Society and a steadily growing interest in natural history and scientific developments."[23]

The inclusiveness in the method of the Anglican religious tradition and the ecumenical impulse to be a *via media* between Protestantism and Catholicism were being renewed in the Oxford Movement during Tuckerman's youth. They provided important foundations for the threefold integrity Witter Bynner described in him, "toward nature, toward his own mind, and toward the unknown God."[24] That inclusiveness also helps explain his success as a mediator in the central conflict of Romanticism, that between head and heart. Such a religious tradition, unique among the American poets of the time, made Tuckerman respond in unique ways to the infusions of the Romantic spirit from Europe, especially because perhaps the single major infusion came from Coleridge, a person energetically committed to that same Anglican religious tradition.

While Wordsworth lapsed into what many consider an uncreative religious orthodoxy after working with Coleridge on *Lyrical Ballads,* Coleridge worked to develop, for what he called "authentic Christianity," the import of the revolution the two had begun. His most influential work, particularly in America, was the 1829 American edition of *Aids to Reflection* (the full title adds *In the Formation of a Manly Character on the Several Grounds of Prudence, Morality, and Religion*). This edition has a fine introduction by James Marsh, whose work as translator (e.g., Herder's *Spirit of Hebrew Poetry* in 1833) and editor and explicator was extremely important in the process of transferring the "spirit of the age" to America. Emerson and others read Coleridge, rapturously but incorrectly, in terms solely of

---

23 Ibid., 12.
24 "Introduction" to Bynner, *Sonnets,* 34.

his emphasis on the transcendent and therefore used him to support a kind of pantheistic Calvinism that would have surely appalled Coleridge. Tuckerman was able to read Marsh's edition, somewhat later, in much better keeping with the intent.[25] The copy in Tuckerman's library belonged originally to his father and was read thoroughly by his brother Edward, who had a strong and complex influence on Frederick.

Edward was one of the first of many who were touched by the proselytizing zeal of Harvard's George Ticknor, who (with Joseph Cogswell and Edward Everett) had studied in Germany in 1815; he was convinced by Ticknor that he should imbibe European intellectual currents directly, and he studied there at different times beginning in 1841. But Edward was one of the few Americans who studied *science* in Europe and thus was exposed to more than the powerful forces of Romanticism in philosophy and art, and his influence on Frederick in this regard was profound. Edward's notes in his father's copy of *Aids to Reflection,* which Edward later apparently gave to Frederick, strongly emphasize Coleridge's distinction between the

---

[25] In *Nature's Nation* (Cambridge, Mass: Harvard Univ. Press, 1967), Perry Miller informs us that another Anglican, writing at the middle of the nineteenth century, recognized this pernicious misreading of Coleridge in an essay that made one of the few objections during that time to the cult of nature:

> The Reverend Caleb S. Henry, an Episcopalian but a student of German, strove valiantly in the only journal of the time which can be said intellectually to rival *The Dial, The New York Review,* to show that Coleridge was no transcendentalist in the Emersonian sense, "denying or refining away the historic truth of Christianity." The *Review* said that Emerson's writings, purporting to be ambrosial food, were in reality poison; in this atheistic perversion of Coleridge it found a striking instance of the inherent lawlessness of the American mind—"the evil and punishment of our age and country." Yet this same *Review,* in less guarded pages, is full of hymns to Nature; it too forgets repeatedly that the Christian should admire in Nature only the handiwork of God, and treats the landscape as a self-sufficient source of morality and law. (158)

"understanding" and the "reason." For Coleridge the understanding was the simple capacity to respond to stimuli, the "outward sense"; but reason was the "inward sense," the universal image of God in men, the source of creativity and insight, an evidence of the harmony of man's essential nature with the attributes of God. It made possible a genuine life of the mind, which (rather than mere sensation) was for Coleridge the most fruitful source of poetry and the means for creating it.

Emerson and others were stimulated by the sense conveyed by Coleridge of man's immense potential and were attracted to the weapons he provided with which to attack the reductionism of commonsense science and materialism. They felt an awakened realization of man's inherent connection, through his resources of emotion and impulse, with transcendent realities. Edward and Frederick Goddard Tuckerman must have felt these influences too. However, at least partly because of the religious tradition they shared with him, they also understood Coleridge's point that man's potential must be *achieved* through rigorous "reflection" and development of the various resources in themselves.

Particularly helpful in this regard was the Anglican emphasis on God as *creator* of nature and man, a maker who remains independent of what he makes, not merged with it. This understanding made it possible to respond in a special way to Coleridge's Romantic reaching for *connection* between the created order and man, between object and subject: Like Coleridge they had faith in a divinely implanted creative reason that is responsive to a rational, though organic, divine creation. Such a view also helped them avoid Emerson's confusion of God with nature and his identification of his immediate impulses and feelings with God's will.

Tuckerman worked out certain implications of this Anglican comprehensiveness in the closing sonnet of his First Series:

> Not the round natural world, not the deep mind,
> The reconcilement holds: the blue abyss

> Collects it not; our arrows sink amiss
> And but in Him may we our import find.
> The agony to know, the grief, the bliss
> Of toil, is vain and vain: clots of the sod
> Gathered in heat and haste and flung behind
> To blind ourselves and others, what but this
> Still grasping dust and sowing toward the wind?
> No more thy meaning seek, thine anguish plead,
> But leaving straining thought and stammering word,
> Across the barren azure pass to God:
> Shooting the void in silence like a bird,
> A bird that shuts his wings for better speed.
>   (Sonnet I: 28, p. 16)

The entire series is an integrated structure. This final sonnet is a specific answer to the anxieties expressed in the beginning poems (which I examine in chapter I) about the usefulness of poetry, particularly its use of natural detail, in the search for meaning. It provides a temporary plateau of assurance in Tuckerman's attempt to reach the unknown but knowable God, though that assurance contains the seeds of further struggle since it suggests that the means of reaching assurance—poetry—must be left behind in that assurance.

Toward the end of the First Series, Tuckerman recognizes that despite the few special visions nature has revealed to his "guarded insight fine," she "breathes contradiction where she seems most clear" (Sonnet I: 26, p. 15). The poet clearly parts company here with the very popular notion that sufficient sources of wisdom and morality could be found in either the "Nature" of the Transcendentalists or the "Heart" of the Revivalists and Sentimentalists. Instead, as we see in Sonnet I: 28, he puts his faith in a rational divine being as the ultimate source of "import."

The style is consistently plain and the didacticism strengthened by a straightforward combination of clarity and supportive imagery, without the device of a moral tag such as we find often in Tuckerman's contemporaries. The tone of anguish

and resolution is supported further by the preceding poems
in the sequence, which have, in their fully realized details of
his struggles, by this point earned Tuckerman the use of gen-
eralities such as "agony to know" and "reconcilement." The
import of a natural order that hints at meaning but does not
furnish it, that gives both beauty and pain, is not to be found
in that order itself nor in the mere effort to know.

The sophistication Tuckerman had reached in conceptual-
izing this dilemma and also the skill he had achieved in the
use of poetic syntax—his power to compress great energy into
his lines through taking full advantage of the rhetorical concision (yet completeness) that the conventions of language make
possible—are revealed in two lines from an earlier sonnet in
the First Series. He both anticipates Albert Camus's famous
realization of the most poignant absurdity of the universe—
that it arouses a lust for meaning which it never fulfills—and
also gives us the existential quality of feeling that such a tragic
understanding should evoke:

> Still craves the spirit: never Nature solves
> That yearning which with her first breath began.
> (Sonnet I: 20, p. 12)

Tuckerman perseveres beyond Camus, as we see in Sonnet I:
28, to recognize that though the universe cannot answer that
yearning for meaning that it painfully calls forth in us, it has
within it means to help us reach a point where answers might
be possible from its Creator and ours. We can yield to the possibility of meaning posed by the possibility of a creator God;
we can find trust sufficient for us to accept our condition and
limitations as creatures; and we can patiently rejoice in the degree of momentum that the grief, the toil, the seeking have
provided (Hooker: "Such as the evidence is . . . such is the
heart's assent thereto"). Then we can, in an image gleaned
from precise observation of nature, stop—temporarily—the
questioning and the struggle before they impede the insight

they have prepared us for, like "A bird that shuts his wings for better speed."

Of course, Tuckerman by no means left behind what he characterizes as "straining thought and stammering word." The sonnets continue in four more series. The faith advocated in this early sonnet becomes more complex and integrated, more powerfully expressed, and thus, though perhaps somewhat tempered, more convincingly mature in later sonnets and in "The Cricket." Tuckerman goes on in the Second Series to describe the life that continues for him while he turns his "joyless verse" and "courts his grief," and he is capable of rather maudlin retelling of the specific events and feelings surrounding his wife's death before working through to a magnificent elegy (Sonnets II: 15–20) at a higher stage of resolution. The "circuitous journey" is a continuing and real growth for Tuckerman.

The influence of the poet's Anglican perspective also continues: In the third sonnet of the Fourth Series, composed sometime after 1860, Tuckerman expresses, perhaps with more balance than in the poem just discussed, the power of insight of the mind—"by its own impulse deep, / As lightning instantly enlighteneth"—but recognizes that "God lends the light we use, the strength we keep" and trusts that it can so be used

> . . . that the mystery
> Of life we touch: in cloud and wind and tree,
> In human faces that about us dwell,
> And the deep soul that knoweth heaven and hell.
>   (Sonnet IV: 3, p. 52)

In the following poem of that series, Tuckerman continues to advocate the Anglican humility and patience:

> Yes, pray thy God to give, whate'er thou art,
> Some work to be by thee with reverence wrought:
> Some trumpet note obeyed, some good fight fought,
> Ere thou lay down thy weapons and depart.

> Brood on thyself, until thy lamp be spent;
> Bind all thy force to compass and invent;
> But shun the reveries of voluptuous thought,
> Day-musings, the floralia of the heart
> And vain imaginations: else may start
> Beside the portals of thy tower or tent,
> Rending thy trance with dissonant clang and jar,
> A summons that shall drive thee wild to hear—
> Loud, as when in the dreaming conqueror's ear
> Antigenidas blew a point of war.
>
> (Sonnet IV: 4, p. 52)

In the next poem, in an image borrowed effectively from Bunyan's picture of a passage for Christian direct to hell right by heaven's gate, he reminds himself:

> Yet some there be, believers for the nonce,
> Who God's commands unwelcomely obey.
> Lost in the path, they keep the heavenward way
> But trip at absolute heaven and drop at once
> In the red gulf: not so do thou essay
> To snatch the splendor and to see the thrones.

Even if we stood in the presence of angels we could not learn

> More than 'tis love that lifts us near their state,
> And the dear fellow aid of man to man.
>
> (Sonnet IV: 5, p. 53)

Though those passages convey the great value of Tuckerman's temperate common sense about God and his own mind, perhaps the most fruitful balance that his religious perspective helped him maintain was that his view of nature was both non-Calvinist and non-Revivalist.

Perry Miller has shown that the "one clearly given truth" of Tuckerman's society (which was that of Emerson, Thoreau,

Whitman, and Melville) was "the terrific universality of the Revival," and "the dominant theme in America from 1800 to 1860 is the invincible persistence of the revival technique."[26] The Revival was essentially a Romantic phenomenon (though it denounced Romantic literature). The major figure, Charles Grandison Finney, cried, "To the dogs with the head." The revivalists made direct overtures to the *heart,* through their "spontaneous," emotional preaching, and they explicitly appealed to the "sublime." That word had become an amazingly powerful means to evoke the Americans' sense that they were engaged in the task of creating a unique solution to the problems of European Christianity through the unique resources, especially the magnificent landscape, available to them in the nation that was, above all others, nature's own. Miller claims that "it is no longer enough to dismiss the period of Romantic America as one in which too many Christians temporized their Christianity by merging it with a misguided cult of Nature." In the face of the challenge of artists like Thoreau, Melville, and Whitman, who must, "in order to protect [their] savage integrity, reject organized religion along with organized civilization," Miller claimed there still remained in his time, the mid-twentieth century, the grave task of severely reexamining the course on which the nation "so blithely embarked a century ago, when it dallied with the sublime and failed to comprehend the sinister dynamic of Nature."[27]

Tuckerman's religious tradition helped him protect his integrity without rejecting organized religion because it insulated him from the excesses of the Revival and its "cult of Nature." Even in his earlier, somewhat less accomplished, poems he was capable of precocious insights (similar to but somewhat before those in either Melville's or Hardy's poems

---

[26] Perry Miller, *The Life of the Mind in America from the Revolution to the Civil War* (New York: Harcourt, Brace, and World, 1965), 7.

[27] In one of a number of penetrating essays, "The Romantic Dilemma," in Miller, *Nature's Nation,* 207.

on the same theme) into the "sinister dynamic of Nature," which has its own heart of darkness:

> For Summer's darkest green, explored,
>   Betrays the crimson blight,
> As, in the heart of darkness cored,
>   Red sparks and seeds of light
>
> And lightning lurk, ready to leap
>   Abroad, beyond reclaim,
> To bathe a world in splendour deep,
>   Or snatch in folding flame.
>   ("The soul that out of nature's deep," p. 111)

LEGAL TRAINING was another important influence during Tuckerman's formative years, besides Anglicanism, that supported him in his resistance to Revivalist and Romantic America's exaltation of heart over head and its sentimentalization of nature. After a year away from school he returned in 1839 to the Dane Law College at Harvard. The staff consisted of the excellent team of Joseph Story, the former associate justice of the Supreme Court who had revitalized the law school with his acceptance of the Dane Professorship in 1829, and Simon Greenleaf, who came in 1833. Together they founded the present Harvard tradition of studying jurisprudence "as a science and a system of philosophy."[28]

In the popular mind the great nineteenth-century issue of head against heart focussed in part on various forms of antilegalism, particularly James Fenimore Cooper's image of Natty Bumppo, the "natural" American who knew law by instinct, not reason, and had no need for professionals. Joseph Story was one of the main figures in the counterattack that, in the first half of the nineteenth century, carried the ideal of law to a triumph in the American mind and carried the legal profes-

---

[28] Morison, *Three Centuries of Harvard*, 241.

sion to the very highest prestige.[29] Story, James Kent, and the other leaders in the effort saw themselves as saving American civilization by creating a *rationality* for law. They persistently and effectively held up the ideals of comprehensiveness, power to systematize, self-possession, and control of temper by logic—at the same time that Emerson was writing the radically antithetical *Nature*. They emphasized patient learning, not natural genius, and struggled to systematize and legitimize the common law in direct opposition to the Revivalist aim of creating in America a unique Christian utopia with its own intuitive legal formulations. They asserted what Miller calls "the comprehensive rationality of traditional wisdom against the fiat of individual statute, the heritage of civilization against provincial barbarism."

In his 1829 inaugural address at Harvard, Story celebrated the law as the highest form of erudition in America and proceeded through the 1830s to demonstrate his claim with his own massive *Commentaries,* which were overwhelming in their combination of theoretical scope and detailed illustrations, yet written, as one reviewer said, "in a simple and unpretending but pure style." Thus, for three of his most formative years Tuckerman studied in perhaps the most anti-Romantic context of the time, under the constant tutelage of a man whose writing was plain and disciplined and whose mind was comprehensive and orderly. Justice Story was so committed to law as a *"liberal* profession" that he insisted on detailed study of the history of the common law and the Greek and Latin classics, and his and James Kent's systematizing of the law achieved, in the decades before the Civil War, the form and overwhelming authority of what was characterized as "a science of vast extent."[30] Story recognized both the inductive and deductive dimensions of the law as a science and strove to keep them both in proper perspective. He insisted that students

---

[29] Miller, *Life of the Mind in America,* 100–142; my following summary is based on this excellent source.

[30] Ibid., 158–59.

acquire an understanding of how the principles of the law had been and were being formed, through a process of systematizing on the basis of the diversities of human experience. But he also required that they strive for the large knowledge and subtle insight that would allow them to apply those precedents to entirely new cases.

That emphasis on scientific method was apparently more congenial to Tuckerman's mind and therefore more telling in its influence upon him than the attraction of the law itself. After graduating from the law school in 1842, he followed the common procedure of "reading law"—apprenticeship—in the Boston office of Edward D. Sohier and was admitted to the Suffolk bar in 1844. But, as his son reports in his letter to Eaton, "Finding the practice of his profession distasteful, he soon abandoned it, devoting himself thenceforth to the pursuit of his favorite studies—literature, botany, and astronomy."[31]

Van Wyck Brooks tells us that Tuckerman's impulse was common in the younger generation of 1840: "They went off mooning in the woods. They refused to talk about railroads, banks and cotton. They had no use for Blackstone and Justice Story. They were unwilling to be 'mere' lawyers."[32] John Lothrop Motley was another who left behind his training in law for something that was, at least for him, much more important—writing *The Rise of the Dutch Republic*. Neither did Tuckerman go off to mere "mooning." In turning from a "normal" Boston career, despite what he clearly valued in his legal training under Story, he was in part responding to Emerson's important awakening impact on the younger generation, turning with them against the effects of that loss of self-esteem under Puritanism which had caused men to pursue material wealth as an evidence of worth.

Tuckerman had felt, as had many others, what he called the "fear of wrong" and the "coldness everywhere" (in "Elidore")

----

[31] July 16, 1840, Tuckerman Papers, Hugh Clark, Amherst; quoted in Bynner, *Sonnets*, 24.

[32] Brooks, *Flowering of New England*, 178.

of the Boston culture he knew. His younger (and only) sister, Sophia May Eckley, who left early to spend her life as part of the coterie of the Brownings in Rome, where she wrote a volume of poems published in England as *Minor Chords,* wrote Tuckerman after he sent her his 1860 *Poems.* She was delighted, but greatly surprised, at his talent and the person it revealed to her again, or perhaps for the first time:

> I close this volume with a thrill of pain for one thing. How is it that *you and I* so near as we were in childhood, ever lost the keynote of each other's hidden strings. Why did reserve, or timidity shut up those gates which had they been open would have found much for us both. Was it the way we were brought up, to hide our feelings, to be insincere, or was it the crushing atmosphere of Boston influences. I wonder at it all. Why none of us developed earlier, though *your* experience proves it's worth waiting for the harvest rather than to pick at the early fruit before it is ripe.[33]

Tuckerman began to withdraw from that "crushing atmosphere" in 1844, though it was not until 1847, when he found someone who could open up those gates of feeling, that he made the complete break. In the meantime, a continuing influence, his brother Edward, was shaping him in the direction of that break, but through another dimension of experience.

T UCKERMAN'S two brothers were both very close to him—encouraging him, giving him books, sharing trips with him—but Edward, the oldest, seems to have had by far the most profound influence, and he gained Frederick's continuing confidence. Edward, before Frederick, also declined to continue in law after obtaining his degree at Harvard. He had developed an interest in botany at Union College, where his ability had been soon recognized and he was appointed curator of the college museum. He continued his study of New England

---

[33] Houghton Autograph File, dated May 2, 1861.

plants (especially lichens) and in 1839 began to publish reports of his new discoveries and also some systematic studies. Much of his field work was in the White Mountains, particularly along the New Hampshire border with Canada, and he apparently took Frederick with him on some of his trips. Those experiences, together with vacations near Sag Harbor on the southeastern capes of Long Island,[34] are by far the most vivid and persistent memories and sources of images from Tuckerman's youth that he included in his poetry.

In 1841 Edward went to Europe with his family when his father was chosen as a delegate to a Bible Society meeting in England. He stayed on to study philosophy and history (he had already published scores of articles on these subjects, as well as theology and biography, in the New York *Churchman*) and, armed with letters of introduction from his mentors John Torrey and Asa Gray, to work under the most prominent European botanists, especially the famous Swedish lichenologist Elias Fries in Uppsala. Upon his return he did work so important that *The Dictionary of American Biography* judged that "In the field of American lichenology Tuckerman . . . [was] outstanding." Little study of American lichens had been done, and Edward was among the first to explore for them in New England. He did so with great thoroughness, publishing, in 1845 and 1848, progressively more comprehensive catalogues of North American lichens. His work stimulated so much study of lichens by others that the period 1847–86 has come to be known among lichenologists as the "Tuckermanian Period."

One of those who was stimulated by Edward was clearly his younger brother, Frederick, who developed a lifelong passion for exploring nature, not transcendentally but scientifically—*as a naturalist.* Something of the kind of relationship that en-

---

[34] Evidence for the exact location is Tuckerman's mention in Sonnet III:9 of Fire Place (near East Hampton) and Good Ground (now Hampton Bays), which are a few miles south and east of Sag Harbor, and a note in his copy of Bigelow's *Plants* (277) that he had found large patches of mallows on the southeastern shore of Long Island.

couraged this is revealed in a small packet inside the front cover of one of Frederick's "herbariums," scrapbooks full of pressed plants.[35] In the summer of 1851 he made a journey throughout England and Scotland with his remarkably widely-traveled mother and with the other older brother, Samuel (who was also infected with the spirit of observing, collecting, and classifying). Frederick left no journal or letters about the journey but left a book of leaves and flowers (with identifying comments) collected at the homes and graves of poets.

The packet in the herbarium, which seems unconnected to the herbarium because its contents are from the Boston area, is addressed "to F. G. T. from E. T." and contains leaves of *Parietaria pennsylvanica* "identified by E. T.," together with the further note, "This is pellitory. You remember we got it in the cave. It is not in Bigelow. The Orchis is *Gymnadenia tridentata* as I thought." "Pellitory" is a rather colloquial term identifying a plant of the nettle family whose root is used as an irritant; and "Bigelow" is Jacob Bigelow, whose *Collection of Plants of Boston and Its Vicinity* (1840) became an important companion to Tuckerman throughout his life, probably introduced to him by Edward.

Dr. Bigelow, as a young man in 1829, had published, as his first book, *Elements of Technology*. Perry Miller claims that the book "should be honored as a major document in American intellectual development," because in announcing the technological revolution Bigelow proved to be "a prophet more relevant to the later economy than either Emerson or Jefferson."[36]

The colonial mind was subservient to the European Enlightenment's theory of science as a form of natural theology—that

---

[35] Houghton MS. Am 1349 (11).

[36] Miller, *Life of the Mind in America*, 289. Again, I am indebted to the fine work of Perry Miller for much of this background material. Further excellent work, bringing useful perspective on the American ambivalence about science from the early nineteenth century down into the present, is in Leo Marx, *The Pilot and the Passenger: Essays on Literature, Technology, and Culture in the United States* (New York: Oxford Univ. Press, 1988), see especially 160–207.

is, as a calm, adoring contemplation of a grand and perfected universe ("sublime," of course); and the colonials were obsessed with science as a way of escape from provinciality into the culture of western Europe. Astronomy was the *most* sublime science. Much early American thought was characterized by a passive, self-congratulatory wonder that star-gazing evoked on the one hand (a mere man can understand the grand handiwork of the stars!) and on the other the utilitarian inventiveness burgeoning throughout the country. Aspiring naturalists, chemists, and others who wished to give science a base in careful, critical observation had a hard time getting a hearing.

However, mainly through the efforts of naturalists, this tendency in the new nation, either to look for immediate benefits or to revere science without understanding its details, gradually diminished. The new landscape of America provided an opportunity for careful observers and reflectors to contribute to universal human knowledge without being merely amateurish or idiosyncratic. As Perry Miller writes, "If there was a science in which the provincial observer could make contributions to universality by concentrating upon his restricted field of vision, it was botany, and to almost the same extent zoology."[37] In those fields work began to be done that gradually compelled European respect. But this process was complicated by natural pride, exacerbated by orators who insisted that a science equal to America's sublime landscape should be achieved *immediately.* They fostered "the dangerous persuasion that an intellect tutored by nothing more than the grandeurs of Nature could easily dispense with the rigors of Old World discipline."[38] The American inferiority complex became an incentive to greater effort, manipulated directly by those who promoted scientific societies, observatories, and such. However, it also fostered an unfortunate tendency to overcompensate with claims that democratic America's safety from superstition and authority and its sublime landscape and new,

---

[37] Miller, *Life of the Mind in America,* 281.
[38] Ibid., 283.

profuse natural resources would soon produce (already were producing) science and scientists superior to Europe's.

Of course the real superiority that emerged was not in science but technology. The revolution was well under way when Bigelow gave it that name, "technology," with his book in 1829. That same year Tuckerman's future teacher, Joseph Story, the great champion of a humane, scientific systematizing of law and its study, announced to the Boston Mechanics' Institute that the age was happily characterized by "the superior attachment to practical science over merely speculative science."[39] By 1836 a congressional committee investigating the U.S. Patent Office could with good cause claim that the outpouring of "human ingenuity" in America since the War of 1812 had been greater than in any other period of history.

Such apparently blatant nationalism and utilitarianism had been salved in the American conscience. This was achieved by a slow process in which the lure of the huge, untamed continent and the example and claims of men like Robert Fulton transformed the image of the man of science from a worshipper of divine order into that of a self-sacrificing hero who goes out to conquer the unknown for the profit of a community that is usually tardy in recognizing him. For a period, according to Miller, the question was, "Could this technological majesty join with the starry heavens above and the moral law within to form a peculiarly American trinity of the Sublime?"[40] By the time of Tuckerman's youth the real question was whether the dazzling progress of applied science might not leave flowers, stars, and moral law entirely behind.

However, Edward and the brother he influenced were not caught up in the oratory nor the technological impulses of American society. They continued in patient, humble, even joyful observation—though the poet was also able, as we shall see later, to raise questions about such impulses like those raised by Thoreau and Melville (which were, of course, like theirs,

---

[39] Quoted by Miller, ibid., 292.
[40] Ibid., 291.

ignored). He was also capable of creating in some of his poetry a sense of the dark monster being fashioned at the very cost of the American landscape itself.

The assumption that the theoretical and practical could be easily united was lost by the 1830s, and a tone of rancor and defensiveness developed. Partly through the influence of Jacksonian democratizing, pure science was denigrated as elitist and useless to the point that serious scientists realized the new utilitarianism was a threat to their whole enterprise. They had to defend themselves against the Transcendentalist and Sentimentalist attack on technology (and thus science) as vulgar and materialist and at the same time try to maintain a case for basic research on the old grounds of ultimate utility—in the face of a deep-seated aversion in much of the American community to the notion of pure, unproductive science. The defenders of science were finally reduced, in the 1850s, to trying merely to stave off vulgarization, and they joined in the hope for beneficial progress—and even the preservation of the Union—through the development of the railroad and telegraph. But science only put new implements of destruction in the hands of men. As a final irony, in Miller's view, the chief result of the Civil War was not so much an access of liberty for blacks as a great acceleration in exploitation of the American landscape by technology.[41]

The effect of Edward was not merely to make Frederick sensitive to the dangerous directions of utilitarian science and to train him to be a careful, persistent observer. Frederick's classmate, T. W. Higginson, in a memoir, gives us a picture of what Edward was like in 1846, during the time when he was having an important influence on the development of his younger brother's mind:

> I must not forget to add that at all seasons I took long
> walks with Edward Tuckerman, then the most interesting

---

[41]I am indebted, in the quick survey in this paragraph, to ideas from Miller, ibid., 321–26, and Irving H. Bartlett, *The American Mind in the Mid-Nineteenth Century* (New York: Thomas Y. Crowell, 1967), 25–31.

man about Cambridge, leading a life which seemed to us
like that of an Oxford don, and already at work on his
Latin Treatise on lichens. His room was a delightful place
to visit,—a large chamber in a rambling old house, with
three separate reading-tables, one for botany, one for the
study of Coleridge, and one for the Greek drama.[42]

Edward's friend, the preeminent biologist Asa Gray, says of
him, in a memorial written for their professional colleagues,
that he "was much more than an excellent specialist."[43] He
lists a number of central characteristics that must have been
part of Edward's influence on Frederick: "The wide reach and
remarkable precision of his knowledge, his patience and thoroughness in investigation, his sagacity in detecting affinities,
and his philosophical and rather peculiar turn of mind." He
also describes Edward's "insight":

> He caught from Fries, or he developed independently,
> and cultivated to perfection, that sense of the value of the
> indefinable something which botanists inadequately ex-
> press by the term "habit," which often enables the system-
> atists to *divine* much further than he can perceive in the
> tracing of relationships.[44]

That kind of "insight" encouraged in Frederick the transition
from the young amateur's simple but accurate observation to
the poet's search for larger significance and made it easy for
him to look to his brother not only as a mentor in botany and
religion but as a critic of his work in the years of his poetic
apprenticeship.

Asa Gray's opinion is of particular significance, because he
was a leader in the important movement to reformulate
Bacon's inductive method in dynamic terms, a movement opposed by Louis Agassiz, the famous Harvard biologist who had

______

42 Thomas W. Higginson, "Cheerful Yesterdays" (Part 4), *Atlantic Monthly*
79 (1897): 242.

43 Asa Gray, "Edward Tuckerman," *Proceedings of the American Academy of
Arts and Sciences* 31 (1886): 544.

44 Ibid., 542.

aroused much of America (including Thoreau) to an interest in observing and collecting biological specimens. Gray fought for a "natural" system reflecting organic comprehensiveness in biology rather than artificial classification. This new inductionism aimed at getting behind facts to governing forces and relating them to the human mind—but not in the simplistic forms of Agassiz, for whom glaciers were "God's great plough" and who felt nature could be fully understood by man merely because he has "an immortal soul."[45]

Gray's approach to science and nature, mediated through Edward, was crucial to Frederick's intellectual development amidst the Romantic influences: It emphasized *analogy* as an intellectual device, but it was explicitly hostile to Transcendentalism; it rejected *a priori* correspondences and preserved a balance of intuition and logic. Yet this prepared the way for some to respond, as Edward did, to the idealism of Hegel and of Coleridge, because it suggested, in Miller's words, a "dialectical process in Nature to which [the] key is found in [the] working of Mind."[46] Gray therefore praises Edward's publication on sedges in 1843 as an early evidence of his genius as a systematizer as opposed to a mere classifier, and Edward's continuing broad scholarship and writing and teaching in a variety of fields throughout his life suggest the perspective he gave his brother on the objects of nature: They are independently real but genuinely related to the human mind by a Creator of both, and they are at least potentially capable of being approached for meaning by the reason as well as the understanding.

THESE WERE THE important early influences—a personally vital religious tradition that assumed that the natural order is an orderly creation of a rational God in whose image man is created; formal training in the law under a powerful

---

45 Bartlett, *American Mind,* 29.
46 Miller, *Life of the Mind in America,* 320.

figure who emphasized broad and deep erudition and a combination of induction and deduction (and had a straightforward, simple style); and informal but thorough training in science and an accurate introduction to Coleridge, both of these provided by the same beloved and trusted brother, who was a skilled naturalist and also a devout Anglican and who sought both the accurate fact and the more general truth that might flower from it through the powers of the mind. Tuckerman, assisted by those influences, developed resources that, combined with his own gifts and intelligence, enabled him to work his way between the horns of philosophical and aesthetic dilemmas that gored most of his contemporaries; and in that process he developed the poetic craft to express and to some extent resolve those dilemmas artistically in unique ways. But his most powerful achievements had to wait for a ten-year apprenticeship that began shortly after his marriage to Hannah Jones, of Greenfield, Massachusetts, and ended with her death.

"at the moated grange resides this dejected
Mariana." m for m.

Tennyson considers this his
best poem —

(MARIANA.)

"Mariana in the moated grange."— *Measure for Measure.*

I.

WITH blackest moss the flower-plots
  Were thickly crusted, one and all,
The rusted nails fell from the knots
  That held the peach to the garden-wall.
The broken sheds look'd sad and strange,
  Unlifted was the clinking latch,
  Weeded and worn the ancient thatch
Upon the lonely moated grange.
    She only said " My life is dreary,
      He cometh not," she said ;
    She said " I am aweary, aweary ;
      I would that I were dead ! "

I am aweary. give me leave a while,
                Shaks,

Stanza I of Tuckerman's annotated copy of Tennyson's poem "Mariana." Used by permission of Houghton Library, Harvard University.

III

APPRENTICESHIP

> My father had a fine telescope and for several years he kept a journal of astronomical and meteorological phenomena and from time to time published his observations on eclipses, etc. He was a pioneer in the flora of Franklin County and the adjacent country and was recognized as an authority in that region. Twice in the fifties he visited Europe. During the second visit he was the guest of the Poet Laureate at Farringford.
>
> Dr. Frederick Tuckerman
> (Letter to Eaton, 1909)[1]

WE know nothing directly of the years between Tuckerman's admission to the bar in 1844 and his purchase of a home in Greenfield from his future father-in-law in February 1847. There is much evidence in the poems, however, that, in spite of—perhaps even partly because of—the salutary influences of his brother and of his training in law and science and his careful and extensive reading, those years were full of a growing sense of discrepancy between the young man's yearnings and the opportunities he was able to find or use in his Boston surroundings. He developed serious and very painful, nearly disabling, doubts about the purpose and potential of his life. "Elidore," a thinly disguised tribute to Hannah (whom he called Anna), ends this way: " . . . so sweet surprise / Brightened his look as that strange beauty beamed / To illume a heart, that had its grace, its power, misdeemed" (p. 97). Acquaintance with Anna (a slight, dark woman of unusual

---

[1] Copy kept by Dr. Tuckerman, in Hugh Clark papers, Amherst, Mass.

beauty, from the evidence of two small portraits) and with her rural town on the Connecticut River in the Berkshires ("No spot so fair in all the fair Estate"), later seemed a literal salvation to Tuckerman: "Such was the Beauty that dispersed his fear / And smiled, and said, 'O world-sick heart believe!' " ("Elidore," p. 97). In "The soul that out of nature's deep," a poem written sometime in the fifties, probably before Anna's death, Tuckerman describes at length the progress of his inner life:

> A soul that out of Nature's deep
>   From inner fires had birth;
> Yet not as rocks or rosebuds peep:
>   Nor came it to the earth,
>
> A drop of rain at random blown,
> . . . .
>
> Nor fortune-crowned with benefits:
>   The life was larger lent,
> Made up of many opposites
>   In contradiction blent. (p. 105)
>   ("The soul that out of nature's deep," pp. 104–105)

Though the poem is marred somewhat by the inappropriateness of the stanza form to the theme and a consequent tendency to padding, relieved only occasionally by powerful imagery and strength of statement, it nevertheless provides an insight into Tuckerman's view of himself. It also shows his clear rejection of certain Emersonian ideas about nature that had proved increasingly unsatisfactory to him. He reviews the blent contradictions within himself: "A nature affable and grand, / Yet cold as headland snow"; "liberal . . . / Though . . . to proffer slow"; "genial" but unwilling "to share the roaring cup"; "courage mild," "savage wit," and a wisdom from nature "like an Indian child." He admits his early temptation to draw from natural details "a larger import" than their revelation of such things as weather and time—that is, to find prophetic significance and moral feeling there. But his integrity and the influences I have reviewed had clearly worked together to prevent a surrender to that temptation: "He saw only a glory lost, / And what he might have been," because

> Too late he learned that Nature's parts,
>   Whereto we lean and cling,
> Change, but as change our human hearts,
>   Nor grow by worshipping;
>
> And that her presence, fair or grand
>   In these faint fields below,
> Importeth little, seen beyond
>   Our welfare or our woe. (p. 115)

The pain of this growing realization of nature's indifference, which came late if at all to Emerson, seems to have been at the heart of Tuckerman's melancholy before meeting Anna, casting as it did a terrible shadow on his naively Romantic expectations about his life and writing. His witty early portrait of himself in "A Sample of Coffee Beans" informs us that he "strangely strove to be unhappy" (p. 129). In one of his first published poems ("Picomegan," 1854) he describes his sense of a "life small grace adorning, / With lost aims and broken powers," based on the painful recognition, despite the attraction of the river and its surrounding landscape,

> That I could not gather something
>   Of the meaning and belief,
> In the voice of its triumphing
>   Or the wisdom of its grief. (p. 86)

Anna and their children brought something new to what had become an impasse. They brought a new source of faith in himself, and they brought a new kind of caring for other mortals, what he came to value as love of "the Creature." The loss of one of the children in 1848, and then especially of Anna in

1857, brought very specific forms of insight into the anomalies of nature—the existence of real pain and grief despite deep desires and good intentions. That insight almost destroyed him but brought about what was to inform his greatest writing, a continuing but fruitful struggle to resolve the ambiguity in nature. In the meantime the new situation also stirred him to embark upon activities that were to turn into a genuine apprenticeship for that later time.

THROUGH HIS early twenties, Tuckerman had been at most a poetic idler. In a letter of introduction, intended to be used on a European tour in 1844 that never materialized, Justice Story referred to "his literary attainments"; but the making of verses during this period most likely was for him, as for other well-born youth in Boston, a rather self-indulgent pastime, of which nothing has been preserved. The bracing, challenging influence of his brother, who created confrontations with real nature on real mountain slopes, helped develop a sense of the cliffs in himself ("Dim gulfs and solitudes / Of the deep mind"["The soul that out of nature's deep," p. 108]). It began a process later completed in Greenfield—a painful, maturing repentance, the slow attainment through deliberate withdrawal and isolation of what Bynner rightly calls an "austere, ennobling, gracious sobriety."[2] The record of that change, and the results in poetry, make clear that it was one of the most profound inner pilgrimages of the century.

The future poet began in an unlikely direction. He had been freed from vocational concerns by a maintenance from his father, and, as his son Frederick says, he took up with full-time effort the avocations of astronomy, meteorology, and botany. After receiving his *Poems* in 1861, Tuckerman's sister, Sophia May Eckley, wrote him, expressing delight that "you have not been 'vegetating' out your life in your Greenfield home, as

---

[2] Witter Bynner, ed., *The Sonnets of Frederick Goddard Tuckerman* (New York: Alfred A. Knopf, 1931), 23.

some people thought," making a gentle pun on his well-known botanical pursuits.[3] Indeed, he seems to have been invigorated not only to a new happiness, by the new life he began with marriage, but also to disciplined activities that at first seemed unrelated to poetry but that continued to involve him in the essential confrontation with nature and its meaning.

The journal Tuckerman started in 1847 begins with extremely detailed and knowledgeable astronomical observations made with his own fine 4.6-inch refractor telescope as well as on occasional visits to the new observatory at Cambridge.[4] (Thanks to the goading of Josiah Quincy and interest in the comet of 1843, Boston citizens had furnished the observatory with excellent equipment, including a fifteen-inch telescope, one of the largest in the world.) Accompanying the astronomical records are finely detailed, well-conceived, and nicely executed drawings of the observed phenomena, which are intended to make clear the terse symbolic notations. Tuckerman knew the language, the symbols, and what to look for; obviously he had progressed beyond the basic astronomy texts that remain in his library, and occasionally he cites explicitly the great English astronomer Sir William Herschel. By early 1848 he had established a daily schedule of observations of weather, wind, and temperature (at 9:00 A.M., 3:00 P.M., and 9:00 P.M.), which he assembled into comprehensive monthly summaries and averages, and was spending two or three hours in the very early morning of almost every day observing with his telescope. He saw Uranus, the moons of Saturn, various conjunctions and eclipses, "lunar valleys, mountains, and shadows displayed in utmost perfection,"[5] and the aurora borealis in such rare strength that, as he notes later after seeing newspaper accounts, it was also seen in Cuba, Odessa, and San Francisco.

---

[3] Dated at Florence, Italy, May 2, 1861. Houghton Autograph File.

[4] MS. Am 1349 (8), Houghton, entitled "Journal Astronomical & Meteorological for 1847 Greenfield."

[5] Ibid., May 27, 1848.

Meanwhile, other interests were working in Tuckerman, energies that moved him beyond neutral observation: A note in late 1847 reads, "Venus, at the time of observation, preceded the sun by about 35 degrees and a fine opportunity was obtained for examining this planet under high power, in the pure and still atmosphere of autumnal mornings." By the spring of 1849 there are fewer and fewer astronomical reports and, though the meteorological records continue, a new kind of note appears in September: "Blue fringed Gentian and ladies tresses." It is not certain how much it was because of his amazingly intense reading, at this time, of various poets (particularly Tennyson, as I review later) and the long walks, at all seasons and hours, in the woods and fields of Greenfield, but Tuckerman's attention clearly shifted to the more organic forms of nature: "13 Mar. 1850 Arbutus, no flowers"; "19 Mar. 1850 First Martins"; "11 April 1850 First Mayflowers Prospect Hill, snow about gone"; and in May many notes, using both common and scientific names, on the first appearances of flowers. There are no astronomical observations and only sporadic weather reports, interspersed with this other kind of note, to the end of 1850, when the journal ends.[6]

------

[6] Tuckerman continued his interest in astronomy, but he evidently combined it with a desire to go beyond mere scientific observation and to put his knowledge to various human uses. He later co-invented an ingenious apparatus for viewing the sun with a telescope; used it to observe, on May 26, 1854, a rare "annular" eclipse (one which leaves, at its maximum, a ring of the sun around the moon, rather than totally obscuring it); and published an account in the *Greenfield Gazette*. He describes the apparatus in clear, spare prose and then continues:

> The advantages of such a plan consist in the great softness of the definition, with sufficient sharpness, and an utter absence of glare and heat, so that the eye may rest unweariedly upon it for hours; the silver-white orb of the sun, as seen through flying clouds, being, apart from astronomical observation, a spectacle of no ordinary beauty.

The account—a clipping is in MS. Am 1349 (9), Houghton—mentions only the day and date, Friday, May 26; but the year must be 1854, because that is the only date during Tuckerman's life in Greenfield that such an eclipse

Despite all he had in common with Thoreau, by way of concern and achievement, Tuckerman seems at this time to have been moving in an almost opposite direction. In 1847 Thoreau *left* his retreat at the pond with an explanation that would have served as well that same year for Tuckerman when he left Boston and *entered* his retreat at Greenfield: "It seemed to me that I had several more lives to live, and could not spare any more time for that one."[7] In Thoreau's words, Tuckerman had decided not to range the world for meaning, but "to maintain himself in whatever attitude he [found] himself through obedience to the laws of his being,"[8] "not to live in this restless, nervous, bustling, trivial Nineteenth Century, but stand or sit thoughtfully while it goes by."[9]

However, Thoreau's course led to increasing *involvement* with the nineteenth century, eventually to an almost hysterical defense of John Brown that undermines the insights of *Civil Disobedience.* In the 1840s Thoreau developed his *Journals* into a powerful tool for exploration of the relation between accurate observation of nature (he also had his Bigelow and made herbariums) and his own inner life as a representative man. By the early fifties entries in the *Journal* begin to limit themselves increasingly to notations of rather sterile memoranda for the history of Concord he planned but never wrote. Perry Miller observes:

> The later portions of Thoreau's *Journal,* those after 1854, with their tedious recordings of mere observations, of measurements, of statistics, seem to attest not only the dwindling of his vitality but the exhaustion of the theory upon which he commenced to be an author in the first place.[10]

---

passed over Massachusetts. See Ritter von Oppolzer, *Canon der Finsternisse* (Vienna: n.p., 1887), 292 and plate 146.

[7] Henry David Thoreau, *Walden and Civil Disobedience,* ed. Owen Thomas (New York: W.W. Norton, 1966), 213.

[8] Ibid.

[9] Ibid., 218.

[10] Perry Miller, *Nature's Nation* (Cambridge, Mass.: Harvard Univ. Press, 1967), 182.

That "theory" is the assumption that moral law and natural law are in part analogous. Miller calls this the Romantic balance, or its "Idea" of combination, of

> fusing the fact and the idea, the specific and the general. . . . Thoreau was *both* a transcendentalist and a natural historian. He never surrendered on either front, though the last years of the *Journal* show how desperate was the effort to keep both standards aloft.[11]

Tuckerman was meanwhile moving *toward* that balance, but to a uniquely complete form of it made possible by the resources of poetry as distinct from prose. There was an easy transition from the last stages of his "Journal Astronomical and Meteorological" to beginning his first herbarium in the summer of 1850.[12] The marvelously preserved specimens of flowers and plants are identified and accompanied with notes about where they were found and about their unusual characteristics, comparisons with Bigelow's and others' earlier identifications, and so on. The entries slowly increase in frequency and then become extremely numerous in the summer of 1852, when Tuckerman spent nearly every day collecting in various places near Greenfield and, for an intense week in late August, at Phillips's Beach, apparently the longtime family vacation spot on the southeast coast of Long Island. Then the entries gradually decrease (with occasional notes alongside preceding entries indicating later findings of the same specimen) until there are only a few for 1866. The last one is dated 1868.

Such careful observation and recording of detail were of course a natural development from Tuckerman's experiences with his brother Edward. An entry in the herbarium for what must be the year 1850, "Poet's Seat Nov. 10th with E. T.," indicates that Edward visited Greenfield and joined him on his walks. In this case they walked to the western slope of Rocky

---

[11] Ibid., 183.
[12] MS. Am 1763, Houghton.

A sample from Tuckerman's well-preserved herbarium. Used by permission of Houghton Library, Harvard University.

*Poet's Seat Tower, Greenfield, Massachusetts,
erected as a memorial to Tuckerman.*

View of Greenfield, Massachusetts, from the Poet's Seat Tower.

Tuckerman's lap desk. Used by permission of Hugh Clark, Amherst, Massachusetts.

Mountain, just east of Greenfield, where Tuckerman had already designated a favorite view spot, which he continued to visit often, as "The Poet's Seat." The name survives and the place is now marked with a stone tower (with a bronze plaque about Tuckerman) reached by a paved road, but most citizens of Greenfield no longer know who "the Poet" was.

SCIENTIFIC observation continued to be an important concern for Tuckerman, but the evidence in his journal of growing attention to the seasons, and then his intense involvement with collecting and identifying for an herbarium, seem to have coincided with his first giving really serious attention to his poetry. In late fall of 1849 his first published poem, "November," appeared in Evert Duyckinck's *Literary World* and then in April 1850 came the companion piece, "April," in this same influential New York journal. In October 1850 (in the most prestigious Boston journal, Littell's *Living Age*), he published a poem about the "Mayflowers" he had noted in his journal the previous spring.

A sort of nature-sampling, and the making of herbariums to record particularly "romantic" experiences, became a Sentimentalist cliché in the fifties. Douglas Branch reports, as one example of this, a poet who, on a walk in the woods, exclaimed with so much delight over every prospect and discovery that his companion, Henry Tuckerman (Frederick's cousin and a popular essayist and art critic), was "transported with appreciation."[13] Van Wyck Brooks states that many of the young men of Tuckerman's generation wanted, in their quest, stimulated by Emerson, to reaffirm the sense and the soul, to have "a flute, perhaps, a little telescope . . . a book of Tennyson's poems to sing and recite on long walks over the . . . hills."[14]

---

[13] E. Douglas Branch, *The Sentimental Years: 1836–1865* (1934; reprint, New York: Hill and Wang, 1962), 145–48.

[14] Van Wyck Brooks, *The Flowering of New England: 1815–1865*, rev. ed. (New York: E. P. Dutton, 1937), 182.

However, Tuckerman's observations—and his reading of Tennyson—were unique in the seriousness and comprehensiveness with which he proceeded, as well as in the eventual results. For one thing, he, more than any other poet of his time and most since, achieved a basis for his claim to *know* nature. He was thus able, from the beginning of his apprenticeship, to integrate nature, with all its detail and contradictions as well as its attractiveness and "import," into his verse. He developed the "quick savage sense" that gave him confidence in the natural settings around him, and at the same time he came to know "nature's secrecies." These insights gradually increased his anxiety about the contrariety of nature, the difficulty of getting at its meaning, and at the same time they slowly became a means for him to reach and convey such meaning as was possible. At the end of his last sonnet series, written near the end of his life—an end he quite clearly anticipated—Tuckerman asked that his poetry be able to tell of one

> Whose strife was this: that in his thought should be
> Some power of wind, some drenching of the sea,
> Some drift of stars across a darkling coast,
> Imagination, insight, memory, awe,
> And dear New England nature first and last.
> (Sonnet V: 25, p. 66)

Tuckerman cultivated such skills that his poetry from the first began to realize those hopes.[15] In the meantime another pre-

---

[15] His careful self-training and consequent attentiveness to accuracy of detail not only provided resources for his own poetry but gave him a basis for responding, both critically and appreciatively, to that of others. As one example, in his copy of Browning's *Men and Women,* next to "My Star" (87), which begins "All that I know / Of a certain star, / Is, it can throw / (Like the angled spar) / Now a dart of red, / Now a dart of blue," Tuckerman has the following note: "Sirius—When the star is low and twinkles strongly, the prismatic colors may always be seen; this has not escaped other observers—And as the fiery Sirius alters hue / And bickers into red and emerald—Tennyson" (Tuckerman Papers, Hugh Clark, Amherst).

occupation—his study of the poetic tradition, especially of Tennyson—was intensifying in ways that would also profoundly affect the nature and quality of his writing.

In this period of close observation of nature, Tuckerman made that other herbarium referred to earlier, "Wild flowers gathered in Scotland and England during the Summer of 1851," which combined his desire to collect and classify with a pilgrimage in memory of his favorite authors: "Ground ivy, Gray's Grave, Stoke, May 14 . . . jessamine, Scott's cottage, July 2 . . . violet pansies, near Wordsworth's cottage, Grasmere, July 9 . . . Mallows, Stratford-on-Avon, July 15 . . . Milton's mulberry, Christ College Gardens, Cambridge, July 23." He took a sprig from a yewtree at Borrowdale on July 9, a "tree said to be over 1000," and quotes a long passage from Wordsworth about the trees of Borrowdale. From comments written in his set of Tennyson's *Poems* (1842) and in a copy of *The Princess* he purchased in London, it is probable that he had these volumes with him, noting when he visited various places Tennyson refers to in the poems (Railroad Station, Coventry, July 14, 1851; Cock Tavern, London, June 9, 1851; Trinity College Cloisters, Cambridge, July 23, 1851).

Family tradition, as Tuckerman's granddaughter relayed it to Bynner, was that Tuckerman met Tennyson on this trip. Certainly he was able to move in social and artistic circles where that might have been arranged. He was invited, for instance, to a "conversazione" at the Society of Arts and given honorary membership in The Royal Society of Literature.[16] This was probably arranged by his brother Samuel, who had just been honored with the Lambeth Degree of Doctor of Music by the Archbishop of Canterbury and was developing a fine reputation in England. However, there is no direct evidence of a meeting with Tennyson as early as this, and Mrs. Clark apparently had the two trips confused. She claimed Anna accompanied Tuckerman on the first trip and not the second,

---

[16] Tuckerman Papers, Hugh Clark, Amherst; Emerson met Tennyson at a meeting of the Royal Society of Literature in 1848.

though a set of letters from Anna to her mother, written from Europe in 1854–55 (preserved at the home of Hugh Clark in Amherst), makes it clear that was her first trip abroad. At any rate Tuckerman returned home in 1850 to a careful study of Tennyson and of the local flora and to an increasing amount of writing.

The early development of Tuckerman's poetry is difficult to chart, because it is still nearly impossible to date individual poems with certainty. Tuckerman left no personal journals or precisely dated manuscripts, and only one known letter survives that tells when he was writing what. The notebooks at Harvard do not help because the only one dated, Houghton MS. Am 1349 (2) ("Litchfield, Eng. 1854"), is a printer's copy for the 1860 publication of the *Poems* and was transcribed from other sources. The one working notebook, Houghton MS. Am 1349 (3), is a hash of fragments of poems known to be early, plus copies of "The Cricket" and other poems I assume to be late because they were not published in 1860, plus the first twelve sonnets. But under all of this, erased but mainly decipherable, is what is apparently Tuckerman's original plan for his book. It contains fewer poems and a somewhat different order that demonstrates that he probably did not write the poetry, especially the sonnets, in strictly the order we find in *Poems.*

This confusing situation led Bynner and Golden to assume that some of the sonnets in the first series were written before 1854, and it led Momaday to assume that they were all written from 1854 on. Neither case is certain. The only certain evidence of dates for the early poems is the *terminus ad quem* of their first publication and in one case a manuscript note. On that basis the latest dates for the poems that we can be certain were written a significant time before the first book was published are as follows: "November," Nov. 1849; "April," Apr. 1850; "Mayflowers," Oct. 19, 1850; "Hymn. Written upon the Dedication of the Green River Cemetery," Oct. 7, 1851; "Poesy," Jan. 1, 1852 (never published but included in a letter to Edward); "Inspiration," "Infatuation," and the sonnet,

"Again, again, ye part in stormy grief," May 22, 1852; "Hymn to the Virgin," June 1853 (not published before *Poems* but date noted in manuscript); "Picomegan," July 1854. Most of the publications are listed in a genealogical notebook written by Tuckerman's son Frederick.[17] Apparently Golden and Momaday did not see that notebook, because they did not include all of these in their references to publications. Clippings of the printed copies are in a commonplace book compiled by Tuckerman.[18]

For further evidence we must look at the poems themselves. Indications there, which we shall look at more closely later, are that the two early sonnet series were written generally in the order printed, but the underwriting in MS. 1349 (3) shows that Tuckerman structured the sonnet series for artistic rather than chronological purposes. Clear references to Anna's May 1857 death, the principal external event that enters the poems, begin about a third of the way through the first sonnet series and more vague ones occur before that. Some of the poems in other forms, which were printed together at the beginning of the *Poems* in 1860, were of course written before Anna's death, but not all of them. If we assume they are in general chronological order, that event definitely begins to affect them with "Coralie," about two-thirds of the way through, with clear references also in "Refrigerium" and "When the dim day" of the poems following.

Before 1860, then, it seems that most of the non-sonnets were written before most of the sonnets, but they cannot be entirely separated chronologically—nor, I believe, qualitatively. Tuck-

---

[17] Tuckerman Papers, Hugh Clark, Amherst.

[18] MS. Am 1349 (10), Houghton. Jeffrey D. Groves, as part of his research for his dissertation, "Frederick Goddard Tuckerman in the Canon of American Literature" (Claremont Graduate School, 1987), found the original publication in the New York *Literary World* of "November" and "April." He also did the extremely valuable work of deciphering the "underwriting" that had been erased by Tuckerman in MS. Am 1349 (3) so that changes from the original plan for *Poems* could be noted (pp. 44, 186, 192–97).

erman started early and continued throughout his life to do excellent work in both the sonnet and other forms. Tuckerman's contemporaries tended to underrate the sonnets as unskillful or too personal; more modern critics have underrated the others (except "The Cricket") as merely derivative or immature. Both attitudes are unfortunate. The sonnet, especially because of the unique variations Tuckerman introduced into it, is the poetic form in which his writing is most consistently distinguished. But "The Cricket" is only one evidence that he could do other things with great skill and power.

Undoubtedly, the earliest poems have weaknesses, and some of those weaknesses recur throughout Tuckerman's work—in his sonnets as well as elsewhere. But perhaps the most persistent impression the published poems give, from the very beginning, is of intense seriousness and integrity and steady competence throughout. There is no triviality, no irritating sense of mere conventionality nor easy sentimentality nor a consistently defective ear, such as can be found in Thoreau and Melville—or even in Emerson, who, more than those two, thought of himself as a poet. There is no sleight-of-hand with moral tags like that common to the schoolroom poets, including even Bryant; no coy idiosyncrasies, no flirting with impressive obscurities, no warped syntax, as can be found fairly often in Emily Dickinson; no ballooning rhetoric, unchastened by a metrical norm, as is common in Whitman. Most important, there are strengths throughout to match most of the strengths of those others.

The faults in Tuckerman's work are not grievous or numerous enough to explain his being neglected, though it has been commonly asserted that this is the case. The faults are there, all right, and they matter; but they are comparatively minor. There is a certain blurring that occurs because of the occasional use of formulary phrases and outright clichés (something, as with that other isolate, Dickinson, that might have been easily corrected if Tuckerman had had the benefit of good contemporary criticism). In dealing with the central subject of his grief he sometimes veers off on the one hand into Romantic vagueness or on the other into Sentimental explicitness.

Tuckerman runs into greatest trouble, in his early work, when he is experimenting with new stanzas and meters (usually taken from Wordsworth or Tennyson) and persists in them even when they are clearly not appropriate to his material. This is perhaps most evident in "Mayflowers," where the anapestic meter in the first section is too rapid for the tone and forces bad inversions ("As the sigh of the wind through the foliage heaves"), and the steady use of beheaded tetrameter in the remainder becomes painfully hammering in such a long poem. In the very long poem, "As sometimes in a grove," the alternating pentameter and dimeter, especially since Tuckerman uses a lilting two-syllable feminine rhyme on the dimeter, constantly undercuts his serious theme ("Yet ever running on the earth his course, / And sometimes into, / Chasing false fire, we fare from bad to worse; / With such a din too—"). Since he simply alternates them, he does not use those different line lengths to give effective change of pace or slight modification of tone, as he later learned to do for "The Cricket" (though he used the two-syllable rhyme quite effectively for straightforward, mild irony in "A Sample of Coffee Beans").

"The soul that out of nature's deep" has four-line stanzas in alternating rhymed tetrameter and rhymed trimeter. The short lines and insistent rhyming seem to inhibit efficient development of complex ideas and distinctions in that meditative reflection on the progress of the soul. The poem probably would have gone much better in iambic pentameter, a measure that Tuckerman learned to use with increasing subtlety and power, both in the sonnets and in other works.

Another source of difficulty in the early work is Tuckerman's use of certain Romantic and pre-Romantic conventions in the very process of rejecting others. For instance, in "The Schoolgirl" he uncritically uses the devices of mindless poetic reverie in a natural setting and of progression by free association of ideas, and he includes an apostrophe to the girl that is sententious and sentimental ("Sleep, sister! let thy faint head fall / Weary with day's long-fading gleam; / And blessed Gloom"). At the same time he rejects the common Romantic notion "That in the unreasoning progress of the world / A wiser spirit is at work for us" and effectively creates a sense of the attraction and danger of the realms of nature and the unconscious, themes that he was able to develop surely and magnificently in "The Cricket."[19] Most of the blemishes in Tuckerman's early work, then, seem to be those inevitable in apprenticeship: experimental modes not adequately worked through and forms of influence not yet fully digested nor fitted to his own proper voice.

T U C K E R M A N ' S early process of working with models and trying to find his own voice is revealed most directly in a unique letter to Edward dated January 1, 1852. The full significance of this letter has not been previously noticed. The reason is that in the extremely unfortunate mishandling of Tuckerman's effects after his death,[20] or many years later when the papers were sorted and some given to the Houghton Library, the two parts of the letter became separated from each other. One page—which includes the date, the address to Edward, and Tuckerman's initials—was placed in the Autograph File; but a second page, probably because it contains a copy of a poem Tuckerman was asking Edward to criticize, was placed in Houghton MS. Am 1349 (7).

Momaday published most of the second part of the letter in his description of the Houghton Manuscript items in Appendix II of his edition of the *Complete Poems,* but he was unable to

---

[19]I am indebted here to Janet A. Mueller, "Frederick Goddard Tuckerman: A Critical Study" (Master's thesis, Stanford Univ., 1960), 16–20, for her analysis of "The Schoolgirl."

[20]According to his granddaughter; see Samuel A. Golden, *Frederick Goddard Tuckerman: An American Sonnetteer,* Univ. of Maine, Bulletin 54, no. 12 (April 1952): 11.

date it or identify its addressee, information which greatly increases the significance of the letter. The entire letter is quoted below as it should be read (including parts that Momaday omitted from the poem and the letter and two typographical corrections of Momaday's version—"gleaming" for "gleaning" in line 6 and "beheld" for "behold" in line 15). This dates precisely a certain stage of Tuckerman's writing and analysis and also indicates more fully Edward's role in Tuckerman's development. In addition to internal evidence, a comparison of ink and writing indicates that the parts definitely go together.

[Part 1, Houghton Autograph File]

Greenfield, Jan 1st 52

Dear Edw,

Anna and myself wish you a Happy New Year this pleasant Morning—nothing *new* excepting this has occurred since I wrote, except a letter from Parkman stating that he is anxious to get home. I send a Sonnet written a little while since. I thought of sending it to one of the magazines, but am not sure regarding the best way of concluding it. I have also retouched a previous piece, please glance over them and let me know what you think, this week if possible, as I shall probably not be here next, and believe me in haste

Yr aft bro,   F G T   over...

I do not wish to hurry your critical examination but the longer piece you have already—and the sonnet is a small matter.[21]

[Part 2, Houghton MS. Am 1349 (7)]

I have endeavoured to retouch these lines, as I do not believe I can recast them in better shape—and do not want to waste the stuff.

---

[21] Though the copy of the sonnet in the letter has been lost, it was quite likely "Again, again, ye part in stormy grief," published in *Living Age,* May 22, 1852.

Poesy

Thou are not fled—
Stunned by the din of this mechanic age;
Nor chilled by wayward stress,
Of wind and cloud to silentness:
Nor in a poet's hermitage,   [5]
Hidest thy gleaming head;
Though still unwooed thy form the sight evades;
But here amid our glens and dark blue scenery,
And rivulets frilled with fern, and soft cascades,
Rustling down steps of sandstone ceaselessly,   [10]
And rocks and banks of pines,
Thy solemn beauty wanes and shines;
Have I not seen thee in the river glades?
Or from a mountain gallery leaning down,
Mid depths of green beheld thy starlike crown,   [15]
And vaguely caught the wonder of thy song?
While crag and stream and foliaged throng,
Glittered as tinted by the morning's wand;
When the fair West with breath the sense o'erpowers,
From orchards blanched with bloom, and all   [20]
    the grassy land,
Is dashed with flowers—

[page break]

Or on a wild hillside
Tanned with the fallen fibres of the pine;
Have I not found thee in the year's decline,
When waste and wide,   [25]
The winds have shattered October's pride
In the weak sunshine sitting mournfully? etc. —

The first six lines I have not touched, the 7th is perhaps an improvement,—8th—"dark blue scenery" I cannot improve, "cascades" I do not like very well but I suppose may be allowed for rhyme's sake at least, "Rustling" you may disapprove of (10th). I retain this word because in the first place it suggested itself naturally, when listening to

the "soft cascade," secondly because I find upon examination that Mr. Emerson has observed it

> By Fate, not option frugal nature gave,
> One sound to pine grove and to waterfalls,

and thirdly because I discovered the other day in an old
ballad "The Worme of Lambeton" a beautiful use made
of this identical expression.

> The monster slept on an island crag
> *Lulled* by the *rustling chear*
> Which eddied turbid at the base,
> Tho elsewhere smooth and clear.

There I think I have beaten you on that—same line
"ceaselessly" I must have an adverb here and cannot find
a better one—without "restlessly" or "tremulously" may
do. Your objection that the current *cannot* always flow I do
not think fair—"I watched the streamlet's ceaseless
flow"—"And the great River over its rocks ceaselessly
bursts and raves" Shelley. I suppose the writer means
while he is looking at them, or listening, 11th, "banks of
pines"—I mean by this not only "piny banks" but real
banks as they appear in the distance—"Like the sweet
South, Which breathes upon a bank of violets." And
Ossian talks about "hills of grass"—"upland throng,"
line 17th I have changed, but why is the original expression more obscure than "mountain throng" which is in
common use. I do not understand your objection to the
20th and 21st lines as it originally stood—"When the fair
West with breathings overpowers"—is it "From orchards
blanched with bloom"—because overpowers is an active
verb? Then may not the substantive be understood? Or
may it not be used as a neuter verb, as is often done in
poetry—as, the picture pleases—"ripe with flowers," I
have altered—23rd line "Tanned with the fallen fibres"—
you do not like. I can only say that it seems to me new
and expressive. Some poet I forget who, Shakespeare I
think, speaks of the pines as "waving their fibrous tops."
Mr. Emerson calls the leaves "strings" and Longfellow

> speaks of the "carpet of golden threads," and I think in
> all humility mine as good as either. 26th line is designed
> to be shorter by one syllable than the succeeding. 27, the
> verb here is "sitting" not "flitting." The greater part of
> the remainder I mean to re-write, but do you think the
> above is improved, or worthy of being preserved from the
> burning.

We have here a large part of one of the earliest poems, one
Tuckerman decided not to publish, written at an important
stage in the development of his thinking and his craft. The
theme is a simple, rather common one: Poetry has not been
defeated by the burgeoning of utilitarian science in this
mechanic age of America nor has it given itself over to the
popular Sentimentalists—"a poet's hermitage"—but remains
in potential, "still unwooed," here in New England's "dark
blue scenery." It is an important theme in Tuckerman's working out, at this early point, of his own purposes and means.
Tuckerman here turns some of that scenery where "Poesy" resides into poetry, with some amateurish fumbling but also with
some of the developing skill that he later used in his lifelong
work to realize the potential that he believed to be latent in the
New England landscape.

The letter implies that this is one of a series to Edward in
which Edward was probably playing a unique role, related to
and developing from his past influences on Tuckerman's reading and scientific study of plants: Edward was the one confi-
dant and critic and encourager in this vocation to which
Tuckerman was now applying himself with a great intensity.
The poet was at a stage (revealed even more fully in his reading, which I examine later) where he was very conscious of the
poetic tradition and the authority of its practitioners, his
models, especially regarding images and language. He valued
his brother's opinions. But he was also clearly beginning to
develop some confidence in his own instincts and judgment,
and with good reason.

There are problems with this fragment of "Poesy," evidence
that Tuckerman was still heavily influenced by the conven-

tional formulations and poeticisms and the cumbersome per-
sonifications of his models:

> Nor in a poet's hermitage,
> Hidest thy gleaming head;
> Though still unwooed thy form the sight evades.

These models include Keats, whose "Ode to a Nightingale" is
strongly echoed here—and awkwardly so, not with the supportive subtlety he later used to echo that same poem in "The
Cricket." But Tuckerman's own voice, which predominates
more and more as his poetry matures, is beginning to emerge:
"Rustling down steps of sandstone ceaselessly."

That emerging maturity is most apparent in the last nine
lines, which Momaday did not print. In the letter, Tuckerman
is right in his judgments that differ with his older brother's,
especially about the lines that are the most surely in his own
voice. However, as he is anxious to show, he is also supported
by precedent in the poetic tradition and accepted uses of the
language: As he claims, "rustling" *does* work for the sound of a
small, cascading set of falls, and it is particularly effective in
this line because it helps achieve a slight imitative effect, both
as a trochee in the first position to give a run and fall to the
first four syllables and in adding to the uneven rustle of the
sibilants throughout the line—which means that Tuckerman is
again right in thinking that "ceaselessly" is the best adverb for
the line end.

Tuckerman is also right about the acceptable use of "o'erpowers" as a "neuter verb" (though the line itself is not a good
one), and he is right that his image of the hillside "tanned with
the fallen fibres of the pine" is "as good as either" of the precedents he cites. (It seems, in fact, superior, an evocative as
well as an accurate description of a unique pinewoods detail.)
He is right that the twenty-sixth line should be read as iambic
pentameter, with "shat-ter-ed" prolonged and given two accents.
That reading achieves the best imitative effect (isolating the
explosion of "shat-") and gives him further opportunity to ex-

periment with juxtaposing of lines of varying length (2-, 3-, 4-, and 5-foot lines in this fragment)—a device, I repeat, which he uses to exceptionally good effect much later in "The Cricket." Certainly these are not major achievements; but they are rare enough to invite our respect, and they reveal a poet in the making who has considerable talent that is being carefully developed.

A MORE finished performance from what must be almost the same time as "Poesy" is "Inspiration," probably written in the next few months, before being published on May 22, 1852. The voice is assured, calm, direct. The use of natural details is restrained and precise and complements the clearly developed theme, which is carried both discursively and through one fully developed and effective metaphor: the great poets as luminaries in the heavens, overwhelming him with hopelessness that he can measure up as well as inspiring him to faith in the possibilities of poetry and of himself. Tuckerman has already learned, we see here, the use of strongly run-over lines ("we walk and wind / Unheedful") and varied placement of the strongest pause within each line to give fluidity and sufficient forward motion to the rhymed couplets and to help create the feeling of the movement of the thought. He is also able to make effective and unusual use of a short stanza in a new meter and line length at the end of each section, both as a change of pace and to summarize and bring to an end the line of argument:

> The common paths by which we walk and wind
> Unheedful, but perhaps to wish them done,
> Though edged with brier and clotbur, bear behind
> Such leaves as Milton wears or Shakespeare won.
> Still, could we look with clear poetic faith,
> No day so desert but a footway hath,
> Which still explored, though dimly traced it turn,
> May yet arrive where gates of glory burn:

> Nay, scarce an hour of all the shining twelve
> But to the inmost sight may ope a valve
> On those hid gardens where the great of old
> Walked from the world and their sick hearts consoled
> Mid bowers that fall not, wells which never waste,
> And gathered flowers, the fruit whereof we taste:
> While, of the silent hours that mourn the day,
> Not one but bears a poet's crown away,
> Regardless or unconscious how he might
> Collect an import from the fires of night,
> Which, when the hand is still, and fixed the head,
> Shall tremble starlike o'er the undying dead;
>
>   And, with a tearful glory,
>   Through the darkness shadowing then,
>   Still light the sleeper's story
>   In the memories of men. (pp. 80–81)

Speaking, as almost always, directly in the first person, Tuckerman reviews how the great models for his thought and writing (which as I later demonstrate he had been reading, criticizing, comparing, and building upon with great, possibly unique, thoroughness) have used common paths like those available to himself. By this means they finally reached into Platonic realms of perfect, incorruptible reality to "collect an import"—from which they could produce poetry that through their victories in thought and language improve our own paths. We can in each hour of the day find avenue into those realms, but (and here Tuckerman introduces the poem's energizing ambiguity) the night bears these "crowns" away. Though we may gain an import from the fires of night, it will "*tremble* starlike" with a "*tearful* glory" to the dead poet's memory. For Tuckerman in this poem the Platonic realms are real and deeply attractive but not adequate to account for experience in nature. The rest of the poem shows precisely why the import *he* collects also trembles:

And such are mine: for me these scenes decay:
For me, in hues of change, are ever born
The faded crimson of a wasted day,
The gold and purple braveries of the morn,
The life of Spring, the strength that Summer gains,
The dying foliage sad September stains;
By latter Autumn shattered on the plain,
Massed by the wind, blent by the rotting rain;
Till belts of snow from cliff to cliff appear,
And whitely link the dead and newborn year.
All these, to music deep, for me unfold,
Yet vaguely die: their sense I cannot hold,
But shudder inly as the years drop by
And leave me lifting still a darkened eye.
Or if from these despondingly I go
To look for light where clear examples glow,

Though names constellate glitter overhead
To prompt the path and guide the failing tread,
I linger, watching for a warmer gleam,
While still my spirit shivers and I seem

> Like one constrained to wander
> Alone till morning light,
> Beneath the hopeless grandeur
> Of a star-filled winter's night.

The reality of change and decay are too great for this student of actual, not ideal, nature. The poem both convinces us of his feeling and establishes that reality in a marvelously full but concise evocation of the seasons. A comprehensive image of mortality is contained in two lines that tell of the "dying foliage" that is

By latter Autumn shattered on the plain,
Massed by the wind, blent by the rotting rain.

Such usage enlivens and empowers language, not through increasing the ingenuity or amount of its metaphoric usage, but by such skillful choice and placing of words as to control their denotations precisely to the purpose at hand. It is, as Samuel Johnson said in his classic definition of "strength" in the poet Denham, to "exhibit the sentiment with more weight than bulk."[22]

Tuckerman knew Denham and Goldsmith and Pope and other eighteenth-century poets who preserved such values in their writing. He also knew Johnson's criticism and, likely enough, this specific commendation. He was already working his way out from under the influence of the later pre-Romantics and Romantics who, in trying to open poetry up to new realms of feeling, engendered a breakdown in the poem's rational structure and a loss of respect for the nature and potential of language as intrinsically bound to such a structure. They turned to an associational progression and piling up of uncontrolled images which brought the vague, easy feelings of Sentimentalism or the blankness of obscurity. Tuckerman, as part of his anti-Romantic reaction, does not move backward in his poetry toward didactic plainness. He is susceptible to the Romantic yearning to connect meaningfully with nature, with the detailed world outside "the inmost mind" of Platonic ideals, and thus he cannot eschew metaphor. He develops in this poem an early form of the combination of pure diction and strong syntax with metaphoric effectiveness that he was later to develop into an instrument that gave unique unity and power to these qualities.

---

[22] Quoted in Donald Davie, *Purity of Diction in English Verse* (1952; reprint, New York: Schocken Books, 1967), 63; in this book and in his *Articulate Energy: An Enquiry into the Syntax of English Poetry* (1955; reprint, New York: Harcourt, Brace, 1958), Davie describes with admiration and convincing examples the purity of diction and strength of syntax that were among the chief glories of English verse until the later eighteenth century, that then came under neglect and attack in much Romantic and Symbolist verse, and that have been defended or practiced by only a minority in the modern period.

Tuckerman shows, already in "Inspiration," that he has the weight without bulk, the careful thinking, graceful concision, and artful arrangement that win the mind to consent. But he also has the images that win the heart. Both kinds of qualities are carried in certain recurring two-word combinations, self-contradictory oxymorons like "tremble starlike," and "tearful glory." If read carefully (especially the *second* time when, as we should, we know the end from the beginning and feel the quiet irony that starts even with the title), these phrases build our anxiety to that perfect climax of ambiguity, "hopeless grandeur," at the end.

Tuckerman's anxiety is no formulary pose; the details of the objective, ever-changing world of particulars are unavoidably real, but "their sense I cannot hold." The past achievements of "names constellate" may "glitter overhead" out of the "darkness shadowing," but they are objects too—cold, alien as the stars under which his spirit shivers and watches for a warmer gleam, for some meaning that he might be able to connect himself to in the rising sun. But the sun's warmth—though it, too, is a star—brings corruption: As we have already been reminded earlier in the poem, "The gold and purple braveries of the morn" are ephemeral.

The further analogy with religious faith is made explicit in the final, summarizing stanza and deepens our feeling for the seriousness of the ambiguity. The stars in their ancient orderliness may argue for faith in an ultimate meaning in the universe and thus for a purpose for man, but just as powerfully their immense, impersonal momentum argues against such meaning and chills the soul. The argument of the poem and the supporting metaphor are deceptively straightforward but exceedingly subtle in implication and emotional shading. The theme and tone are very similar to that of Dickinson's "The Moon upon her fluent Route." Tuckerman's poem is less directly powerful than hers in pursuing the analogy with religious faith, but it uses its greater length effectively to achieve richer development and complexity of feeling, and to explore the analogy with *poetic* faith as well.[23]

One line of the poem, descriptive of the "undying dead" who have written great poetry, is particularly reminiscent of the Dickinson of poems like "The last Night that She lived" and " 'Twas warm—at first—like Us." As are the best lines in those poems, Tuckerman's line is marked by diction and syntax that are the work of genius:

Which, when the hand is still, and fixed the head,

The two synecdoches for death release enormous energy through the conveyed sense of words excluded or immutably arranged, after long struggle, by the discipline that meter requires and brilliant inventiveness with syntax allows. Tuckerman does not give us, for instance, "When the hand is stilled and the head is fixed," as Whitman with his free syntactical rhythms might well have had it. The rich suggestiveness of the descriptive "still" and "fixed" is chastely controlled by perfect placement: "still" gives the end of activity—peace—but it also gives impenetrable, alien immobility, an image of the body in the coffin, its hands adamantly placed. That feeling is made certain and exact by "fixed," which suggests the finality of both the mortician's adjustment of the head in the coffin and his earlier cosmetic grooming to retard and mask the head's irrevocable decay. "Fixed" also denotes the mind's incomprehensible cessation—but without any intrusion of the other meaning of "fixed" (ministrations from the psychiatrist), such as the line I imagined for Whitman surely invites through its very small difference in syntax.

This all seems simple enough—that is, until one has worked long hours to pack that kind of energy into a line. Such are the

---

[23] Emily Dickinson, *The Complete Poems of Emily Dickinson,* ed. Thomas H. Johnson (Boston: Little, Brown and Co., 1960), 639. A short but helpful analysis is in Yvor Winters, *Forms of Discovery: Critical and Historical Essays on the Forms of the Short Poem in English* (Denver: Alan Swallow, 1967), 270–71.

subtle victories that language in metered verse makes possible and that a good poet must care to win. Such a line wins life for the whole passage, for the poem, and for the poetic tradition; it lives in the mind and on the page for other minds in such a way that it is in itself the reason why the absolutely dead poets are still undying. Great poetry is one form of "import from the fires of night,"

> Which, when the hand is still, and fixed the head,
> Shall tremble starlike o'er the undying dead.

The theme of "Inspiration" is one of the great ones, but it is seldom handled this masterfully. Another place where it is well handled, and with a remarkably similar syntax and feeling, is in the closing passage of "Time and the Garden" by Yvor Winters (who had not read Tuckerman's poem):

> The passion to condense from book to book
> Unbroken wisdom in a single look,
> Though we know well that when this fix the head,
> The mind's immortal, but the man is dead.

But Winters's faith is more certain at this point than Tuckerman's; it does not admit the tremble.[24]

---

[24] Yvor Winters, *Collected Poems* (London: Routledge and Kegan Paul, 1960), 120. While Winters's faith is more certain here, Tuckerman's is not absent, though it is based on a very subtle consolation. John Raymond Getz, in his dissertation on "The Originality of Frederick Goddard Tuckerman" (Univ. of Pennsylvania, 1977), uses the work of Harold Bloom to identify a sophisticated form of allusion ("transumptive") which does not merely include or suggest a source but possesses and modifies it (i.e., "The precursors return in Milton, but only at his will, and they return to be corrected," Harold Bloom, *A Map of Misreading* [New York: Oxford Univ. Press, 1975], 142). Getz argues that "Inspiration" is a testament to Tuckerman's "alienation from both nature and the poets who have gone before," that his "picture of the shattered and shattering world is so convincing that in seeming to undercut himself he actually undercuts his predecessors" (38–39). But this is perhaps making Tuckerman *too* modern, almost an early deconstructionist, and

T U C K E R M A N ' S search for an acceptable poetic faith was conducted in isolation and with an integrity that brought great anguish as he struggled, beyond the resources provided by his literary and cultural training, to respond truly to his full experience. He was not entirely alone nor inclined to be self-sufficient. We have seen the influence of Edward, which continued into these years. Tuckerman's rather idiosyncratic use of classical allusions and private coinages and his occasional lapses, in even the finest work, may make us wish he could also have been part of a supportive *literary* culture, with a few friendly critics to point out problems and help him think certain things through more fully. Yet it is impossible to imagine who among his contemporaries, except possibly Dickinson, could actually have been helpful. Like Dickinson, he needed and deserved to be alone.

However, even more than Dickinson, Tuckerman was extremely well-read, and his notes on his reading reveal a highly unusual mind and tell us a great deal—more than anything else except the poetry—about that mind and its resources and the processes by which it became the mind of a fine poet. In

---

Getz's very language participates in a self-deconstructive ingenuity of which Tuckerman would never have been guilty ("In this final use of the star image Tuckerman tropes his predecessors' trope to make it his own," [39]). Tuckerman's anxiety is the central Romantic one, related to the poststructuralist ones, but not exactly the same or as extreme. More helpful in understanding its operation in this poem is M. H. Abrams's description of a characteristic Romantic poetic form (see "Structure and Style in the Greater Romantic Lyric," in *Romanticism and Consciousness: Essays in Criticism,* ed. Harold Bloom [New York: Norton, 1970], 201–29), which Tuckerman uses in many of his poems (see my later discussion of "The Cricket") and which Bloom summarizes in a way that seems to me exactly descriptive of the sophisticated combination of anxiety and faith in "Inspiration":

> First, an initial vision of loss or crisis, centering on a question of renewal or imaginative survival; second, a despairing or reductive answer to the question, in which the mind's power, however great, seems inadequate to overcome the obstacles both of language and of the universe of death, of outer sense; third, a more hopeful or at least ongoing answer, however qualified by recognitions of continuing loss. (Bloom, *Map of Misreading,* 96)

the front of the copy of Irving's *Beauties* that Edward gave Frederick when he was fourteen, the older brother advised, "Read, mark, learn, and inwardly digest." That is precisely what the young Tuckerman did, with Irving and a remarkable number and variety of other authors.

When I first began to examine the surviving volumes from Tuckerman's library—especially the Tennyson, on which he lavished the most attention—I soon noticed his unusual ability to pick out allusions and cite their sources. My awareness advanced to astonishment when it gradually became apparent that he was operating almost completely from memory and with nearly unique perspective on the poetic tradition.[25] For example, on page 17 of his copy of the 1851 edition of *The Princess*,[26] Tuckerman underlines *twinn'd* in the line "Together, twinn'd as horse's ear and eye"; then he quotes Milton's similar usage of that unusual word, "true liberty / Is lost, which ever with pure reason dwells / Twinn'd . . ."; and finally he adds "this word has an older signification also, i.e., parted,—made two of."

As other examples pile up, some extremely recondite, it seems certain he had *The Oxford English Dictionary*, or at least some good concordances, at hand—but of course none of these was available in the 1850s. The only other possibility is an incredibly retentive mind and long, careful study. As one

---

[25] N. Scott Momaday first called these volumes to my attention. He had been visiting in Amherst when Mrs. Orton Loring Clark, the poet's granddaughter, died; he then helped make certain these books were retained in the family when there was real danger that another careless estate settlement might have again resulted in the loss of precious materials vital for an understanding of Tuckerman. Most of the Tennyson volumes (both editions of the 1842 *Poems*, the 1848 Boston edition of *The Princess*, and the 1855 London first edition of *Maud and Other Poems*) had already been placed in the Houghton Library by Mrs. Clark, but the 1851 London copy (the most significantly marked) of *The Princess* and thirty-three other volumes—clearly only a small part of Tuckerman's original library—have remained in the family, until now not examined by students of Tuckerman. These volumes, and other informative memorabilia and letters at the home of Hugh Clark in Amherst, are in the process of being donated to the Houghton Library.

[26] This is the one (London: Moxon, 1851) still in the Tuckerman Papers, Hugh Clark, Amherst.

ponders these notes, which demonstrate and refer to the work of many years of pious apprenticeship to the craft of poetry and its tradition, an unusual intellect and spirit are revealed. I will now review a substantial sampling of this material in order to provide a better base for responding to the poetry which that mind and spirit produced.

In his markings Tuckerman shows an abiding carefulness about the meaning and use of words, and thus he anticipates important qualities in his own poetry. He compares Tennyson's use of "fulmined" with Milton's.[27] Longfellow's claim that "the farm was enclosed by . . . the flowing *wall* of a river" moves him to comment, "There seems to be no authority for this, in any derivation; when the Israelites crossed the Red Sea the waters were like a wall upon the right hand and upon the left, but that means really like a wall, which a river is not."[28] At the side of Tennyson's "You . . . have . . . wrong'd and lied and thwarted us—" he writes, "I do not remember to have seen this verb before used actively."[29] By 1857 Tuckerman's confidence is such that he responds to Browning's "such an One" with, "Why, such *an* One? We say an hour, because hour has the vowel sound, so *one,* having the sound of wun, should be prefixed by a"; and when he comes across the usage a second time thirty pages later he jots "*a* you cockney!"[30] He marks Tennyson's use of "many-sided mind" thus: "This expression (from the German, I believe) has for a long time been appropriated to Shakespeare," and he comments on his use of "myriad-minded" thus: "This epithet is Coleridge's applied (from the Greek) to Shakespeare"—and then he quotes the Greek.[31]

----

27 Tennyson, *Princess* (London, 1851), 35.

28 Henry Wadsworth Longfellow, *Kavanagh* (Boston: Ticknor, Reed, and Fields, 1849), 74, in the Tuckerman Papers, Hugh Clark, Amherst.

29 Tennyson, *Princess* (London, 1851), 101.

30 Robert Browning, *Men and Women* (Boston: Ticknor and Fields, 1856), 74, 105, in Tuckerman Papers, Hugh Clark, Amherst.

31 Tennyson, *Poems* (Boston: Ticknor and Fields, 1842), 1, both on page 37; the two-volume set is in the Houghton Library.

One of Tuckerman's notes reveals his conviction, which he conforms to in his poetry over the objections of his contemporary critics, that Americans should write poetry true to their own language and its sources in the American landscape and experience. W. E. Channing has a line, "As this wide sun flows on the mere," which moves Tuckerman in 1853, when he is midway in his apprenticeship, to exclaim, "What a pity for New Englanders to use these foreign and intensely local words, as linn, mere, wold, etc., which represent nothing here—whereas run, pondhole, and plain *have* a significance however humble."[32]

The many notes in his copy of Bigelow's *Plants*[33] show that Tuckerman continued his observation of natural detail with the same extraordinary care as in his reading, sharpening his multisensual perception. That trained ability, combined with careful analysis and thinking through of distinctions and relationships, makes his images in the poetry fresh but not esoteric or obscure—unusual but convincing. Under Bigelow's description of "Chequer Berry" (p. 54) as having four segments in the corolla, he writes, "sometimes five and even six"; under "Painted Trillium" (p. 151) he notes, "I have found this plant, actually contradicting its nature and name, in three instances: i.e., the petals, sepals, and leaves were in fours; otherwise resembling the genus: Wood[34] recounts a still more singular metamorphosis."

Tuckerman sometimes, on the evidence of his observation, contradicts Bigelow; more often he adds information, particularly by opening up new means of identification, often through the unusual means of smell and taste: "Water Avons" (p. 236)—"The most noticeable feature in this plant, the plumose

---

[32] W. E. Channing, *Poems* (Boston: Little, Brown and Co., 1843), 11; copy in Tuckerman Papers, Hugh Clark, Amherst. This is one of the few volumes in which he clearly dates the time of his reading.

[33] Jacob Bigelow, *A Collection of Plants of Boston and Its Vicinity*, 3d ed. (Boston: Little, Brown and Co., 1840); copy in Tuckerman Papers, Hugh Clark, Amherst.

[34] Probably Alphonse Wood, *A Classbook of Botany* (Boston, n.p., 1845).

[feathery] style, is not mentioned in this description"; "Spotted Pyrola" (p. 186)—"This species is fragrant while the others are not"; "Caducous Polygala" (p. 282)—"The root of this plant has an aromatic taste and smell not noticed by botanists, I believe"; "Yellow Ladies' Slipper" (p. 350)—"Two species of this I believe; at any rate the flowers differ in size: the small being slightly fragrant." Botanists tell me he was later proven right about the "two species."

Tuckerman was not merely spending his time looking and tasting and smelling with botanical precision. His notes indicate that plants were brought to him for identification from a large area around. In addition to his careful preserving of dried specimens, he expertly developed a garden that a letter by his son implies was magnificent and precious to him, and the garden was in part made up of wild species. "Tall Ladies' Slipper" (Bigelow, p. 51)—"This plant I took from a mountain swamp in 1852; and after the second year, it has flowered every season up to the present period 1866; the spot is cold, wet and shaded, with a north exposure, and receives the drainage of the garden."

Tuckerman was continually alive to a larger perspective. "Tall Orchis" (p. 342)—"For a description of this plant which is beautiful see Wood"; "Vipers Bugloss" (p. 73):

> Last summer in riding over the Shelburne Range I came, for the first time, upon a great quantity of this flower, filling and bordering the road; and was delighted with its beauty; remembering and recognizing St. Pierre's description of the plants, "rising like superb candlesticks from a central vacuum, and rearing towards Heaven their prickly arms, loaded with lamps of violet-coloured flowers."

Through the notes in various books we also see something of the development of Tuckerman's poetic judgment. Apparently quite early he aptly criticizes John Gay for "false meter" and excessive alliteration; beside W. E. Channing's horrible line, "For O death stands to welcome thee sure" (in iambic pentameter verse!), which someone else (probably Edward) had suitably changed to "For O death surely stands to welcome thee," Frederick has the tart comment (written in 1853) that merely adding an accented "ly" "would be more Channingiannesian" ("For O death stands to welcome thee surely"). And Channing's (serious) line, "The Bible is a book worthy to read," moves him to suggest, "This as a *line of poetry* should stand beside that ethereal one in Festus, 'It is time that something be done for the poor.' "[35] As for Longfellow, the copy of *Kavanagh* he received in 1849 is carefully read and marked, but somewhat critically as cited above; *The Golden Legend,* given him by Anna in 1852, seems little read and has no notes; and *The Song of Hiawatha,* received in 1855, was barely opened.

On the other hand, Tuckerman gave *increasing* attention to Tennyson. Tennyson was extremely popular in America. Even before he was well known in England, his work was pirated by American newspapers, and Tuckerman probably began to read him at Harvard, if not earlier. Tuckerman's commonplace book includes handwritten copies of some of Tennyson's poems, especially sonnets, that had been published in 1832 and 1833.[36] In 1845 Tuckerman purchased a copy of the two-volume American edition of Tennyson's *Poems* (Boston: Ticknor and Fields, 1842), and in 1850 he received a copy of the identical British edition (London: Moxon, 1842) from his brother Samuel. These two sets, heavily marked over a period of years, with some comments copied or repeated from one to the other, are especially interesting because they record Tennyson's own comments about several of his poems, made during Tuckerman's three-day visit to the famous poet in January 1855.

Samuel Golden, for his 1967 study, only noticed the Moxon edition, which was then in the possession of Mrs. Clark in Amherst.[37] Tuckerman's copy of the American edition of *The Princess* (Boston: Ticknor and Fields, 1848), inscribed with his signature and the date, February 10, 1848, is in the Houghton Library, as is the autographed copy of the first edition of *Maud*

---

[35] These two examples are from Channing's *Poems,* 136 and 36.
[36] MS. Am 1349 (10), Houghton, apparently completed in the 1850s.
[37] Golden, *Tuckerman: An American Sonnetteer,* 43.

and Other Poems (London: Moxon, 1855) given him by Tennyson. But neither of these volumes has any particularly valuable notes (mainly marks alongside certain—favorite?—passages). However, a very extensively marked copy of the fourth edition of *The Princess* (London: Moxon, 1851), inscribed June 27, 1851, and, on the evidence of the notes, probably carried by Tuckerman on his literary pilgrimage through England that summer, remains with the Tuckerman Papers at Hugh Clark's home in Amherst. Internal evidence in these volumes shows that Tuckerman also had available to him earlier and later publications, both of individual poems in various periodicals and of the books. For instance, he copied in the back of his copy of volume two of the 1842 Ticknor and Fields edition of Tennyson's *Poems* the full text of Tennyson's "To E. L. on His Greece," which appeared first in the 1853 *Poems,* and also "Buonaparte," which was published only in the 1832 *Poems,* or possibly also in American publications.

T U C K E R M A N ' S notes in the surviving Tennyson volumes from his original, much larger library yield a great deal of information about both Tuckerman and Tennyson. First, there are the records of comments made by Tennyson as they read his poems together in 1855.[38] For example, by "Mariana" (Tennyson's *Poems* [Ticknor and Fields, 1842], 1: 10) Tuckerman writes, "Tennyson considers this his best poem." Next to a stanza of "The Miller's Daughter" (Moxon, 1842, 1: 113), which begins, "In idle sorrow set me not / Regret me not, forget me not," Tuckerman comments, "Tennyson said his brother Charles wanted to know if he could get in something here about 'tare and tret'!" (These terms were common in the nineteenth century; "tare" is a deduction, in weighing a commod-

---

[38] Most of these from the London edition are quoted in ibid., 38; I have included in my examples all that are only in the Boston edition, which Golden did not see. From this point I refer to Tuckerman's two 1842 editions of *Poems* in the text, by publisher.

ity, for the container, and "tret" is a deduction for wastage.) In a note at the beginning of "The Lotos-Eaters" Tuckerman indicates that "in reading this poem aloud the author was quite struck by [my] suggestion, that he might have written strand for land in the first line" (Moxon, 1842, 1: 175).[39] Later on in the same poem, by the line "Is there confusion in the little isle?" Tuckerman notes that "Tennyson in reading this poem to me, remarked that it was not usual for people to ask and answer their own questions."

Tuckerman's annotations also augment our knowledge and understanding of Tennyson's "parallelisms" to his own and others' works. The exhaustive notes on allusions and sources in Christopher Ricks's definitive edition of Tennyson's works sustain many of Tuckerman's identifications.[40] For example, Tuckerman implies a borrowing by quoting a passage beginning, "But I the mirror sweet would be," alongside Tennyson's very similar lines in "The Miller's Daughter," "That I would be the jewel / That trembles at her ear." Ricks refers to the same passage, which is from Thomas Moore's *Odes of Anacreon,* but Tuckerman also points to many other sources not noted by Ricks nor, it seems, by other scholars. At the beginning of Tennyson's "The Palace of Art," Tuckerman writes, "There is an old poem by [Stephen] Hawes (1505) called 'the Palace of Pleasure' of which I have only seen a portion but which commences . . . ," and then quotes the first stanza, apparently from memory (Moxon, 1842, 1: 136). He goes on to quote a number of stanzas alongside passages in the poem that Tennyson had obviously based on those passages.

---

[39] Sometime later Tennyson commented, " 'The strand' was, I think, my first reading, but the no rhyme of 'land' and 'land' was lazier"; Alfred, Lord Tennyson, *The Poems of Tennyson in Three Volumes,* ed. Christopher Ricks (Harlow, Eng.: Longman, 1987), 468.

[40] I am greatly indebted to Ricks's edition of *Poems of Tennyson* for this kind of information. Ricks provides the complete (English) publication history for all the individual poems, dates all the internal variants, and traces all sources known to Tennyson scholars.

But there is something going on in Tuckerman's notes besides the tracing of allusions or borrowings. In "The Palace of Art" Tuckerman discovers, besides the obvious debt to Hawes, a number of subtle relationships to other works. He quotes, beside "O soul, make merry and carouse" (p. 136), Shelley's "And I and you / My dearest soul will then make merry." Then he adds that the passage is "also scriptural" and of course knows that Shelley and Tennyson were both working from the same common legacy. Tuckerman notes Tennyson's appropriation of "grateful gloom" from Dryden but also points to a number of passages—from Wordsworth, Byron, Shakespeare, Chaucer, Milton, The Wisdom of Solomon, and others—that he clearly did not think were directly borrowed but thought it important to note were in some way related. I think he is interested in noticing that those passages were probably working in Tennyson's mind just as they obviously were in his own—that is, as real possessions from long acquaintance. He also seems to be noticing that the Tennyson passage and the reference are both based on a third source in the great wealth of the poetic tradition—the rich accumulation of human thought and feeling won out of chaos and preserved through the use of language. At any rate the noted relationships express Tuckerman's confidence—and also give evidence—that such a winning and accumulation is possible, because men's minds work toward each other, coming independently to similar ideas, images, expressions that become their shared glory and inheritance.[41] Tuckerman would have marked Winters's

---

[41] At one point Tuckerman makes this quite explicit: In his London edition of *The Princess*, 98, he marks a passage describing a group of people fluctuating to and fro "as flowers in storm." He writes,

> There is a curious coincidence here, between this passage and one in the early writings of Hawthorne showing how two men of high genius have hit independently upon the same image, though the American Author was not then acknowledged— "This time the party wavered, stopt, and huddled closer together; thus tossing to and fro they might have been fancifully

"Time and the Garden" with a reference to his own "and fixed the head."

There is direct evidence that Tennyson himself would have agreed with Tuckerman's views on poetic tradition. In 1880 he attacked an essay by J. Churton Collins that had described the laureate's supposed "borrowings." Declaring Collins's essay accurate in pointing to parallels but mostly "nonsense" in its conclusions, Tennyson insisted that his own images were "made" from nature, not copied from other books. Obviously he thought of himself as a rediscoverer of what others may have known independently. He concluded, "I will answer for it that no modern poet can write a single line but among the innumerable authors of this world you will somewhere find a striking parallelism. It is the unimaginative man who thinks everything borrowed."[42]

Tuckerman was not such an "unimaginative man." Although his mind was gifted with a highly unusual retentiveness, it was not a merely mechanical "photographic memory" triggered by key words. He could pick up with ease the direct borrowing or parallel but more often was concerned to note the similar feeling or tone (e.g., "Compare the manner of this with the close of the 2d act in Cymbeline" [Moxon, 1842, 1: 36]). Sometimes he called attention to a similar meter and movement, even though the matter was different. Tuckerman was not interested in source scholarship or in showing his own erudition but in expressing, and demonstrating, a particular view of poetry, of its tradition, and of the human mind. He was pointing to the power of the human mind to relate to other minds, and to the value of poetry as a great accumulation of those

---

compared to a splendid bunch of flowers suddenly shaken by a puff of wind."

The Hawthorne passage is from "The Wedding-Knell," published in 1836 and collected in the first volume of *Twice-Told Tales* (1837).

[42] Quoted in H. P. Sucksmith, "Tennyson on Genius," *Renaissance and Medieval Studies* 2 (1967): 88, which is the source of the information used in this paragraph.

relationships and of the nuances of development within and beyond them, the power of those nuances being dependent in part on the strength of the common heritage from which their slight departure is clearly seen and felt.

Even if Tennyson had not consciously intended, or perhaps even realized, that certain ideas, words, feelings, or perceptions from others resonated in his poetry, Tuckerman in his notes does. At times Tuckerman even seems to be *adding* to Tennyson's work a resonance important to himself as a development of the thought or feeling. Thus, the note itself becomes a connection, part of the heritage. Such a view is Anglican; it is not Romantic. The poet is rather one of many anonymous links in the series of builders of a cathedral than an isolated, independent hero, Emerson's "endless seeker, with no past at my back." And Tuckerman's perspective was shared with Tuckerman's fellow Anglican, Tennyson.

In a comprehensive essay on "Tennyson's Methods of Composition,"[43] Ricks traces some of the poet's numerous "self-borrowings," how he moved portions of only slightly changed earlier poems into later ones, often with great effectiveness. Ricks argues that these passages, nearly always dealing with the subject of change through time, reflect Tennyson's anxieties about time and change:

> [In] a world of unending flux, a world where all seemed ephemeral (even the works of the greatest poets), a world where personal identity was a mystery and often a burden, Tennyson found some rallying point in the continuity of his own creativity. . . . To revise a published poem was to show that the past was not done with, irrevocable, immutable. To quarry from his unpublished work was to show that the past was indeed a quarry, its geological obduracy the source of its riches.[44]

Tuckerman had similar anxieties, a nominalistic sense of

---

[43] Christopher Ricks, "Tennyson's Methods of Composition," *Proceedings of the British Academy* 52 (1966): 209–30.

[44] Ibid., 228.

flux, and a vision of unrecoverable loss through time ("for me these scenes decay"). But with his acquired understanding of his tradition and by virtue of his own poetic efforts, he developed a faith in philosophical realism and in the power of that creation of the human mind, language, to make bridges across the subject-object void. Tuckerman believed language to be a substantial and necessary, though tragically limited, connector of mind to objects because language is the inspired creation of human minds, which are similar to the mind of the divine Being who is Creator both of those minds and of objects. Tuckerman's notes to Tennyson's poems establish Tennyson as able, in Ricks's words, to demonstrate—against the "ephemeral"—a "rallying point," not only in "the continuity of his own creativity" but also in "the works of the greatest poets." The notes also demonstrate a similar capability in Tuckerman himself—that he understood that being part of such a tradition required a serious, painstaking apprenticeship.

Beginning with what is apparently the earliest of his surviving personal copies of Tennyson volumes, the 1842 Ticknor and Fields *Poems,* we find Tuckerman carefully writing in the margins all changes from the earlier printings he had seen. Even the slightest isolated word changes are noted, such as "to" to "the," indicating he was either remembering all of Tennyson's work in exact detail or comparing each line or a combination of both. Comparing Tuckerman's emendations to the dated variations in Ricks's edition of Tennyson's works reveals that Tuckerman not only reviewed editions published earlier than those he possessed but that he continued to incorporate revisions from later editions, so that he ends with a compact picture of the processes of Tennyson's revisions up through about 1855. By this means, at least by soon after 1850, he appears to have been instructing himself in his chosen craft: He writes beside one such passage, "Compare the improvement of this verse with the original" (Moxon, 1842, 1: 140).

At this time, when Tuckerman was reading his second set of Tennyson's *Poems* (Moxon, 1842), given him by Samuel in 1850, he was also able to go a step further into mild criticism,

PROLOGUE.

With tilt and tourney; then the tale of her
That drove her foes with slaughter from her walls,
And much I praised her nobleness, and ' Where,'
Ask'd Walter, (patting Lilia's head (she lay
Beside him)) ' lives there such a woman now ? '

    Quick answer'd Lilia ' There are thousands now
Such women, but convention beats them down:
It is but bringing up; no more than that:
You men have done it: how I hate you all!
Ah, were I (something great!   I wish I were
Some mighty poetess, I would shame you then,
That love to keep us children!   O I wish
That I were) some great Princess, I would build
Far off from men a college (like a man's,
And I would teach them all that men are taught;
We are twice as quick!'   And here she shook aside
The hand that play'd the patron with her curls.)
and I would teach them all Things: you should see.

    And one said smiling ' Pretty were the sight

A page from Tuckerman's copy of Tennyson's
The Princess, *showing his proposed cuts—the sections
inside handwritten parentheses—and substitutions,
also written in his own hand.*

catching Tennyson using the feminine pronoun for his soul, though he had earlier called it "king" (1: 146). By the time he went through *The Princess* for at least the second time (apparently in the summer of 1851, using the fourth edition he purchased in London), he was actually engaged in a tentative kind of *rewriting* of Tennyson, using the best versions of words and lines from former editions but also indicating a great deal of cutting of lines and even whole sections. These cuts seem skillfully to remove the fat in flabby passages and thus provide increased muscle to the syntax (see facing page for example). Tuckerman thereby reduces the vague luxuriance that makes the poem, despite its great lyrics like "Tears, idle tears," finally a failure, what Ricks calls a "therapy of evasion," a kind of smokescreen for Tennyson's unresolved ambiguities.[45]

Tuckerman did not presume to rewrite Tennyson. He had simply matured to a point where he could make self-instructive judgments about how some things his mentor was doing both *had been* and also *might be* improved. He could also venture by this time to criticize Tennyson's diction. By "An eagle *clang* an eagle to the sphere" (*The Princess,* 1851, p. 59) he has, "This word is used as a good poetical word, but not very expressive, I suppose of an eagle's cry, which is said to resemble a dog's" (later he cross-references "Lean-headed Eagles yelp alone" to Wordsworth's "Thou too be heard lone eagle . . . / The hungry barkings . . . ," p. 167). When Tennyson slips badly with a pronoun reference, he remarks drily, "It seems in this College of Women that the neuter gender was under an interdict also, even the messages were feminine" (p. 62).

However, what we see most is the development in Tuckerman of singular admiration for Tennyson and increasingly close attention in the early 1850s to the details of the laureate's craftsmanship as a model. This is evidenced both by the nature and quantity of notes in Tuckerman's various copies of

----

[45] "Tennyson wrote it after the worst five years of his life, and he created a complicated series of evasions such as could temporarily stave off his dilemmas and disasters" (Tennyson, *Poems of Tennyson,* ed. Ricks, 190).

Tennyson's works and also by the rare appreciative comments, of which there are none in the surviving copies of the work of other authors. By "And eyes grow dim with gazing on the pilot stars," in "The Lotos-Eaters," he writes, "What a solemnity is in this line" (Ticknor and Fields, 1842, 1: 182). Concerning a passage near the end of "The Departure" ("And o'er the hills, and far away / Beyond their utmost purple rim") he notes, "I can scarcely ever read or recite these two lines without a sensation of tears, partly from their exquisite expression, but chiefly from an association, undefinable but utterly pathetic which the imagery always brings up" (Ticknor and Fields, 1842, 2: 159).

T U C K E R M A N ' S special feeling about Tennyson and silent apprenticeship to him led him to visit the famous poet, at the conclusion of the European tour Tuckerman began in the summer of 1854. This encounter was immensely successful and served both to increase his admiration for Tennyson as a model and also to give him the self-confidence to recognize his own abilities and to follow them, eventually in new directions beyond Tennyson's influence.

The direct information that survives concerning Tuckerman's second trip to Europe (apart from the Tennyson-Tuckerman letters about their visit) is in the form of some additions to the herbarium he had started on his first trip and some letters from Anna to her mother.[46] Anna and Frederick sailed from New York (July 26, 1854) to Liverpool (August 6) and then traveled across Scotland (Tuckerman took specimens of plants from Kenilworth and Roslin) and down to London. There they met Frederick's mother, who continued the trip with them, and stayed for a while at Windsor, where Samuel was studying music.

------

[46] These letters, apparently unexamined by Bynner, Golden, or Momaday, I found in family papers at Hugh Clark's home in Amherst; the originals are still there but will soon, I trust, be donated to the Houghton Library at Harvard. I have photocopies in my possession.

Anna's letters, though clearly gauged to the interests of her mother and reticent on personal matters, nevertheless reveal a close relationship with Frederick and the deep attachment of both to their two young children, Edward (4), and Anna (1), whom they had left with Anna's parents. While at Windsor the two "talk long and often about the children," and Anna confides that Tuckerman "has missed the children more than I have; I do believe this second trip he is so less interested in traveling." They seriously discussed returning home but decided to go on to Italy through Switzerland (Frederick collected crocus in the snow at Jura on October 20 and plants from Keats's and Shelley's graves in Rome on November 19). Tuckerman climbed Vesuvius without Anna, commenting that he would like to have seen an eruption, "a slight one, of course," and after visiting Florence and Venice (Lord Byron's palace) they returned via Paris to Windsor. On January 21 (a Sunday) Anna wrote her mother that "The Dr. [Samuel] and Mr. T. went to the Isle of Wight on Thursday, return tomorrow."

That extended weekend as guests of Tennyson and his wife (and young child, Hallam), at their isolated retreat at Farringford on the Isle of Wight, was a remarkable and deeply affecting experience for Tuckerman. Other American poets visited Tennyson, notably Emerson in 1848, but Tuckerman seems to be the only one who was able to have long talks alone with him and to draw him out fully concerning his poetry. Tuckerman's granddaughter related a family anecdote that "when he first came to Tennyson's door, he was rather gruffly received. But when Tennyson realized that Tuckerman was more than casually familiar with his poetry and could quote at length from it, he adopted a more cordial attitude."[47] This

---

[47] Golden, *Tuckerman: An American Sonnetteer*, 18. Mrs. Clark told Golden that this occurred in 1851, and he therefore posited *two* meetings, the second in 1855. However, as I noted earlier, all the direct evidence, especially the letters from Tuckerman's wife Anna to her mother, indicates that Tuckerman traveled alone to Europe in 1851 and met Tennyson only on the second trip he made, with Anna, in 1855. The visit is corroborated by Emily

anecdote is confirmed and elaborated upon by Charles K. Tuckerman in his *Personal Recollections of Notable People.* He includes a summary of a letter (apparently now lost) from Frederick, who was his cousin, about the visit:

> Tennyson's manner was not uncivil, but it clearly indicated that the visitor was regarded by him as one of those innumerable bores who intrude upon the retirement of literary men for the sole purpose of gratifying a morbid and idle curiosity. My cousin felt that, under the circumstances, the shorter he made his visit the better, but he was determined to let Tennyson know that he was an ardent admirer of his poetry, and that he had come to see him as a pilgrim comes to a shrine where his heart and sympathies may find expression. He therefore, in a few words, thanked the great man for the privilege of meeting one who had so largely contributed to his intellectual enjoyment. Tennyson scanned the features of his guest, as if searching to know how much sincerity there might be in his avowal, and, to test the matter, asked which of his poems he preferred, and what particular passages he chanced to remember. My cousin could not have desired a more gratifying question, and thereupon referred to his favourites and quoted line upon line, and then longer passages, with such unfeigned enthusiasm that it was evident the poet had before him a pure and unadulterated disciple.
>
> Tennyson's manner and tone suddenly exhibited a magical transformation. His face relaxed its inquisitorial

---

Tennyson in *Lady Tennyson's Journal,* ed. James O. Hoge (Charlottesville: Univ. Press of Virginia, 1981), 42. There are, however, serious contradictions in the evidence about the *exact* dates of the visit. Emily Tennyson dates Tuckerman's arrival on January 12 (*Journal,* 42), and letters of hers and Alfred's mention three days together with him. Emily's redacted "journal" is notoriously untrustworthy, however, and is contradicted by the letters of Anna Tuckerman to her mother (especially January 21), which clearly indicate that the visit took place the same days of the week as Emily notes but one week later, Anna's husband being gone from her, on his trip to Farringford, from January 19 to 22. A further complication is that Tuckerman himself alludes to the journey as just recently completed in a letter to his brother Edward, but it is unclear whether the date of that letter is January 20 or 26.

severity; he settled himself in his chair, as if desirous of further acquaintance with the young American, and fell into a free and easy conversation on matters and things in general. When his guest rose to take leave, Tennyson would not listen to it, but insisted upon his remaining for dinner and passing the night.... After dinner the poet armed himself with smoking-pipes and a bottle of spirits, and conducted his guest upstairs to his study, where he threw himself at full length upon the rug before the fire, and the two passed the evening, well into the night, discussing poetry—chiefly the Laureate's own poems—which he recited with sonorous junction, as if no greater compliment or source of enjoyment could be afforded to his companion than to supply him with unlimited draughts of poetic inspiration from the very fountainhead.[48]

As we have already seen, Tuckerman was thoroughly familiar with Tennyson's work (probably able to quote all of it, including revisions), and we can understand how impressed the laureate was. Tennyson invited the young stranger to return for three full days to his "smoking attic," where he seems to have become convinced of Tuckerman's depth of appreciation and critical judgment as well as his remarkable memory. A friendship developed that matured quickly and seems to have persisted for some time.[49] Although the correspondence from 1855 is all that survives, the length and unconstrained ease of the few extant letters from Tennyson, who hated the chore of letter writing, is strong evidence itself of the depth of the relationship.[50]

----

[48] Charles K. Tuckerman, *Personal Recollections of Notable People* (London: Richard Bentley and Son, 1895), 22–26.

[49] In addition to several letters to Tuckerman, Tennyson's wife, Emily, who handled much of the poet's correspondence, wrote a letter of sympathy to Tuckerman's sister, Sophia Mae Eckley, after his death in 1873. See *The Letters of Emily Lady Tennyson,* ed. James O. Hoge (University Park: Pennsylvania State Univ. Press, 1974), 301; see also 72, 86, and 146 for other relevant letters.

[50] Charles K. Tuckerman also notes the continuing strength of this relationship; in the book referred to above, he quotes from a letter to him from

Besides that exchange of letters, there are the notes that Tuckerman made in his copies of Tennyson's work (he evidently had them with him, and Tennyson perhaps even read from them and saw the previously made notes and comparisons of editions). Together these show that during their time together Tennyson, in his singular chant, read through all or most of his poems, commented on them, and freely discussed Tuckerman's comments, even taking very seriously suggestions from him. Tennyson included his newest work, some of the "Idylls" and "Maud" (which Tuckerman commented on then and again when Tennyson sent him published copies). When they parted Tennyson gave Tuckerman the original manuscript of *Locksley Hall,* which, as Tuckerman reported in a letter to Edward a few days later, was "a favour of which I may be justly proud as he says he never did such a thing in his life before, for anybody."[51]

Tuckerman was, of course, deeply affected. His letters to Tennyson following the visit are somewhat effusive, but they also show that Tuckerman was not intimidated by the laureate and that the poets dealt with each other quite openly. Tuckerman's first letter, sent from Windsor just before the return voyage (January 31, 1855), praises "the surpassing beauty of your Idyll [and] of Maud, scraps of which are floating through my head like 'fragments of the golden day.'" Tuckerman's ability also to remember an obscure line from the pirated editions read years before is revealed in another comment:

> The Locksley Hall, your most valued gift, contains also a
> part of The Golden Year; . . . In reading this fragment I
> have discovered a curious substitution of sound for sense.
> You remember the line, "Yet seas that daily gain upon the

Tennyson, "very many years" after the visit: "I remember with great pleasure your cousin's visits to me, and I am glad to find in yourself something of the interest in the old country which distinguished him" (25–26).

[51] Frederick to Edward Tuckerman, January 26(?), 1855, Houghton Autograph File. The *Locksley Hall* manuscript was given to Yale University Library by Mrs. Margaret Tuckerman Clark, the poet's granddaughter.

shore." In the American editions this is printed, "Yet seize the daily gain upon the shore."[52]

Tuckerman trusts that Tennyson "will yet see America, for where else can I repay you."

> Should the Russian overrun Europe, or the "auri sacra fames" of publishers become insatiable you will there find one (among many) who will proudly serve you to the extent of his influence and fortune. May this feeling, the growth of many years, the flowering of a few days, yet bear fruit.

Tennyson responded quickly, on February 6, 1855. He reports that he was worried that Tuckerman's ship (which sailed on February 3) might have been caught in a bad storm that had passed and that he would not be "easy" until he had heard that his friend had "safely arrived at your pleasant sounding Greenfield, Mass." He recalls their "talks over my little fire in my wind-shaken attic," thanks him for his gifts (a fine meerschaum pipe, which "I sit and smoke to your memory," and Webster's *Dictionary*), and hopes "that if ever you come back to us you will put up at no hotel but in my house and if I come to you will likewise find you out and we will be as happy together as two friends may on either side the Atlantic."[53]

---

[52] Tuckerman to Tennyson, January 31, 1855. Typed copy in Houghton Autograph File. The original is at the Tennyson Research Centre, Lincoln, England, and is published in *The Letters of Alfred, Lord Tennyson,* ed. Cecil Y. Lang and Edgar F. Shannon, Jr., 2 vols. (Oxford: Clarendon Press, 1987), 2:104. Tuckerman apparently could remember whole poems from a single hearing, because in this letter he promised Tennyson not to repeat in America "the unpublished poems, which you did me the honor to read me . . . until I see them printed."

[53] Tennyson to Tuckerman, February 6, 1855, original in Houghton Autograph File. As an additional gift, Tuckerman promised to send some volumes of Poe, whom they had discussed; but in the meantime Tennyson received those very books from another friend and had Emily hastily write Tuckerman (February 8) to save his effort. On February 23 Tennyson wrote Tuckerman's mother, Sophia May Tuckerman (who had written him about her son's report of the visit), "I can assure you that I have seldom met any

This friendliness further encouraged Tuckerman, and his response of February 22 is barely restrained. It even uses one of Tennyson's own images in ultimate tribute:

> How often . . . in the solitude of the sea did my thoughts return to Farringford; how often did I think of all that I would have said to you. . . . Since my return to America a warm and eager interest has been manifested in my personal knowledge of yourself, one young friend said to me "You have seen Tennyson, it is the event of a lifetime." Another, "I hope you told him what we think of him in New England." In fact your fame in America among the names of the age seems to stand alone, as sometimes in the very ardour of sunset we see a single keen star.[54]

Tuckerman had learned that, unknowingly, he had been somewhat presumptuous in one of his critical comments:

> Do you remember my quoting some lines one evening from a newspaper and objecting to the rhymes "blunder'd" and Hundred," thinking it should read blund*ered*?" I had then seen exactly *three* lines, and knew nothing of the connexion. Judge then of my surprise at discovering the whole poem in an American paper, with your name attached.

He continued (in what seems a bit of overcompensation) that he had read "The Charge of the Light Brigade" with "astonishment and delight," thought it "a most noble performance, the finest irregular Ode ever written upon the

---

man whom I should be more glad to meet again. My house is always open to him whenever he chooses to revisit England." See Lang and Shannon, *Letters of Alfred, Lord Tennyson,* 2:104. This letter also provides evidence that Tennyson knew something of Tuckerman's own work. Apparently his mother had sent a copy of one of Tuckerman's poems with her letter, and Tennyson responds, "I do not wonder that you are pleased with your son's poem but I cannot think of retaining it as it seems to have been so carefully treasured amongst you."

[54] Tuckerman to Tennyson, February 22, 1855, typed copy in Houghton Autograph File. The original is at the Tennyson Research Centre, Lincoln, England, and is published in Lang and Shannon, *Letters of Alfred, Lord Tennyson,* 2:108–9.

grandest subject" and hoped "that this poem will not receive any alterations. (Of course I refer to your general habit of retouching your poems and not to any remarks of mine.)"

Tennyson had probably enjoyed keeping quiet about the authorship of those three lines when Tuckerman attacked them during the visit, but he took the criticism seriously. When he wrote back in July, promising a copy of *Maud and Other Poems* which would include "The Charge of the Light Brigade," he reported that it would come with "The 'blunder'd' that offended you and others omitted. It is not a poem on which I pique myself but I cannot help fancying that, such as it is, I have improved it."[55] But Tennyson, as he often did, went too far in trying to please "others," and Tuckerman, who had not wanted the *line* omitted but only the self-conscious *syncope*, "blunder'd," apparently told him so. On October 17, responding to a letter of Tuckerman's not now extant, Tennyson wrote: "Many thanks for your critique of *Maud*. She has been very roughly treated on this side of the water. You are quite right about the *Charge*. I was overpersuaded to spoil it."[56]

-----

[55] Tennyson to Tuckerman, July [8], 1855, original in Houghton Autograph File. Bynner, in his introduction to Tuckerman's *Sonnets*, 29, and Samuel Golden, *Frederick Goddard Tuckerman* (New York: Twayne, 1966), 20, both misread this passage; they substitute "blunders" for "blunder'd" and thus encourage the mistaken notion that Tuckerman objected to more than the artificiality of the *syncope*.

[56] Tennyson to Tuckerman, October 17, 1855, original in Houghton Autograph File. This is a note written across the top of a letter from Emily accompanying a "soldier's copy of the *Charge*" that Tennyson requested she send to Tuckerman. Charles Tennyson, in his *Alfred Tennyson* (London: Macmillan, 1949), 288, assumes, because of Tuckerman's criticism reported in his February 22 letter and Tennyson's references in his July 8 and October 17 letters, that the laureate "had been overpersuaded by Tuckerman and other friends to alter the first version for publication in the *Maud* volume . . . by omitting the key line 'someone had blundered,' " and had then reconsidered and gone back to the original version for the "soldier's copies" and subsequent publications. But Tuckerman had no objection (as others did) to the rhyme or to the political criticism; consistent with his own developing poetic practice at this time, he merely wanted Tennyson to avoid an archaic

Tennyson's influence—"the growth of many years, the flowering of a few days"—did indeed "bear fruit." Tuckerman recorded, in one or the other of the sets of *Poems,* the comments Tennyson had made to him concerning specific works and returned to his close study of those poems and then of the new ones Tennyson sent. He was convinced he had been given in particular a new feeling for the "music" of poetry. In his February 22, 1855, letter, Tuckerman wrote to Tennyson:

> I have been reading the "In Memoriam" since my return and never has its solemn music affected me so deeply for how could I help hearing a
>
> > "voice the richest-toned that sings"
>
> chanting these strains
>
> > "From point to point with power and grace
> > And music in the bounds of law."
>
> Your reading in truth made a deep impression upon me....

In his January 31 letter he had said:

> In regard too, to your manner of reading or chanting, I feel that it must be the true one; at all events I cannot recite your lines—the exquisite ones for instance—
>
> > "Came glimmering through the laurels
> > In the quiet evenfall,"
>
> in any other way.

At this period (despite his earlier criticisms of Tennyson's language), Tuckerman's tendency toward the kind of diction in this passage increased. "Glimmering," for instance, occurs with almost embarrassing frequency for a while in his manu-

---

poeticism and to accept the perfectly good slant rhyme of "blundered" (instead of "blunder'd) with "hundred."

script poetry.[57] Tuckerman also began to use Tennyson's chant in reading his own poetry.

News of Tuckerman's good fortune and the continuing relationship spread through literary circles in America. Emerson in 1861 refers to "your friend Tennyson"; and a reviewer of Tuckerman's 1860 *Poems,* in noting the influence of Tennyson, alluded to the friendship. But the most profound effect of the visit, I believe, was to begin to move Tuckerman, in important and beneficial ways, beyond the influence of Tennyson into his own independent realm. The most respected and popular poet writing in English had spent long periods of time with Tuckerman. He had shared—in many ways as with an equal— ideas, judgments, and responses concerning poetry.[58] That poet obviously continued to feel affection for Tuckerman and to value his judgment. This experience ultimately helped Tuckerman gain the confidence to depend less on models, including Tennyson, and to begin to develop his own unique poetic talent.

However, a single event was to catalyze the most profound changes.

---

[57] An interesting token of Tennyson's strong influence, and then Tuckerman's independence from it, is the frequency with which "glimmer" and "glimmering" appear in the early manuscript versions of the poems— only to be revised at a later time, probably in the late fifties, before the publication of Tuckerman's *Poems.*

[58] There is no evidence that Tennyson read or heard any of Tuckerman's poetry during the visit—or indeed that he even knew, until Tuckerman's mother sent him a poem in February, that he wrote poetry, apparently because Tuckerman was diffident about his own work. In a letter dated October 22, 1855, which includes quite extensive comments on *Maud,* Tuckerman wrote, "I remember once saying to you that I was no poet. The remark perhaps should have been that in your presence I dared not claim such a title, for it seems to me only poets can fully appreciate and enjoy the singular beauty of 'Maud.' " This letter is reproduced in [Hallam Tennyson], *Materials for a Life of A[lfred] T[ennyson],* 4 vols. (n.p., [1895]), 2: 152–53; one of the very rare copies of this set of materials is in the Houghton Library. Lang and Shannon, in *Letters of Alfred, Lord Tennyson,* 2: 132n, suppose that the date has been mistranscribed from October 2, because the letter from the Tennysons, dated October 17, seems to them to be an answer to this one.

Hannah Lucinda Jones. Used by permission of Hugh Clark, Amherst, Massachusetts.

IV

MATURITY: A SONNET

The older religions are fully aware that the heart...
is untranslatable, whatever may be true of the soul, and
that one can escape from the claims of the world only
by understanding those claims and by thus accustom-
ing oneself to the thought of eventually putting them
by.... The attitude is humane, and does not belittle nor
evade the magnitude of the task: it is essentially a tragic
attitude.

Yvor Winters *(In Defense of Reason)*

TUCKERMAN'S thoughts, during the years 1855 and 1856, were probably full of memories of the visit with Tennyson. He was rereading Tennyson's poetry and adding further notes, including reminiscences of the visit and Tennyson's comments, reading the new poems Tennyson sent him, and responding at length and with his new-found assurance. There is no direct evidence about the poetry he was writing, though he was probably working on some of his imitations of Tennyson, like "The School Girl: An Idyll" and "Rhotruda," and perhaps beginning to try new things with the sonnet form, producing early versions of some of the first ones in the initial series. Edward had taken a position at Amherst College, eighteen miles away, and the two no doubt often spent times together in the field. Many entries in the herbarium and penciled notes in Frederick's copy of Bigelow are dated 1855 and 1856, far more than during any other time after 1852.

By the spring of 1857 Anna was well along with her fourth

pregnancy. On May 7 a son was born[1] and on May 12 Anna died of complications from the birth. Tuckerman was afflicted permanently, even overwhelmed for a time, by a haunting, vague guilt (perhaps for some failure to provide medical care), by a deep personal grief at the loss of the person who had changed and sustained his life, and by a shaking of the foundations of his religious and poetic faith.

We must look to the poetry itself for a sense of Anna's qualities and significance to Tuckerman and of the effects of the loss; there is little else to go on. The small paintings of her, the letters to her mother from Europe, and a reference or two in Tuckerman's letters suggest a remarkably beautiful young woman and a remarkably loving wife and mother, but they give no direct evidence of the particular qualities of mind and spirit that Tuckerman obviously found and depended upon. Her letters are full of rather trivial domestic detail and instruction, apparently aimed at her mother's concerns, but she does tell of long talks with Tuckerman about their children, notes that Louis Napoleon was "a very great man if not a very good one," reports speaking French with villagers in the Jura Mountains and preferring the religious services in Naples where there were "beggars and the rich seated together."

How much his wife shared directly in Tuckerman's interest in poetry is not known, though she gave him at least a few of the books surviving from his library. Late in 1855 he wrote to Tennyson that although he himself tended to feel that only a poet could fully appreciate *Maud,* "my wife who is now reading it could hardly assent to this."

While no complete or clear picture of Anna can emerge from such fragmentary evidence, the force of her personality and evidence of her significance to Tuckerman pervade almost all of his poetry and directly motivate his mature work. The

---

[1] He was named Frederick and became the heir; the first child, a daughter, died at birth (1848), Edward (1850) died while a student at Harvard in 1871, and Anna (1853) lived in Boston well into the twentieth century but never married.

essential movement of the five sonnet series is a repeated, circuitous journey progressing out from the fact of his irreducibly final loss. The pattern moves through the doubts which that loss raises about himself, about his work, finally about the rationality and goodness of nature, of existence, of life itself, and then to a grappling in poetry with those doubts and a return to a kind of resolution, which in turn is challenged as insufficient by the intensified memory of loss so that another level of doubt and resolution must be worked through.

In the next three chapters I examine closely Tuckerman's best poems (which span perhaps ten years of his fully mature writing), using examples all dealing with Anna's death, but at three levels of increasing complexity and generality and three levels of increasing poetic scope and power. First I examine a single sonnet, which appears early in that first series and was written, I believe, the autumn after Anna's death. It exhibits, in its intuitive groping for a new form of imagery, a hypersensitive acuteness of perception and an almost irrationally overpowering strength of suggestiveness, qualities one might expect at that first stage of reaction. Later, after falling back into more direct (and less effective) attempts to deal with his grief in subsequent sonnets and other poems, Tuckerman creates an elegy in six connected sonnets (probably in 1858 or 1859) that places his experience in a larger context of change and loss, particularly man's intrusion upon the natural landscape. The poem gains additional artistic distance by transforming Anna and placing her in a created mythic context. Finally, in "The Cricket," written, I believe, in the middle or late sixties, Tuckerman is able to deal at length, in full possession of a great range of skills and conceptual insights, with the whole group of forces and facts—the animal world, the sea, his own primitive nature—that belong to a realm that lies beyond our rational, alienating minds. Anna's death is a part of that realm, and suicide or a lapse into mindlessness is a powerfully tempting response.

ONE OF AUDEN'S many complaints about Tennyson is that "There was little about melancholia that he didn't know; little else he did."[2] Christopher Ricks has traced with great insight the sources, the development, and the effects of Tennyson's melancholia, including his longing for death, particularly in the period after his greatest loss (the death of his friend Hallam), which was the period of his most remarkable achievement.[3] A somewhat similar mood affects Tuckerman's poetry from the first and may have then been something of a Romantic affectation picked up from Tennyson and others. That melancholia persisted, intensified by real losses like that of his infant daughter in 1848 and compounded by a growing disenchantment with easy Romantic notions of the beneficence and easily perceived correspondences of nature. However, it is a mistake to let this generalized melancholy mask very specific references in the poems. Perhaps because some Tuckerman scholars have done so (and because they did not see the sonnets as an integrated sequence with one central theme), they have erroneously dated the first series of the sonnets too early and some have misread single sonnets that refer to feelings or details connected with Tuckerman's greatest loss.

Though Tuckerman had worked with the sonnet and had published three poems in that form in the early fifties there is no manuscript (or other) evidence that he began the First Series, as such, before his wife's death. And the internal evidence (once we admit the possibility) seems quite clear that he conceived of the series as it was finally organized and published (if not all the individual poems) as a *response* to that event. The last sonnet of the Second Series (Sonnet II: 37), which is the last one of the sixty-five which were printed in sequence in 1860 (and at one point in manuscript were numbered consecutively rather than in two groups), refers to the preceding poems as "these offspring of my sorrow." There is

---

2 Quoted in E. E. Smith, *The Two Voices: A Tennyson Study* (Lincoln: Univ. of Nebraska Press, 1964), 6.

3 Christopher Ricks, *Tennyson* (New York: Macmillan, 1972), 118–24.

no reason to believe Tuckerman meant anything other than the single over-whelming sorrow that possessed him. There is instead very good reason to believe—in what reveals itself increasingly on closer observation as a highly integrated structure of poems and not a mere collection like most other sonnet sequences—that this reference ties directly back to the line in the third sonnet of the First Series, "Has fruitful sorrow swept thee with her wing?" Not only is the whole sequence of the first two series an answer, but that question itself is followed directly (still in Sonnet I: 3) by an example of sudden and intense experience of sorrow by the poet that was, I believe, motivated by the still raw pain of his wife's recent death. (The "sweet voice" quite probably belongs to his daughter Anna, named after her mother and four years old in 1857.)

> Today I heard a sweet voice carolling
> In the woodlot paths, with laugh and careless cry
> Leading her happy mates: apart I stepped
> And while the laugh and song went lightly by,
> In the wild bushes I sat down and wept.

To read this as "general" melancholia is to impute to Tuckerman an affliction quite literally bordering on madness, and that is not supportable.

The passage might legitimately be read as a specific response to the death of the Tuckermans' other daughter in 1848, but that event is too remote in time and lacks any evidence of having carried sufficient emotional weight to justify this intensity. This remains true even at the earliest possible composition date—1850—when, as we have seen, Tuckerman was just beginning his serious writing. As the series continues it becomes increasingly clear that he is concerned with one specific, fresh, overwhelming sorrow as the subject of his struggles and successive resolutions, and the only possible source seems to be the loss of Anna. In the fifth sonnet he stands "struck in grief," unable to find a haven. He is clearly reaching for answers, "Laboring to reconcile, content, assuage," as he says in I: 6, where his grief reappears as a "dark apparelage." He finds some relief in a Romantic retreat into a suitably melancholy natural setting, where "Fresh griefs beat tranquilly," in Sonnet I: 7. But in I: 8 he realizes that there is no answer to be found in the effort "to read the secret" in the environment, neither by brooding "among / Dead graves," as he says in I: 9, nor through teasing "the sunbreak and the cloud / For import." He wonders if it might not be better "To follow those that go before the throng" and accept some simple analogical lesson in his loss, "easily / Exampling this existence," or whether, given his skepticism, he might have any reason at all to hope to

> Come into light at last? or suddenly
> Struck to the knees like Saul, one arm against
> The overbearing brightness, hear a voice?

The answer to these questions, the response at this early stage to the quest for import, is implicit in the next sonnet, number I: 10:[4]

---

[4]This version departs from Momaday's edition in one instance—"cup" instead of "lot" (which Momaday chose from a manuscript version) in line 3—but thus it actually returns to Tuckerman's choice for all the printed editions of his *Poems*. I think Tuckerman had good reasons for the change from manuscript; "cup" both enlarges the important reference to Christ, intrinsic to this sonnet (see also "upper chamber"), and makes the tie more explicit to Sonnet I: 25, which describes Tuckerman's "wild grief" when he actually held and kissed Anna immediately after her death,

> Gathered her close and closer to drink up
> The odour of her beauty, then in tears
> As for a world, gave from his lips the cup.

> An upper chamber in a darkened house,
> Where, ere his footsteps reached ripe manhood's brink
> Terror and anguish were his cup to drink;
> I cannot rid the thought nor hold it close
> But dimly dream upon that man alone: [5]
> Now though the autumn clouds most softly pass,
> The cricket chides beneath the doorstep stone
> And greener than the season grows the grass.
> Nor can I drop my lids nor shade my brows,
> But there he stands beside the lifted sash;   [10]
> And with a swooning of the heart, I think
> Where the black shingles slope to meet the boughs
> And, shattered on the roof like smallest snows,
> The tiny petals of the mountain ash.

This poem is remarkable for many reasons. It stands out immediately from the First Series as unusual in tone, imagery, and syntax. It also emerges, upon careful examination, as a unique struggle—uniquely successful considering its date in Tuckerman's development and in the history of poetry—to use natural description in the process of both creating and understanding perception and feeling.

Tuckerman was certainly heavily influenced to emulate what Arthur Hallam very early recognized as Tennyson's "picturesque" capability. In a remarkably perceptive and historically premonitory essay, "On Some of the Characteristics of Modern Poetry, and on the Lyrical Poems of Alfred Tennyson," which appeared in *The Englishman's Magazine*, August 1831, Hallam draws a sharp and crucial distinction. It is the same one that Poe was later to make, with profound implications for modern poetry because it was taken up and carried to its ultimate conclusions by the genius of the French Symbolists:

> It is not true, as [Wordsworth's] exclusive admirers would
> have it, that the highest species of poetry is the reflective:
> it is a gross fallacy, that, because certain opinions are

> acute or profound, the expression of them by the imagination must be eminently beautiful. Whenever the mind of the artist suffers itself to be occupied, during its periods of creation, by any other predominant motive than the desire of beauty, the result is false in art.[5]

According to Hallam, it is possible to "find beauty in those modes of emotion, which arise from the combinations of reflective thought," but "hardly probable," because if "a poet's reveries take a reasoning turn," he "will be apt to mistake the pleasure he has in knowing a thing to be true, for the pleasure he would have in knowing it to be beautiful" and thus try to convince rather than enrapture. Thus, much of Wordsworth is "good as philosophy, powerful as rhetoric, but false as poetry." On the other hand, Keats and Shelley are "poets of sensation rather than reflection. . . . Other poets seek for images to illustrate their conceptions; these men had no need to seek; they lived in a world of images; for the most important and extensive portion of their life consisted in those emotions which are immediately conversant with sensation. . . . Hence they are not descriptive; they are picturesque."

H. M. McLuhan, in his discussion of this essay,[6] reviews the relation of Hallam's distinction between poetry of sensation and poetry of reflection to aesthetic experiments, from the eighteenth century on, that led from mere description and interest in immediate sensation to more abstract appreciations—to impressionism and cubism in art, in poetry to Symbolism and to T. S. Eliot's "objective correlative." According to McLuhan, Eliot's working backward from any particular emotion to a formula of "external facts, which must terminate in sensory experience," and which alone, without reflection or rhetoric, can infallibly evoke the emotion, was an-

---

[5] A. H. Hallam, "On Some of the Characteristics of Modern Poetry, and on the Lyrical Poems of Alfred Tennyson," *The Englishman's Magazine,* August 1831, 616.

[6] H. M. McLuhan, "Tennyson and Picturesque Poetry," in *Critical Essays on the Poetry of Tennyson,* ed. John Killham (London: Routledge and Kegan Paul, 1967), 67–85.

ticipated in theory by Hallam and in practice by Tennyson. Yeats was able to use Hallam's essay to understand the French Symbolists better than perhaps any of his contemporaries could, and Tennyson's "Mariana" (which he told Tuckerman was his best poem) shows "that the most sophisticated symbolist poetry could be written fifty years before the Symbolists."[7]

Tuckerman benefited from what McLuhan calls the "growth of awareness at once psychological and naturalistic," which was a great technical development of the picturesque tradition. For Tuckerman as well as Tennyson, "scientific observation and psychological experience met in landscape," partly because of influences on both of them but mainly, I believe, from Tuckerman's intense study and emulation of the laureate. Hallam's perceptive characterization of Tennyson gives us central qualities evident in the poetry that most affected Tuckerman up to the writing of Sonnet I: 10:

> First, his luxuriance of imagination and at the same time his control over it. Secondly, his power of embodying himself in ideal characters, or rather moods of character, with such extreme accuracy of adjustment, that the circumstances of the narration seem to have a natural correspondence with the predominant feeling, and, as it were, to be evolved from it by assimilative force. Thirdly, his vivid, picturesque delineation of objects, and the peculiar skill with which he holds all of them fused, to borrow a metaphor from science, in a medium of strong emotion. Fourthly, the variety of his lyrical measures, and exquisite modulation of harmonious words and cadences to the swell and fall of the feelings expressed. Fifthly, the elevated habits of thought, implied in these compositions, and imparting a mellow soberness of tone, more impressive, to our minds, than if the author had drawn up a set of opinions in verse, and sought to instruct the understanding, rather than to communicate the love of beauty to the heart.[8]

---

[7] Ibid., 70.

[8] Hallam, "On Some of the Characteristics of Modern Poetry," 621.

One of the remarkable things about Sonnet I: 10 is that while it achieves, as well as Tennyson did, all of the qualities Hallam lists, it is evidence, even a kind of description, of a struggle to transcend the limitations of the picturesque. That struggle, partially successful in this sonnet and fully successful later, makes it possible for Tuckerman to go beyond his mentor. He was able to anticipate by fifty years a new possibility in poetic technique—what came to be called by Winters "post-Symbolism"—that is related but superior to the Symbolist technique that Tennyson had anticipated by fifty years.

The trouble with the notion of the objective correlative is that it leaves out the mind and language. McLuhan's particular prejudices made him miss some hints in the essay by Hallam that indicate even *he* was not entirely happy with the anti-rational implications of the dichotomy he had drawn. Hallam's talk of the "powerful tendency of imagination to a life of immediate sympathy with the external universe" has lying behind it Coleridge and the rationalistic Anglican traditions.[9] "Imagination" is not the power of ingenious invention supposedly necessary for Donne's conceits or Eliot's correlatives, nor is it the unique sensibility of the Romantic poet-hero. It is that faculty of human beings that is capable of being manifest in unusual strength in certain people but, more important, capable of being *developed* so that they can be called poets. Imagination, in Coleridge's view, allows humans to use the resources of their minds, their rational and verbal capabilities, to reach out in meaningful relationship to an external universe whose "sympathy" derives from its creation by a rational being related to them—the original Word.

Hallam is heir to the Lockean associationism which in the eighteenth century had been popularized by David Hartley into *the* theory of poetic composition. However, for Hallam, influenced by Coleridge, poetry is not *free* association of

---

[9] This tradition was receiving, through the beginnings of what became Newman's reform movement at the universities, a powerful new impetus in the late 1820s when Hallam and Tennyson were at Cambridge.

ideas derived from sensations received in passive reverie but "a regular law of association." It is therefore necessary for the reader and the poet not to engage in "indolent impulse" but "clearly to apprehend the leading sentiments in the poet's mind, by their conformity to which the host of suggestions are arranged."

In his list of Tennyson's "distinctive excellencies" quoted above, Hallam hints at matters important to the kind of discipline that he obviously senses is necessary for poetry, and they are matters to which Tuckerman ultimately gives greater and more effective emphasis than Hallam, or even Tennyson. Such crucial elements are "accuracy of adjustment" so that "the circumstances of the narration seem to have a natural correspondence with the predominant feeling," "variety of . . . lyrical measure, and exquisite modulation of harmonious words and cadences to the swell and fall of the feelings expressed," and most crucial, as is clearer on a rereading, "elevated habits of thought, *implied* in these compositions, and imparting a mellow soberness of tone, more impressive, to our minds, than if the author had drawn up a set of opinions in verse, and sought to instruct the understanding"—which is fine, but the conclusion gives Hallam away—"rather than to communicate the love of beauty to the heart."[10]

That last phrase brings us back to Poe and the ultimate failure of the noble Symbolist experiment—a failure McLuhan is not prepared to see, as the following passage proves:

> There is in all these [modern Symbolist] works a vision of men and creatures which is not so much ethical as metaphysical. And it had been, in poetry, due to the technical innovations of Baudelaire, Laforgue, and Rimbaud that it was possible to render this vision immediately in verse without the extraneous aid of rhetoric or logical reflection and statement. The principal innovation was that of *le paysage interieur* or the psychological landscape. . . . Whereas in external landscape diverse things lie side by

---

10 Hallam, "On Some of the Characteristics of Modern Poetry," 618–21.

> side, so in psychological landscape the juxtaposition of
> various things and experiences becomes a precise musi-
> cal means of orchestrating that which could never be ren-
> dered by systematic discourse. Landscape is the means of
> presenting, without the copula of logical enunciation, ex-
> periences which are united in existence but not in con-
> ceptual thought. Syntax becomes music, as in Tennyson's
> "Mariana."[11]

The "vision" achieved is neither metaphysical nor ethical, but
mystical. When it is cut off from the "extraneous" aid of rhetoric and statement, it becomes—*became,* as Mallarmé seemed
finally to recognize—essentially as contentless as a mystical
vision, pure as music itself. It thus gives us what Susanne
Langer calls "the morphology of feeling"—that is, only a *sense*
of meaning (because words unavoidably retain general cognitive denotations) without *precision* of meaning, and thus no
precision of emotion either.

That phrase from Langer is quoted by Donald Davie in his
discussion of her excellent treatment, in *Philosophy in a New
Key,* of the question of meaning in the arts.[12] Elsewhere she
says of music: "Articulation is its life, but not assertion; expres-
siveness, not expression. The actual function of meaning,
which calls for permanent contents, is not fulfilled; for the
assignment of one rather than another possible meaning to
each form is never explicitly made." Langer, as Davie is quick
to point out, does not mean that music is meaningless but that
it uses "presentational" rather than discursive symbolism—
the latter, since it has "permanent contents," being used in
speech and prose. In her writings, Langer realizes that poetry
can, like music, use meaningful arrangement or articulation—
in poetry's case made possible through syntax—to communicate "what it feels like to feel." She views poetry, as an art, as
being essentially like music; but it seems to me that she (like
the Symbolists) has failed to see that poetry can do other

---

[11] McLuhan, "Tennyson," 74, 75.

[12] Donald Davie, *Articulate Energy: An Enquiry into the Syntax of English Poetry*
(1955; reprint, New York: Harcourt, Brace, 1958), 17.

things as well. Proper use of syntax can allow poetry to be *both* discursive and presentational. Limiting it to the latter is a great disservice because poetry does not have sufficient flexibility and precision of sound quality, tone, or even rhythms to "aspire to the condition of music" (as Pater—unfortunately, since he was influential—said all arts should). Poetry, I believe, had best leave purely presentational articulation to music (which is so abstract that it unavoidably excludes discursive meaning and can move us to powerful impressions of feeling without specifying them and thus is free to deal more effectively with *structure* of feeling, *sense* of order). Poetry should use its unique combination of powers to do something music cannot do—that is, both present the structure of a specific feeling and also convey that feeling's moral and cognitive meaning.

Davie, in *Articulate Energy,* has analyzed the effect on modern poetry of the widespread loss of faith in the power of language to make meaningful connections and the consequent aspiration that poetry move toward the condition of music. Many modern poets treat syntax, if it is used at all, as something "wholly different from syntax as understood by logicians and grammarians"; that is, those poets tend to reject syntax as a tool of conceptual thought based on conventionally accepted symbols that allow us to understand each other. Davie provides a basis for understanding that McLuhan's case for Symbolism depends directly on such a nominalistic distrust of conceptual thought. It requires a loss of faith in systematic discourse and the positing of an ultimate faith, with what seems to me even less justification, that experiences are "united in existence" and that mere details of landscape can present them precisely to the . . . what?—consciousness? Davie reminds us that Coleridge opposed such a "delusive notion, that what is not imageable is likewise not conceivable." He recommends that "the power of abstraction . . . be called forth" to "emancipate the mind from the despotism of the eye" and admonishes Wordsworth that "the best part of human language comes

X

An upper chamber in a darken'd house,
Where, ere his footsteps reach'd ripe manhood's brink
Terror & anguish were his cup to drink —
I cannot rid the thought nor hold it close:
But dimly dream upon that Man alone;
Now though the autumn clouds most softly pass,
The cricket creaks beneath the doorstep stone,
And greener than the season grows the grass;
Nor can I drop my lids, nor shade my brows
But there he stands beside the lifted sash,
And with a swooning of the heart I think
Where the black shingles slope to meet the boughs,
And shattered on the roof like smallest snows,
The tiny petals of the mountain ash.

*Holograph of Tuckerman's Sonnet I: 10 from Houghton
MS. Am 1349(3). Used by permission of Houghton
Library, Harvard University.*

from the allocation of fixed symbols to internal acts of the mind."[13]

A major reason for Tuckerman's value to poetic theory, as well as of the greatness of his poetry, is his isolated, unique, but exemplary struggle with these two faiths—the Coleridgean, Anglican, realist faith in conceptual thinking and use of syntactical abstractions for precision in language, and the early Tennysonian, Symbolist, nominalist faith that images are superior to concepts. He is beginning to work out a unique resolution of this dilemma in Sonnet I: 10.

THE FOUR or five years of Tennyson's greatest influence on Tuckerman naturally came to a climax in the year of their visit together, 1855. However, that visit marked both a high point and the beginning of a decline in that influence: Tuckerman found the self-confidence, partly through Tennyson, to begin to rely more on his own resources and judgment; he then, in 1857, experienced an overwhelming but "fruitful" sorrow that gradually called forth all of those resources in order to cope with his grief, both personally and artistically. In the view of a number of critics, the year of the visit, 1855, and the publication then of *Maud and Other Poems,* marks the end of Tennyson's most important lyrical writing.[14] According to Ricks, it is a time when "his greatest achievements were behind him" and "he was successful, famous, secure, and the Poet Laureate."[15] Tennyson took on the public, didactic voice of a mid-Victorian laureate and wrote nothing approaching the quality of the earlier work until the last few years of his life. He did not move on from the "picturesque" capability (what from a historical perspective might be called pre-Symbolism), which he had achieved and had maintained to some extent up through *Maud,* to the more intense and complex forms that

---

[13] The Coleridge quotations are from ibid., 153.
[14] See Smith, *Two Voices,* 2.
[15] Ricks, *Tennyson,* 236.

Baudelaire and his Symbolist successors then created in France. Tennyson did not find a new form of resolution to the tension between his picturesque capability and his "anti-Romantic bias" (the interest in larger issues that only cognitive reflection and statement could satisfy). Instead, he retreated into rather dull if graceful occasional poems and a long struggle with the narrative *Idylls* (without the help of a narrative gift).

Tuckerman, fortunately, did not follow Tennyson along that route. He continued to struggle with the two capabilities Tennyson had helped him develop: the heightened sensual perceptiveness, which enabled him to create imagery related to human "sensation," and faith in the powers of the mind, particularly through language, to create cognitive meaning. Despite Hallam's dichotomy, Tennyson was a poet of both sensation and reflection. And so was Tuckerman, though he resolved the tension more completely. A crucial stage in that resolution is Sonnet I: 10:

> An upper chamber in a darkened house,
> Where, ere his footsteps reached ripe manhood's
>   brink,
> Terror and anguish were his cup to drink;
> I cannot rid the thought nor hold it close
> But dimly dream upon that man alone: [5]
> Now though the autumn clouds most softly pass, . . .

The first three lines evoke in quite general terms a situation which is in some sense (exactly what sense is not important at first) separated from the "I" and "Now" of the following lines. Lines 4 and 5 make clear that the speaker (who we know from the convention of the entire sonnet sequence is Tuckerman himself) is remembering something from the past—a past perception of which he is exploring the meaning and its present power over him. The speaker is both possessed and repelled by the perception ("I cannot rid the thought nor hold it close") and is at the same time both remembering it and developing its meaning for him. The time is now autumn, and we have enough hints to know that we have the traditional use of the passing seasons as a vehicle for thinking about, feeling, the passing of nature's forms and of life itself. During this time when winter and death are approaching, the person speaking focuses on the held-over claims of life—the pervasive summer cricket now moving inside the house, the grass still growing green though the leaves are turning:

> Now though the autumn clouds most softly pass,
> The cricket chides beneath the doorstep stone
> And greener than the season grows the grass.

Despite these images of life persisting in the face of approaching death, the speaker cannot ignore their opposite. From sometime in the past an image of death in the midst of renewing life also persists. The poet looks up, probably from a yard or roadway, at a window where someone (surely himself from the acuteness of the details) once stood seeing and feeling something that now is felt with greater intensity and more powerful claim on him—and now is capable of being expressed in a form of imagery that successfully completes his quest in the mind for meaning:

> Nor can I drop my lids nor shade my brows,
> But there he stands beside the lifted sash;   [10]
> And with a swooning of the heart, I think
> Where the black shingles slope to meet the boughs
> And, shattered on the roof like smallest snows,
> The tiny petals of the mountain ash.

The time of that earlier experience is made precise with the detail of the falling of the petals of the mountain ash, which occurs in late spring, the time as well of Anna's death, when, it seems, Tuckerman looked out from an upper window of their home, darkened by death and mourning, possibly turning from her very deathbed, in terror and anguish. He now remembers that scene in imagery that creates for us its continuing power over him, a recovered reality so intense he can entirely separate himself as present "I" from past "he": Even in that time of spring there were the black, dead shingles sloping down to meet the living boughs and there were delicate, new-fallen petals prefiguring the snows of seasonal change to death. What was then only dimly felt is now thought through in precise imagery, so that he cannot drop his eyes from that remembered vision, because he also *feels* it even more intensely, more precisely and with larger understanding. The power of the mind to transcend time is both liberating and terrible: Tuckerman in the same moment can now literally look up at the window where he once suffered fresh grief and also mentally look out of the window again, now with both renewed intensity and increased understanding, all captured in the same imagery.

The poem is remarkable in many ways, even strange in the impression it makes, because of the intensity of feeling communicated without immediately obvious motive. Individual lines and images, particularly the concluding one, take hold of the mind and live with increasing power in a way that is new in Tuckerman's work. But there are problems. Some of the Romantic vagueness that persisted in Tuckerman is to be found here, particularly in the second line, where bad diction, phrasing and awkward crowding of rhythm and sound produce a line so inferior to the compact, complex, but deceptively simple fourth line, "I cannot rid the thought nor hold it close," that it is hard to believe they have the same author. "Swooning of the heart" is a similarly unfortunate Sentimentalist cliché; "Terror and anguish" (though I will argue otherwise) have also been objected to as imprecise and excessive in their emotional claim.

Yvor Winters was very early attracted to some of the excellent lines and fine descriptive detail in this sonnet but remained throughout his years of teaching it (and in his last book of criticism) convinced that it is marred by typically

Romantic forms of obscurity. In his essay on Emerson and Jones Very, written in the 1930s, he included a footnote that mentioned the recent rediscovery of Tuckerman by Bynner and called him a "distinguished poet," but then he qualified his praise:

> He is, however, romantic in the essential sense; he divorces feeling from motive as far as possible. The beautifully executed sonnet beginning "An upper chamber in a darkened house" is a perfect example of the procedure: a man is imagined in a tragic, but impenetrable, setting, to serve as the symbol of a feeling with which he has no connection and the source of which we are not given.[16]

After seeing "The Cricket" in 1950 and acclaiming it one of the greatest poems in the language, Winters's judgment of Sonnet I: 10 remained essentially unaltered. However, he then began to view it as only a stage in Tuckerman's remarkable development: He saw the poet as moving, within a short career, through successive poetic modes that took three generations to achieve in France and did not occur in England—from derivative and merely competent Romanticism in the early non-sonnets, to Symbolist precision of detail but obscurity of meaning in Sonnet I: 10, and then on to a particularly fruitful combination of rational theme with that precise description in "The Cricket." Winters was convinced that Tuckerman at the fairly early stage of this sonnet is still indulging his Romantic tendencies sufficiently to be led into what Winters elsewhere calls "pseudo-reference"; he felt that, though obsessive "terror and anguish" are claimed, the poem provides no explicit justification for those emotions and, though the precise description of the landscape is such as to convey intense feelings, the source of those feelings is obscure. He also

---

[16] Yvor Winters, *In Defense of Reason* (Denver: Alan Swallow, 1947), 262. Getz, in his 1969 dissertation at Columbia, demonstrates the persistence of Winters's influence on the reading of this poem. Getz tells of a graduate seminar devoted to arguing whether the man in the poem is simply insane and then reads the poem as if he were.

found the grammar and syntax of the last lines obscure and considered them further evidence of Romantic indulgence.

Winters is right, I think, that Tuckerman is engaged here in something much like the Symbolist struggle to let images speak directly, as what Pound called "adequate" symbols, for ideas and feelings. However, I will argue that Tuckerman, even in this fairly early poem of his mature period, is working his way through to a more successful resolution of that intrinsically questionable effort than the Symbolists ever found.

First, it is important to recognize that this sonnet is part of a sequence; and Tuckerman, perhaps more than any other sonneteer in English, took the idea of a sequence seriously. He saw at least each series (and certainly the first two series together) as a fully integrated whole. Many of his sonnets continue directly from one to the next, some in mid-sentence. Direct and indirect references backward and forward in the series are common, with clear intent to assist understanding and response. Thus the context for determining whether Tuckerman is providing adequate motive for the emotions he claims, or for the intense feeling of the description, is larger than this fourteen-line part of the whole "poem" which is the sequence. Furthermore, we can assume that Tuckerman was fully aware that any serious work of literature is created for the second and successive readings, the first reading so often being dependent on, and distracted by, specious forms of suspense. Such a work can thereby take advantage of various forms of dramatic irony and other such devices which depend on the reader holding the whole work in his mind as he reads. Thus, Sonnet I: 10 can, and does, depend for its full resonance on explicit references throughout the First Series (whether before or *after* this "stanza") to Anna's death and to the feelings and perceptions which that event triggered in Tuckerman. In that context there is nothing obscure about the emotions claimed and suggested in this sonnet.

In addition, it is important to realize that Tuckerman is struggling to develop a new poetic technique here. The poem refers specifically to the struggle, and that unusual closing syntax is a kind of definition of the technique. It is a way of making general, remembered, feelings, those associated with sensory details, achieve the precision of integrated—that is, properly motivated—feeling in relation to cognitive understanding. The poem defines its own motivation for the feeling it claims, in a new form of imagery that carries precise meaning. The development is not from specific details to general theme but from general feeling to the specific. A past premonition that can at first be only vaguely described as terror and anguish is now being rethought in the present with perceptions from the past, using past sensations informed by present understanding. The perceptions, thus, are now capable of being precisely recreated for us in the poem, in part through the use of that somewhat mysterious (music-like) power of rhythm and rhyme to affect our feelings in their relationship to the expression of particular images. We are given a specific realization of the terror and anguish that a particular man felt in the face of mortality and is now feeling again with new understanding.

This is not merely a meditation on death—a linear, inductive argument—nor is it simply reverie over strong feelings recollected in a free association of sensory images. It is not thinking *about* something but *rethinking* it by way of selected and empowered verbal images; it is the most mature form of expression of a mature poet, experiencing and creating for us a new experience of combined idea and emotion. Thus it is probably the earliest and certainly one of the most interesting achievements of what Winters described, in discussing other poems, as post-Symbolist imagery—speaking, of course, in an epistemological, not a historical, sense.

TO A GREAT extent, in Tennyson's "picturesque" poetry, and certainly in Mallarmé's Symbolist work, the interest is not in apprehension or idea but in feeling—in the strength and unusualness of human emotions, not in the understanding of or even accuracy in relation to them. To satisfy their nominalist skepticism about the ability of language to approximate the rapid flux of experience, the Symbolists aimed for a "pure" poetry, cleansed of denotative reference, of ideational content; they yearned for a language with the "freedom" of music. But post-Symbolist imagery depends for its effects not only on the Symbolist sophistication about perception of details and evocation of strong or unusual feelings; it depends as well on language that retains its syntactical categories and takes advantage of the denotative power of language. It thus increases rather than decreases its ability to be accurate in relation to experience and also increases its scope to include—as well as sensory perception—the life of ideas, judgment, and the like, that goes on *within* the mind.[17]

If the logical syntax and denotative content of words are not retained, language loses its function of providing what St. John Perse calls "fiduciary symbols like coins as values of monetary exchange."[18] These are the conventional, or agreed-upon, values that thus can be related and controlled in such ways as will achieve precise communication of content. However, that function can be retained only if we can summon enough philosophical realism to have faith that minds are sufficiently alike for fixed conventions of any kind to be justified, a faith that seems *necessary* if language is to be used at all seriously

---

[17] Davie, in *Articulate Energy,* quotes T. C. Pollock from *The Nature of Literature* (Princeton, N. J.: Princeton Univ. Press, 1942): "Abstract and generalized linguistic forms are more useful than are concrete for making specific references" (13). Davie shows—conclusively, it seems to me—that the efforts of some poets (in hope of being more "concrete" and true to experience) to destroy logical syntax or to turn it to other uses are certainly understandable and that those efforts are even fruitful for the achievement of certain resources in poetry. But whenever such poets have succeeded, they have removed from language and poetry its chief source of power to deal with the basic concretions—that is, our experiences and our total intellectual and emotional response as part of those experiences. Davie also quotes Pollock's demonstration that what we call "objects" are, psychologically speaking, *abstractions from experiences* and concludes that the effort to "purify" language, to make words directly embody things, makes language *more* abstract rather than less (108).

[18] Quoted in ibid., 97.

or effectively. That again is a faith held by Tuckerman's fellow Anglican, Coleridge:

> The educated man chiefly seeks to discover and express those connections of things, or those relative bearings of fact, from which some more or less general law is deducible. For facts are valuable to a wise man, chiefly as they lead to the discovery of the indwelling law, which is the true being of things, the sole solution of their modes of existence, and in the knowledge of which consists our dignity and our power.[19]

Such a human possibility can only be approached if language is used in a way that preserves its powers of syntax and denotation ("fiduciary symbols"), a way that takes advantage of its ability to make connections and to articulate and precisely control a context of meaning which has specific intellectual and moral content. But, as Davie also reminds us, poetry uses language in ways that take advantage of additional resources: "Not all of the words in a poem should be 'fiduciary symbols.' . . . We want, for objects as for actions, words which partake of the denseness and the tang of the things they stand for . . . loosely but usefully called, in our criticism, images."[20]

It is only in this combination of words as images and words as counters or signs (together with the special powers of rhythm and rhyme to affect emotion in relation to idea, which I examine later) that poetry can exploit its special power to use *all* of the resources of language. It is the special achievement of post-Symbolist poetry to draw most completely on these resources in order to create forms uniquely compact and integrated. The post-Symbolist image, though remaining as precise at the level of sensory detail and as evocative of feeling as the Symbolist image, grows out of a quest for a larger reality than the Symbolists had faith in reaching. It is, in Winters's phrase, the ultimate in poetic "forms of discovery"

---

[19] Quoted in ibid., 109.
[20] Ibid., 122.

and leads specifically, as Coleridge put it, to "the discovery of the indwelling law, which is the true being of things." But it retains a specific fidelity as well to nominalist concern for "the denseness and the tang" of externally originating experience.

Tuckerman's editor, N. Scott Momaday, observes, in an analysis of "The Cricket," that "for Tuckerman the ultimate question is not how to die but how to live in the face of death."[21] The values Tuckerman affirms in "The Cricket," and in some ways even more clearly defines for himself in Sonnet I: 10, achieve a realization of one of the most significant and difficult themes of the great religious poets, the one expressed definitively by Winters in the epigraph for this chapter: We can only transcend the world's claims on us by fully comprehending, appreciating, and preparing to leave them—not by either ignoring the world or pretending to merge with it. Sonnet I: 10 is about a struggle to understand a perception about those claims of mortality. It is not about what caused the perception except as that is made clear in the struggle and by images forged from the crucible of that struggle. The *subject* of the poem is not a specific loss but what Edgar Bowers has called "the form of loss."

Tuckerman's achievement is a successful move beyond the "dimly dream" of line 5 to the "think" of line 11 and the following image, which is a remarkable creation of the thought which he "cannot rid." Those last lines are an example, probably the earliest in literary history, of a fine, powerful technique used in modern poetry. That special technique attempts to bring the means of the rational mind for dealing with reality—that is, conceptional language with all its resources in the poem— to as close a reconciliation with the particulars of existence as may be possible without denying the very nature of language and thought. The technique is characterized by a special use of description in which the details themselves are charged with

---

21 N. Scott Momaday, in the introduction to "An Edition of the Complete Poems of Frederick Goddard Tuckerman" (Ph.D. diss., Stanford Univ., 1963), 43.

meaning both through selection and through an expressed relationship to the total context of the poem.

Natural detail does not itself contain meaning or moral significance (the pathetic fallacy of the Romantics must be avoided; there must be no imposition of meaning or emotion on a physical realm not capable of knowing or feeling). However, meaning can be made to reach out to detail through selection, concentration, and shaping of the details with the resources of language until meaning and detail are more or less inseparably joined. Thus the details and their relationships are expressed in a certain context and manner that parallels and reveals moral and intellectual—that is to say, human—experience.

In Sonnet I: 10 the vagueness of the speaker's anguish and also his ambivalence are resolved through the language in the latter part of the poem, which actually creates the reality of the beauty he perceives. Such beauty is an antidote to the pain of continued existence in the shadow of death and is therefore increased in its preciousness ("Death is the mother of beauty," Wallace Stevens would say); but simultaneously that beauty is an evidence and reminder of death. The passing clouds and changing seasons and blackening shingles and falling petals are not just like death; they *are* death—but only in a general sense. To describe them in the terms and sounds and rhythms that Tuckerman chooses is both to describe death in a particular way and to evoke powerfully the emotion that the chosen terms of perspective on death in the poem should motivate. The description creates and justifies the tone, which is a moral judgment of an important and understandable content.

Tuckerman begins to achieve in this poem both the emotional immediacy of sensory details and an intellectual context that can communicate the significance of that immediacy. He is able to *control* with precision the powerful suggestions of his descriptive details through his use of poetic form and syntax and by the nature of the images themselves as they are expressed in language. Tuckerman is not attempting to report or to create an obscure or esoteric emotion; he is trying to define for himself and his fellow human beings (who can be reached to that effect only through language), as fully and exactly as possible, the qualities of his specific response to the general human experience with death.[22]

Certainly, "good" or "precise" description must be accurate, detailed, and, in poetry, concentrated. Sometimes the force of uniqueness or newness or simplicity or a combination of these is what assures our "seeing" the details. Yet these difficult accomplishments are not enough. In addition, the description must be so fitted into the full context—which includes meter, rhythm, relationship of syntax to line and to rhyme, and the like—that either idea or emotion are served. In this post-Symbolist method Tuckerman is developing, *both* must be served. The right details must be selected and so expressed that they will give precisely the subject of which the details are a part at both the descriptive and thematic levels. The details will also control the emotion, which carries moral

---

[22] Robert Pinsky, in his fine study of Landor, hints at what seem to me some intriguing similarities, despite the enormous differences, in these two "anti-Romantic" poets. The following characteristic way of operating for Landor—giving acute specificity to a common human emotion—seems exactly what Tuckerman is successfully struggling for in Sonnet I: 10 (though Tuckerman uses a method that was never attempted by Landor):

> The reader, in other words, is to understand that the emotion of the poem — real as it is — exists in its truest, most perfect state on the page, in the tone of the poem. This tone is likely to be the product of many separate, brilliant moments of composition, each fashioning the inert clay of the commonplace. The *exact* emotion is the tone of the poem; unlike the original commonplace, it never existed until the last painstaking revision was completed.
>
> One can say that Landor sees his value as a poet to be that of giving us tones, exact qualities of response to generalized, and therefore familiar experience; he assumes a basic, quite available, and rather vague commonality of human emotion, and he struggles for clarification and definition within this commonality. The definition makes the emotion acute. (*Landor's Poetry* [Chicago: Univ. of Chicago Press, 1968], 32)

judgment with exact appropriateness and conviction that move the reader.

The descriptive details available in nature, though none of them contain cognitive or moral significance in themselves, have a varied *potential* for being used to help communicate a particular human response to experience. This is because of the uses they have been put to traditionally and also because of their own nature. They have an irreducible existence in a dimension not fully amenable to man's rationality. Tuckerman shared the nominalist determination to be true to that irreducibility and the Romantic yearning to cross the void to that dimension, but he also had the rationalist faith that the needed bridges can be made in language. He developed the skill to justify his faith; he learned to have confidence in the appropriateness of certain kinds of detail and relationships for illumination of particular states and processes of mind. And Tuckerman learned to select and shape in language that natural potential, the way a sculptor might shape the "right" piece of wood or stone, to reach his final statement. The meaning is both discovered and invented; it is a shaping of and adjustment to reality.[23]

Tuckerman's method, then, effectively realizes the Romantic quest to relate the inner and outer life—the desire, in René Wellek's words, "to read a meaning into the landscape, but also . . . to find it there."[24] It best responds to what M. H. Abrams calls the Romantic interest in metaphors for "the chief theme of continuity and interchange between outer motions and interior life and powers."[25] However, it does not respond to these yearnings in the Transcendentalist manner of seeing objects only as emblems of a greater, invisible reality and thus falsifying their particularity, nor in the Symbolist manner of

---

[23] I am indebted to Professor Don Markos of California State University at Hayward for helping me articulate this idea of the varied inherent potential for meaning of natural details.

[24] Northrop Frye, ed., *Romanticism Reconsidered* (New York: Columbia Univ. Press, 1963), 125.

[25] Ibid.

exalting the particularity of things until their verbal images partake of the delusory fascination of magic but become merely inscrutable.

Tuckerman's poetic method, then, is the first instance of what Winters defined as post-Symbolism; and to understand better both the method and Tuckerman's poetry, it can be useful to look at Winters' own work. In a discussion of Winters' poetry, Howard Kaye gives an extremely helpful explication of the method and some of the characteristics of its results. I agree with Kaye that Winters overstates when he declares that the simultaneity of concept and sense-perception, of tenor and vehicle, in post-Symbolist imagery is qualitatively different from that in other metaphoric language. The difference is more nearly quantitative, though significant:

> The Renaissance vehicles Winters calls ornamental are not devoid of thematic significance, but may be less closely involved with the articulation of the poem's abstract idea than ... poems which fulfill his ideals.... An abstract style on the one hand, without sensory details, and the metaphoric-ornamental and Symbolist methods on the other, where sensory vehicles eclipse the abstract meaning, bracket ... post-Symbolist imagery.[26]

In the course of some illuminating analysis of Winters' work Kaye points out the tendency of this method to appear "cultish," because the tenor is so bound up in the descriptive details that it may be available only to those with some knowledge of Winters's ideas and concerns. But Kaye is right in saying that such knowledge is certainly no more than is necessary to read Yeats, Eliot, or Pound and in fact is usually less. This is because of the "keys," words which act effectively on both the descriptive and thematic levels but call attention to themselves since they are unexpectedly abstract at the level of the vehicle and thus force the reader to consider their implications for

---

[26] Howard Kaye, "The Post-Symbolist Poetry of Yvor Winters," *Southern Review* 7 (Winter 1971): 181–82.

the tenor. Such a word, if it is working at the level of the method's ideal, always "acquires by association more sensory specificity than it would enjoy by itself"; and the use of such words does not mean that the method produces mere allegories or puzzles, which can be solved as soon as we find the keys by which the meaning can be fully reduced to cognitive terms. The virtue of the post-Symbolist image is that it eludes the limitations of the Symbolist image but still employs Symbolist strengths in its power of suggestiveness about the detailed reality, the mystery beyond fully defined meaning, of the universe beyond the mind.

Nor are such "keys," or descriptive words slightly too abstract for their context, always necessary. For it is quite possible, as Kaye demonstrates in his analysis of Winters's "A Summer Commentary," to use certain concrete details, certain juxtapositions of imagery and of chronological ordering, to advance an argument that is sufficiently cognitive that it can be usefully paraphrased (though not exhausted by the paraphrase). This happens precisely because of the specificity of the details and the form. Sonnet I: 10 requires no more "external" knowledge of Tuckerman's state of mind than does Winters's poetry; and, in fact, if we accept Tuckerman's use of the convention of the sonnet sequence and see Sonnet I: 10 as informed by the specific references to Anna's death made later in the series, there is no need for *any* "external" information. Even without such references from the larger "poem"—standing by itself—the sonnet works powerfully enough. Though "terror" and "anguish" possibly claim too much, too vaguely, at first, and thus are somewhat melodramatic (a slight lapse of taste in diction), yet they are quite appropriate for a Christian's response to his estranged and fallen mortal state (surely as much his bitter "cup to drink" as it was Christ's in the face of isolation and death). They are right enough for any man's anxiety in the face of contingent existence, and eventually they are given an exact specificity.

A good part of the precisely focused energy of the poem is created in the last four lines, and Winters was mistaken in thinking those lines are marred by obscurity. Certainly, the reader's normal expectations about grammatical forms are thwarted. Thus, he is forced to focus particular attention upon the form and content of the speaker's *rethinking* of his terrible confrontation with mortality, and he is prepared for the created tension to be "resolved" with a new, but legitimate, syntactical form:

> And with a swooning of the heart, I think
> Where the black shingles slope to meet the boughs
> And, shattered on the roof like smallest snows,
> The tiny petals of the mountain ash.

The construction of those last lines is not at all a grammatical *lapse* on Tuckerman's part, nor is it unclear. It is an intentional use of an *unusual* syntactical form that in fact describes the new poetic method the poet is using at the same time that it identifies the poet-speaker with his former perception and its completed meaning in the details of present perception. The source of apparent difficulty is that, in modern times, "think" normally takes an indirect object. We think *of* or *about* things. But "think" was used fairly commonly down into the nineteenth century as a transitive verb with a substantive or adverbial object. For instance, in Milton's *Paradise Lost,* "Peace is despaired, / For who can think submission?"; in Shelley's *The Cenci,* "While yet manhood remained, to act / The thing I thought"; in Cowper's *The Task,* "Meditation here / May think down hours to moments." Tuckerman's syntax in these lines is unusual in order to meet his unusual needs. The object of "think" is the imagery embodied in a complex adverbial phrase, the entire last three lines of the poem.[27] The speaker in the poem is thinking

---

[27] It has been encouraging to find confirmation of some of my preceding analysis in an excellent, though rather obscure, essay by Edwin H. Cady, the only published criticism other than my own which makes more than slight reference to Sonnet I: 10 ("Frederick Goddard Tuckerman," *Essays on Ameri-*

through or with the details of the description—the created images—and he makes the grammar not into a limitation but into a tool.

The speaker does not say I think *about* this image, but I *think* this image. He is not thinking *of* something in the past but thinking *again* the images of a past perception, selected and informed with his present understanding—including the full integrity of the rational mind as well as the swooning of the heart. He therefore chooses to think the juncture of life and death in a line that creates a visual focus and depression to define his theme and mood as it brings the dead, fixed shingles down against the living tree: "Where the black shingles slope to meet the boughs." The speaker finally thinks again the beauty of the frail white petals shattered in death on the black roof: "And, shattered on the roof like smallest snows /

----

can Literature in Honor of Jay B. Hubbell, ed. Clarence Gohdes [Durham, N.C.: Duke Univ. Press, 1967], 141–51). Cady, as I do, reprints the poem in Tuckerman's published version (which retains "cup to drink") and calls it "a prime example of his finest poetic genius." He claims, *contra* Winters, that it "is in fact syntactically not notably difficult," though he offers no explanation of the syntax but merely notes the speaker's complexity of vision (both looking up at the window and remembering when he stood there). Cady continues, "The difficulty is not linguistic but one of perspective. When the perspective shifts from the narrator's view to that of the subject, what occurs is a sharp dissociation, a blocking. Suddenly to the mind's eye it is very exactly spring, with the white on black paradox of blossoms like snow on the roof." Cady concludes his essay with a brief but, it seems to me, highly perceptive comment on the overall effect of this poem:

> The poem is confessional for its speaking narrator. Because he cannot be rid of the smitten sufferer lost out of time in his moment of terror and anguish, and because he can unite his vision with that of the sufferer, the two are one. His memory is projective, but he is the sufferer.... Finally, moreover, what is there ever to say of grief? Only perhaps that, while tyrannically overwhelming, it has no meaning. One sees, exactly irrelevantly, beyond comprehension, how time, nature, beauty, and all the rest merely go on. Perhaps the poem is not mysterious because it is not symbolic at all. It is only a perfect way of saying something about the emotionally ultimate. (150–51)

The tiny petals of the mountain ash." If we admit the possibility of thinking in images, if we have faith that we need not merely let sense impressions freely associate but can carefully create a response to experience in language, using the potential of sensory details from landscape, then these lines certainly realize that possibility. The lines therefore create their own precise emotional motive in the context of the general rational theme. The poet is fully sensitive to the claims of mortality but is prepared to put them by. He sees life clearly, with death as an ultimate part of life. The poem increases our appreciation of the possibilities of language even as it refines and impassions our vision of life.

V

MATURITY: AN ELEGY

But unto him came swift calamity
In the sweet springtime when his beds were green;
And my heart waited, trustfully serene,
For the new blossom on my household tree.
But flowers and gods and quaint philosophy
Are poor, in truth, to fill the empty place.

Sonnet II: 9

BETWEEN the tenth sonnet of the First Series, in which Tuckerman creates a new kind of imagery in the struggle to cope with Anna's death, and the elegaic grouping of six sonnets midway through the Second Series, which uses that form of imagery in a sustained mythic context, there are thirty-two sonnets. Each of these sonnets either makes a direct reference—or is explicitly connected to a neighboring sonnet that does—which indicates that the constant background for its theme and tone is Tuckerman's great "sorrow." I have argued that this is true of *all* the sonnets in the first two series, and thus there is an assumed background for Sonnet I: 10 that frees Tuckerman to concentrate on discovering a specific form for his response. This secure base also lies behind the "elegy," freeing Tuckerman to create as vehicle an unusual transposition of Anna into "sister-twins" and to place them, without fear that his tenor might be obscure, in a traditional elegaic context: the changes and losses in human and natural history.

Sonnet II: 9, quoted in part as the epigraph for this chapter, shows Tuckerman developing his unusual device of transforming himself and Anna into more objectifiable forms (the device also appears in some of his non-sonnets written at about this time). In the preceding two sonnets he uses one of his thinly disguised personae, a preoccupied gardener, to describe himself from the outside ("His heart was in his garden; but his brain / Wandered at will among the fiery stars," Sonnet II: 7). He tramps in the fields and woods with this alter-ego (as he does in "The Stranger"), quotes his wisdom ("beauty . . . is seen where'er we look"), but then shifts back to full identity with him (from "him" to "my") in the course of one sentence: " . . . unto him came swift calamity / . . . And my heart waited, trustfully serene / For the new blossom on my household tree" (Sonnet II: 9, p. 23).

After Anna's death, which had followed the childbirth that brought the "new blossom," "undimmed the May went on with bird and bower." However, for Tuckerman, "flowers and gods and quaint philosophy / Are poor, in truth, to fill the empty place." As this passage implies, Tuckerman is indeed fully, desperately, engaged in a theodicy, his own attempt to explain the ways of God to at least himself. The curve of the First Series goes from the shock of initial loss of faith in nearly everything (mitigated only by the assumption that "God were not God, whom knowledge cannot know," which at least leaves him something to work with) to the affirmation in Sonnet I: 28 of that God beyond the natural world and the deep mind that can be reached across "the void." The Second Series moves though a similar arc: Despite his faith in God and an attempt to put Anna's death into the perspective of ongoing life ("whilst overhead / Creation moveth, and the farmboy sleeps / A still strong sleep"), Tuckerman feels deep pessimism about the continued meaning of his life and work ("a joyless verse I turn" [Sonnet II: 2, p. 19]) and the possibility of ever finding solace, of ever being able to move beyond his stunned grief.

However, in the process of this longest of the five series Tuckerman achieves the moving optimism of its last few sonnets, where he explicitly bids Anna final farewell, assuring her

> I would not hide my face from light, nor shun
> The full completion of this worldly day. . . .

> I will not fear to take the path alone,
> Loving for thy sake things that cheer and bless.
> (Sonnet II: 34, p. 35)

He ends the two series with a lovely classical frame (offering them to his Maker as Eponina did her "children of the tomb"), then publishes his *Poems* and goes on, in the remaining three series, which he never published, to other themes. His greatest poem, "The Cricket," which I discuss in the next chapter, is a magnificent working out of the meaning of that promise to Anna to "take the path alone" and not shun the "full completion of this worldly day."

Within these larger movements of the first two series are expressed a number of smaller movements of Tuckerman's soul and sensibility, circuitous journeys of significant growth in understanding and feeling, accomplished in individual sonnets and groups. For example, the intensity of Sonnet I: 10 is followed by a poem of enormous spiritual exhaustion in the face of his "dark household woe." He rouses himself in I: 12 with a "cry for strength," but it is conveyed in the already-defeated image of himself as a boy striking down weed stalks. Then in Sonnet I: 13 he recognizes the bleak condition of his faith in the figure of a marooned sailor who sees the great constellations that he had once used for navigation "through mists that hinder and deform / The dewy stars of home," taunting him in their beckoning uselessness. These movements out into new areas of questioning, in which he discovers new images for the motions of his thoughts and feelings, work constant variations upon the bedrock theme of Tuckerman's grief.

Far from being repetitive, the sixty-six sonnets in the first two series (almost all written soon after and in direct response to what could have been an immobilizing blow) evidence a Tennyson-like outpouring of creative energy. In fact, Tuckerman turned directly, for a model for both form and content, to *In Memoriam,* the extended elegy Tennyson had written as part of his remarkably creative response to his own most immobilizing blow.[1] The similarity to Tennyson's remarkable "flowering" from 1833 to 1835, in a cluster of poems all responding to the loss of Hallam, is increased by evidence that less than a third of Tuckerman's poetry was written before his wife's death, another third was written after the 1860 *Poems* and never published in his lifetime, but the remainder—nearly half of the published poems—was probably written in the three years between the death of Anna and the publication of *Poems*. The work of that short period is more consistently skillful and moving than that of any other time and exhibits particular achievements greater than those of any other poem, with the single exception of "The Cricket." Though nothing quite rises to the overall quality and particular success with a new method of Sonnet I: 10 until we reach the elegy, individual lines and images occur constantly that are amazing. And except for a few sonnets, which were written at perhaps the

----

[1] Of the phenomenon of Tennyson's creative response to grief, Christopher Ricks writes, "A more immediate effect of Hallam's death was a burst of imaginative energy that intensifies and corroborates the achievement of the previous year or so, and makes the years 1833–1834 the most remarkable flowering of Tennyson's genius . . . . A cluster of poems responded at once and directly to Hallam's death" (*Tennyson* [New York: Macmillan, 1972], 119). The obvious formal imitation Tuckerman makes of *In Memoriam* is his use of the *a b b a* rhyme of Tennyson's stanzas for the first four lines of each of his sonnets, which make up the "stanzas" of his own extended elegy. The obvious similarities in content have been summarized by David Seed:

> Both [Tennyson and Tuckerman] are writing their way out of loss through a serial sequence of short lyrics which examine particular stages in the process. Both set up a dialectical relation of self to setting which might mirror mood or agonizingly remind the poet of the lost friend or wife. Both writers broaden their individual sense of loss outward to include religious doubt, and both unify their sequences by local connections or by recurrent images. Finally both poets experience, and then immediately question, a fleeting contact with the dead subject of their sequences (Tennyson in lyric 95, Tuckerman in I: 23). ("Alone with God and Nature: The Poetry of Jones Very and Frederick Goddard Tuckerman," in *Nineteenth-Century American Poetry*, ed. A. Robert Lee (London: Vision Press, 1985), 186.)

greatest ebb of his self-control and thus lose artistry and force in the informed explicitness of their grief, each of the poems written in this period is interesting and powerful.

Above all, the poems are convincing in their clearly communicated purpose: They do bring out "into the light," and give some ordering to the elements of, a shattered life. Tuckerman moves from despair to a kind of certitude (which is then re-examined and reformulated again and again) and from irrational grief to a kind of confidence, not exuberant but sufficient to maintain him through a long and lonely sorrow. He gradually but fully escapes the self-pity that is a constant temptation in the first of the sonnets. The achieved resolution that is the subject of the closing poems of each series, and which is reached in successive small victories throughout, is entirely believable. If we have been through the sonnets with Tuckerman, we know that the resolution is not just claimed but earned.

One of the low points in the journeyings of Tuckerman's spirit is reached after the explicit recounting of his loss in Sonnet II: 9, quoted at the beginning of this chapter. In the next sonnet he recalls, speaking directly to Anna, their hopeful conversations about the expected child and is so distraught that he is careless whether he "fall at once" or "Stand like a charred and fire-hardened trunk, / To break the axe's edge of time and fate." He desperately snatches for any "beam of comfort," but the image he forms is of the "witchlight of the reedy rivershore," the ghostly illusion that fools the engineer into stopping his train and is "not to be left, but with the waste woodland." In Sonnet II: 12 his despair extends again to his poetry:

> How most unworthy, echoing in mine ears,
> The verse sounds on: life, love, experience, art
> Fused into grief and, like a grief-filled heart
> Where all emotion tends and turns to tears,
> Broken by its own strength of passion and need.

The image is of "feverish / Beatings against a gate forever barred." He then compares himself to a lover who "calls o'er his mistress' features hour by hour," and he indulges in just that—dreaming on Anna's beauty in Sonnet II: 13. But next follows Sonnet II: 14, a first-rate poem that belies his despair with writing poetry as he recalls a day on Long Island with Anna, developing the imagery of the sea's primordial identification with death and dissolution that he will use later as a central source of energy in "The Cricket":

> Again I hear the drenching of the wave;
> The rocks rise dark, with wall and weedy cave;
> Her voice is in mine ears, her answer yet:
> Again I see above the froth and fret
> The blue loft standing like eternity
> And white feet flying from the surging surf
> And simmering suds of the sea!

From this springboard Tuckerman thrusts us into an entirely new perspective as he moves into the group of six sonnets I am calling an elegy:

> Gertrude and Gulielma, sister-twins,
> Dwelt in the valley at the farmhouse old;
> Nor grief had touched their locks of dark and gold
> Nor dimmed the fragrant whiteness of their skins:
> Both beautiful, and one in height and mould;
> Yet one had loveliness which the spirit wins
> To other worlds: eyes, forehead, smile and all,
> More softly serious than the twilight's fall.
> The other—can I e'er forget the day
> When, stealing from a laughing group away,
> To muse with absent eye and motion slow,
> Her beauty fell upon me like a blow?—
> Gertrude! with red flowerlip, and silk black hair!
> Yet Gulielma was by far more fair.
>
> (Sonnet II: 15, p. 26)

In *Forms of Discovery* Yvor Winters first identified this and the following five poems as a unified group that could be designated an elegy and in which "the force of the whole outweighs particular faults."[2] In the anthology designed to accompany that book of criticism, edited by Winters and Kenneth Fields, Fields writes that the poems "as a group are more impressive than any single poem."[3] These comments apply to some extent to each of the five series, and to the first two series taken together as a single sequence, but they are particularly apt for this group of six sonnets. Tuckerman is more clearly engaged here than anywhere in a unified effort to objectify his grief through the use of conventions that human beings have developed over thousands of years to deal with their overwhelmingly powerful and difficult experiences and feelings in the face of death. Of course he gives these elegaic conventions the stamp of his own unique invention; as all fine poets have done, he makes his variations on the conventional theme of formal lament tell precisely the quality of his particular response to his loss, within the context of all human loss.

The first poem (or strophe or stanza of the elegy) uses a device similar to that of a special form of elegy—the pastoral—by representing Anna and her mourner as quasi-mythic figures. Anna is in fact divided into *two* figures, representing her spiritual and physical qualities. Tuckerman uses a common convention of romances of his time (developed by Walter Scott and popularized in America by Cooper and his imitators): the tension between the dark, exotic, physically seductive heroine and the blond, "natural," spiritual paragon whom the hero, after trial and gloom, finally prefers. Perry Miller, in an essay on Melville, shows how this convention became for Americans the embodiment of the "issue of the nineteenth

---

[2] Yvor Winters, *Forms of Discovery: Critical and Historical Essays on the Forms of the Short Poem in English* (Denver: Alan Swallow, 1967), 258.

[3] Yvor Winters and Kenneth Fields, eds., *Quest for Reality: An Anthology of Short Poems in English* (Chicago: Swallow Press, 1969), 4.

century," coming to represent "a victory of nature over culture, of simplicity over complexity, of country over city."[4]

The almost frenetic insistence on this convention revealed
the profound American anxiety of the time, its subconscious
fear that nature would not prevail against the ruthless march
of man across the continent. Melville finally despaired at the
shallowness of the Transcendentalist assurance that simple
heartfelt
impulse would lead aright—to the salvation of the individual
and nature. He worked with that despair in *Pierre* through a
deliberate confusion of the romance convention (the hero
chooses the dark heroine—his sister!—by natural impulse and
is pursued by the *blond* to the *city,* where all three go to
their destruction). That convention is surely working in
Tuckerman's mind to a purpose similar to Melville's, since it is
obvious in the remainder of the elegy that he has a similar disenchantment with Transcendentalist optimism. His understanding of the ambiguity in America's at once profoundly
worshipful and yet implacably destructive relationship to nature is being developed as a context in which to comprehend
the loss of Anna.

The quiet overall excellence of Sonnet II: 15 deserves
emphasis. Only the inversion at the close of line 2 is weak.
The writing is consistently impressive and conveys certainly,
if without any extraordinary effects, the qualities of Anna
and her impact upon Tuckerman. But the next sonnet *is*
extraordinary:

> Under the mountain, as when first I knew
> Its low dark roof and chimney creeper-twined,
> The red house stands; and yet my footsteps find,
> Vague in the walks, waste balm and feverfew.

---

[4]Perry Miller, *Nature's Nation* (Cambridge, Mass.: Harvard Univ. Press,
1967), 185.

> But they are gone: no soft-eyed sisters trip   [5]
> Across the porch or lintels; where, behind,
> The mother sat, sat knitting with pursed lip.
> The house stands vacant in its green recess,
> Absent of beauty as a broken heart.
> The wild rain enters, and the sunset wind   [10]
> Sighs in the chambers of their loveliness
> Or shakes the pane—and in the silent noons
> The glass falls from the window, part by part,
> And ringeth faintly in the grassy stones.
>   (Sonnet II: 16, p. 26)

The formality of the pastoral realm of the "soft-eyed sisters" and the aptness and precision of descriptive details and rhythms all work to withhold the sentimentality that could easily intrude. The emotion, whose power comes from the whole series and can be sensed clearly in the background here, is also carefully controlled with understatement and with the post-Symbolist method I describe earlier, using detailed natural imagery to convey the theme. That theme is the irrevocable passing of Anna in the context of the irrevocable deterioration of all human abodes and memories—the mysterious, impenetrable gap between the present and past of what was formerly vital but is now decayed or dead. The *description* of the decaying house is perfectly accurate and "natural," but at the same time it is chosen and ordered so as to convey the *significance* of the loss of house and occupants to the poet. He uses both syntax and rhythm to convey the details of the division within time and existence that he feels and is struggling to understand. As early as line 2 the descriptive details begin to prepare us to see a building merging back into the landscape; but at the beginning of line 3, through the firm iambic rhythm and an almost startling detail of color, Tuckerman shows us that still, for him, "The red house stands" in special importance. However, as the poet gets closer, in an almost abstracted, tentative approach, his footsteps "find" small useful herbs still growing.[5] But before he identifies them he prepares us to feel a certain way about them:

Vágue ĭn / thĕ wálks, / wăste bálm / ănd fév- / ĕrfĕw.

The trochee at the beginning of the line and the heavily stressed, though metrically unaccented, word following the strong caesura emphasize two key words that alert us to Tuckerman's special method: "Vague" and "waste," at the level of vehicle, perfectly describe the random, untended growth now useless to humans, especially the former tenants. At the level of tenor, these words develop the theme of absolute cleavage between that time when the beloved occupants of the house intentionally cared for those herbs and the present when the plants grow wild, beyond human control.

Tuckerman moves back to a strong regular iambic rhythm at the start of line 5 in order to intensify the finality of his loss, but then he immediately develops a more varied rhythm that aids in imitation of the actions of those who are gone—and thus serves to make specific and believable to the reader his feeling about them:

> But they are gone: no soft-eyed sisters trip   [5]
> Across the porch or lintels; where, behind,
> The mother sat, sat knitting with pursed lip.

The fast runover from line 5 to line 6 and the varied speed of the first part of 6, which ends abruptly in mid-foot before the strong caesura, help give the feeling of the light movement of the sisters, in a particular scene from his memory. The rhythm, syntax, and diction of line 7 give us the contrasting mother: This is a regular iambic pentameter line, but Tuckerman plays

---

[5] I am indebted to James McMichael's discussion of this poem in *The Style of the Short Poem* (Belmont, Calif.: Wadsworth Publishing, 1967), 55–60, 64–68, for help with parts of the following analysis of rhythmic effects.

against that norm two strongly *stressed* but *unaccented* syllables, the second "sat" and "pursed," to help give us his sense of the mother's preoccupied stolidity. He intensifies this effect with that repetition of "sat" and also by putting "pursed" with "lip" (rather than the usual cliché, "pursed mouth"), a fine kinesthetic combination because it requires an imitation of the action to pronounce. The poet then returns to the present signs of decay, which register on him with increased subtlety and power:

> The wild rain enters, and the sunset wind   [10]
> Sighs in the chambers of their loveliness
> Or shakes the pane—and in the silent noons
> The glass falls from the window, part by part,
> And ringeth faintly in the grassy stones.

These lines leave an impression that is unforgettable, though impossible to explicate fully. We can notice the effects of the trochee at the beginning of line 11 and the one in the second position of line 13. Used in connection with particular sound combinations, one helps imitate sighs but the other falling glass. A sense of almost imperceptible but nevertheless absolute change is created by the image of the sunset wind loosening the glass panes, which then fall, seemingly without cause, in the silent, windless noons—just as change occurs in the heart, which, in its own time, closes, in Dickinson's words, "Like stone" ("After great pain, a formal feeling comes,") or, to quote her again, "First—Chill—then Stupor—then the letting go—." Indeed, Tuckerman is working throughout this elegy (as he is in many of his poems) with something very close to that device in Dickinson's work, identified by Winters, which she uses to "deal with the inexplicable fact of change, of the absolute cleavage between successive states of being":

> Seasonal change is employed as the concrete symbol of the moral change. This is not the same thing as the so-called pathetic fallacy of the romantics. . . . It is rather a

legitimate and traditional form of allegory, in which the relationships between the items described resemble exactly the relationships between certain moral ideas or experiences; the identity of relationship evoking simultaneously and identifying with each other the feelings attendant upon both series as they appear separately.[6]

In the next sonnet Tuckerman explicitly connects his states of feeling to large-scale changes (and his impressions of change) in the planets themselves, as well as in the weather and in the seasons:

> Roll on, sad world! not Mercury or Mars
> Could swifter speed, or slower, round the sun
> Than in this year of variance thou hast done
> To me: yet pain, fear, heart-break, woes and wars
> Have natural limit; from his dread eclipse   [5]
> The swift sun hastens, and the night debars
> The day but to bring in the day more bright.
> The flowers renew their odorous fellowships;
> The moon runs round and round, the slow earth dips,
> True to her poise, and lifts; the planet-stars   [10]
> Roll and return from circle to ellipse;
> The day is dull and soft, the eavetrough drips,
> And yet I know the splendor of the light
> Will break anon. Look! where the gray is white!

(Sonnet II: 17, p. 27)

The writing is again effectively adjusted to its limited purposes, with one unusually lovely line, number 12.

BEFORE CONSIDERING the fourth sonnet, probably the finest stanza of the elegy, I must explain more fully Tuckerman's use of various forms of rhythmic effect. It is particularly

---

6 Yvor Winters, *In Defense of Reason* (Denver: Alan Swallow, 1947), 294.

useful to do so here, because it is in this elegy that he clearly achieves, through the way he integrates his mature technical mastery with complex thematic development, the sustained individual voice and original style that mark him as a major poet.

Prosody is a dangerous subject, particularly when it is given only the kind of limited explication possible here. James McMichael, in an excellent brief review of this dimension of poetry in *The Style of the Short Poem,* reminds us that "in discussing the function of meter and rhythm, one inevitably exaggerates." He properly advises us, "Please remember that the effects of all facets of poetic style are so particular that they can never be translated into concepts. . . . For the composite effect of the poem's meter, rhythm and meaning you must finally trust yourself."[7] Yet we must venture upon this difficult terrain. It has received deplorably scant attention, and a proper understanding of Tuckerman's artistry depends in large part on our seeing how thoroughly he understood and used the special prosodic tools won for us in the great tradition of English poetry—tools that were neglected by most of his contemporaries and too many of his successors.

Of the major critics in the twentieth century, Yvor Winters has given the most useful attention to explaining how English prosody works. He has constantly tried to understand how it is that the special rhythmic effects possible in poetry (including various forms of rhyme, the interplay of syntax with caesura, line length, and stanza form) are able, as they unquestionably seem to be, to affect feeling and meaning. His work was anticipated by others, notably Robert Bridges (whose important analysis of various kinds of systems of meter in English is marred by his confusing terminology) and Otto Jesperson (whose original identification of the central importance of relative stress within clearly identified individual feet went unknown, partly because it was in Danish). But, in essays like "The Audible Reading of Poetry" and "The Influence of Meter

---

[7] McMichael, *Style of the Short Poem,* 64.

on Poetic Convention" and in short passages of explication and demonstration throughout his work, Winters has expressed what Harvey Gross, who has done the most thorough and effective subsequent work on the subject, calls a "general theory of meter that . . . has never, to my knowledge, been convincingly controverted."[8]

Winters persuasively argues and exemplifies the following propositions: Rhythm is, in a way not fully understood, expressive of emotion, and thus rhythmic language can be used to communicate simultaneously a statement about human experience and the feeling which that statement motivates. Poetry has available an extremely important additional resource (unique to it and music) because it can be written in meters; that is, certain metrical norms have been developed in the history of the language (the most generally useful in English being iambic pentameter) which the poet can establish in the reader's mind's ear as definite measures and against which he can play his rhythms with almost infinite flexibility. Like the beat of the conductor's baton, the formal pattern of the meter is not actually heard, but the degree of departure of every note (or syllable) from that beat is apprehended as an intrinsic part of the poem, precisely qualifying the emotion and thus the total meaning. Proper analysis of traditional prosody (that based on the interplay of meter and rhythm) requires recognition that no syllable is inherently stressed or unstressed according to some absolute scale but that what matters is the "relative stress" of the syllables within each foot as feet are determined by the meter. Proper response to traditional poetry, since rhythmic variations are more precise the firmer the metric structure, requires that poetry be read (even when read silently) in a way that preserves the metric norm as well as the rhythmic departures, that is, in "a restrained but formal chant."

---

[8]Harvey Gross, ed., *The Structure of Verse: Modern Essays on Prosody* (Greenwich, Conn.: Fawcett Publications, 1966), 131; this collection includes essays by Bridges, Jesperson, and Winters.

Despite the obvious dependence of Harvey Gross on some of Winters's insights, he apparently misread him sufficiently to accuse him of seeing meter as "primarily a means of semantic emphasis." He thought Winters failed, like John Crowe Ransom (who believed that metrical textures are to be enjoyed for their own sake, independent of any relationship to meaning), to see "that it is through rhythmic structure that the infinite subtleties of human feeling can be most successfully expressed."[9] Yet it is precisely this infinite subtlety of definition of "meaning" (which includes proper emotion), uniquely available in poetry, that Winters emphasized again and again.[10]

Gross is right to say that Winters does not pursue very far a "theory of rhythm and feeling." We are indebted to Gross himself for taking the fine work of Susanne Langer on music (already alluded to in my earlier discussion of syntax) and extending it effectively to poetry for the development of such a theory, which I will summarize: Prosody, or rhythmic structure, is not simply an extraneous ornament or sensuous element but a symbolic structure, like a metaphor, that is central to the poem's meaning, a meaning that is not simply paraphrasable. Rhythmic structure articulates the movement of feeling in the poem (as it does in that other art of time, music) and thus transmits crucial information about the nature of our inner life, including "empathic human responses to time in its passage." It can also imitate psychological processes such as perception and sensation, which each have characteristic

---

[9] Harvey Gross, *Sound and Form in Modern Poetry* (1964; reprint, Ann Arbor: Univ. of Michigan Press, 1968), 12; this seems to me the best single source on this subject.

[10] I.e., in his essays *In Defense of Reason* on Stevens (439) and Poe (247) and especially "On the Morality of Poetry": "A poem is composed of an almost fluid complex . . . of relationships between words . . . , a relationship involving rational content, cadences, rhymes, juxtapositions, literary and other connotations, inversions, and so on, almost indefinitely. These relationships, it should be obvious, extend the poet's vocabulary almost incalculably. They partake of the fluidity and unpredictability of experience and so provide a means of treating experience with precision and freedom" (19).

rhythms, revealing the mind and nerves as they "grow tense in expectation and relax in fulfillment and quiet." But "a poem's prosody cannot exist apart from its propositional sense." It imitates ideas and emotions but in "non-discursive" symbols— that is, not exactly in ways that simply stand for the ideas or emotions, but intrinsically and educatively, such that in a good poem "neither meaning nor sound can operate independently."[11]

Certainly this theoretical formulation does not answer all the questions; and, as seems unavoidable when someone ventures onto this kind of terrain, the exact meaning of "meaning" remains somewhat indefinite. But Gross is unusually helpful about many important matters. The resources poetry uniquely shares with music, that allow it to get at the "morphology of feeling," are very plausibly explicated by Gross; and he also firmly insists on preserving the resources that poetry uniquely retains to itself, because it is based in cognitive language, not merely in tones and rhythms.

Gross avoids the common error, rooted in Romanticism, of focusing only on how poetry and music are *alike*. He sees that just as natural detail or other metaphoric elements in language can affect specific feeling only when they are embodied in syntactical forms which make sense, the various forms of rhythm can affect specific feeling and meaning only on the same conditions. Every form of metaphor (including rhythmic structure) must have a tenor. Otherwise we have the obscure Symbolist image and nonsense verse like Lewis Carroll's "Jabberwocky," which give us the *impression* of what it is like to feel or think but no definite or specifically articulated feelings or thoughts. (This can have value, the impression of what it is like to think being, in its own right, an interesting and important phenomenon; yet poems which merely try to dramatize this possibility cannot help but be special cases.)

Gross also gives proper attention to the importance of established patterns of expectation set up in the poem (by the

---

[11] Gross, *Sound and Form*, 4–23.

conventions of syntax and diction, the traditions of previous poetry, and so on) and controlled departures therefrom for the establishment of precise poetic effects. He steers carefully a proper middle course between two very common dangers: On the one hand, there is an easy temptation to see rhythmic effects as mere imitation (which we find in somewhat more literal and therefore less valued forms like program music and onomatopoeia) or to suppose that every idea or feeling has its unique rhythm. On the other hand, there is the obscurantist claim that the effects are purely abstract or "mystical," unamenable to analysis in terms of rational content.

James McMichael, himself a fine poet and critic, takes good advantage of the insights of Winters and Gross. In his introductory study of poetic style cited above,[12] he emphasizes the importance of *meter* as something immediately shared between poet and reader (like human experience in general) and of *rhythm* as that element through which the poet can depart from meter in controlled ways to communicate with precision his particular experience and how his insight into it has its own special feeling. Coincidentally, McMichael chooses to demonstrate his point with a perceptive analysis of Sonnet II: 16 of Tuckerman's "elegy." It is therefore disappointing to see him go too far in that analysis—that is, in emphasizing the imitative effects of rhythm in its manifestation as rhyme. After noting that the sonnet begins with a traditional *a b b a* rhyme scheme and saying that it continues with an expected *c d c,* he claims:

> As we enter the description of the house in its present state of decay, the poet employs a highly irregular *efdegf* scheme through line 13 and ends on the only imperfect rhyme ("stones" and "noons") in the poem. Once [Tuckerman] has hinted that he would use a regular rhyme scheme, the subsequent disintegration of the scheme very effectively evokes the disintegration of the house itself.[13]

---

[12] McMichael, *Style of the Short Poem,* 49–72.
[13] Ibid., 68.

XVI.

Under the mountain, as when first I knew
Its low dark roof, & chimney creeper-twined
The red house stands, & yet my footsteps find
Gone in the walks wastobalm & feverfew:
But they are gone, no soft-eyed sisters trip
Across the porch, or lintels, where behind
The mother sat, sat knitting with pursed lip.
The house stands vacant in its green recess
x Absent of beauty as a broken heart,
The wild rain enters, & the sunset wind
Sighs in the chambers of their loveliness,
Or shakes the pane: & in the silent noons
The glass falls from the window, part by part
And tinkles faintly in the grassy stones.

x abstracted

113

Holograph of Tuckerman's Sonnet II: 16. This is from the manuscript made for the printer, Houghton MS. Am 1349(2), which Momaday used as his main authority, with slight editorial variations as can be seen on pp. 158–59. Used by permission of Houghton Library, Harvard University.

This seems to me to impute to Tuckerman the "imitative fallacy," which in its most absurd form would insist that a poet writing about something bad or boring or inarticulate must write bad or boring or inarticulate poetry. This fallacy reduces the extremely subtle tools we have been discussing to the grossest effects. It will just not do to believe that an irregular rhyme scheme can evoke nothing but disintegration or that the theme of disintegration requires an irregular rhyme scheme. On the evidence we have presented thus far, a skilled craftsman like Tuckerman is capable of doing something much better than that with the resources of poetry.

But what about that (according to McMichael) "irregular" rhyme scheme? Tuckerman was chided often by his contemporaries for misusing his chosen form, and even Eaton was impelled to write, "There is not a perfectly formed sonnet in the volume. He either scorned or did not know the rules of the sonnet form."[14] Tuckerman knew the rules, all right; if nothing else, his intense apprenticeship is evidence of that. But in breaking the rules, "scorn" was not his motive. Bynner is much more accurate:

> In the light of Tuckerman's obvious familiarity with the classics, in the light of recent experiments with variations in verse, in the light of present knowledge that Walt Whitman and Emily Dickinson had ears more sensitive than their contemporaries had, we may be sure that Tuckerman knew what he was doing when he ended a sonnet with an Alexandrine or shortened the last line by a foot, or when he shuffled the rhyme scheme to suit the roll and rise and fall of his meaning. . . . Instead of bungling or staling the sonnet-form, he renewed it and, moulding it to his emotion, made it inevitable. Along with the tide of his words flowed the tide of his thought, cresting in breathless images.[15]

---

14 Walter Prichard Eaton, "A Forgotten American Poet," *Forum* 41 (January 1909): 64.

15 Witter Bynner, ed., *The Sonnets of Frederick Goddard Tuckerman* (New York: Alfred A. Knopf, 1931), 17–18.

This is all true, but it does not go nearly far enough. If we look carefully at Sonnet II: 16 we find that the rhyme scheme is not really McMichael's *abbacdcefdegfg'* (I use the apostrophe to indicate what McMichael calls an "imperfect" or partial or near rhyme on the last line). Rather it is:

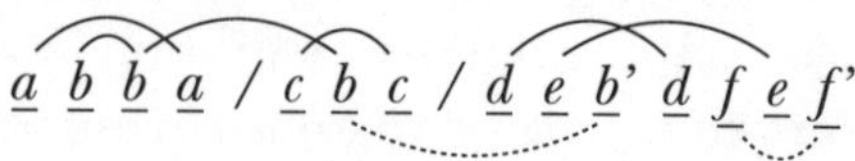

(McMichael missed the continuation of the b rhyme to "behind" in line 6 and then further to a partial rhyme with "wind" in line 10.) Looking at the scheme above that I have made by separating the rhyme groups according to syntactical units and connecting the true rhymes with solid lines and the partial rhymes with broken lines, it begins to appear that this rhyme scheme is not "disintegrated" at all but is closely related to the syntax and integrated in a complex way throughout.

It takes a thorough analysis of all of Tuckerman's sonnets to begin to see his unusual achievement here. From the beginning he uses only the Italian sonnet form (originally *a b b a a b b a/c d e c d e,* with a strict division of thought and syntax between octave and sestet). He, of course, knew the form was modified by Donne and Milton (who included subjects besides the lover's complaint) and especially by Wordsworth (who introduced a new rhyme in the second part of the octave and varied the ordering of rhyme in the sestet, as well as discontinuing the sharp break between the parts and further broadening the subject matter). Tuckerman's first sonnets, published probably in 1850, are quite regular in terms of Wordsworth's practice (e.g., "November" *[a b b a a c c a d e f d f e]*), but even by 1852 Tuckerman was beginning to work unusual variations on this norm ("Again, again, ye part in stormy grief" *[a b b a a b b c d d c d d' c]*). At the beginning of the sonnet series (1857, with possibly a few written earlier), he tried various combinations for the beginning four rhymes, while using increasingly varied forms of partial rhyme in the remainder. He finally settled on a consistent *a b b a* opening, modeled directly on the stanza form of

Tennyson's *In Memoriam* (after the sixth sonnet in the First Series all but a very few begin that way). However, as additional evidence of Tuckerman's growing independence from his mentor, that opening is followed by complex variations in the rhyme scheme. By the time of Sonnet I: 10, which I have analyzed closely in other terms earlier, there is something truly startling.

But because of Tuckerman's unusual techniques, it is necessary, before I give the rhyme scheme of Sonnet I: 10, to establish some new conventions for describing his poetry. First, I must identify and provide distinguishing notations for the various forms of *partial* rhyme, which are not usually discriminated. True rhyme, of course, requires that final accented vowels and all succeeding consonants and vowels of two lines exactly correspond (brink/drink; alter/halter). "Imperfect" or "partial" rhyme has normally meant correspondence of the final consonants but no (or only near) correspondence of the vowels (house/pass). This has also been called consonance and may take the form of "partial" consonance when the final consonants are only similar (grass/brows). Assonance, in this context, may be taken to mean correspondence of the vowels but not the consonants (close/alone); it too may be only partial or near correspondence of the vowels (house/alone).

If we indicate consonance with an apostrophe and assonance with an underline and add single or double apostrophe or underline marks as Tuckerman works variation upon variation, we get a rhyme scheme for Sonnet I: 10 something like this (rhyme words: house / brink / drink / close / alone / pass / stone / grass / brows / sash / think / boughs / snows / ash):

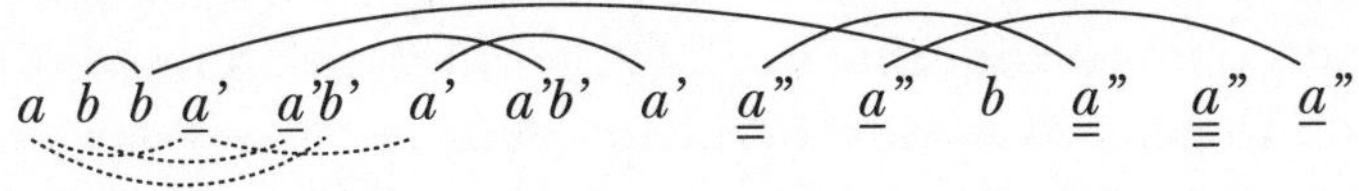

Drawing lines to show the various connections becomes an almost hopeless task which I have only begun to illustrate. Tuckerman is clearly doing something quite similar to what Dickinson did later when she took the common meter and stanza forms of the Protestant hymnal and worked brilliant variations on them to achieve her particular effects. It is intriguing that one of the variations she developed was extensive use of partial rhymes like Tuckerman's, apparently the only other case in nineteenth-century American poetry.

TUCKERMAN probably chose the sonnet form in part for its traditional strengths, which M. H. Abrams has concisely stated: "The stanza is just long enough to permit a fairly complete lyric development, yet so short and so exigent in its rhymes as to pose a standing challenge to the artistry of the poet."[16] It is now clear to us that Tuckerman also recognized what the Italians had valued in the sonnet, defined as follows by the fine English poet and critic, F. T. Prince: "[The sonnet was], by virtue of its limited scope and clear yet complex structure, a form which could be carefully polished, and one in which it was possible to concentrate upon small technical innovations and experiments."[17] Tuckerman's choice of the sonnet form clearly reveals his values and concerns—as a man as well as a poet. With the additional choice of a highly integrated sequence, he was able to develop an essentially new form in English, combining traditionally proven resources and discipline with variations developed through his own insight and experimentation. As a result, he could work within the scope of a single sonnet to examine and express a particular dimension or movement of his spiritual life, as he does in Sonnet I: 10; or he could group the sonnets in combinations of any desired length to explore larger circuitous journeys in the ebb and flow of his perception and feeling, as he does in the "elegy" I am considering here. He could do all of these things within the clearly established context of the five series, which

---

[16] M. H. Abrams, *A Glossary of Literary Terms*, 4th ed. (New York: Holt, Rinehart and Winston, 1981), 181.

[17] F. T. Prince, *The Italian Element in Milton's Verse* (1954; reprint, Oxford: Oxford Univ. Press, 1962), 14.

embody the larger curves in the development of his understanding.

But this is not all. Tuckerman obviously intuited for himself the fundamentals of Gross's theory of "rhythmic cognition." He discovered, in his chosen struggle with the sonnet form, that he could use the properties of rhythm and rhyme, particularly his original variations on rhyme, to provide images in the poem of the whole process of thinking and feeling in time. He broke away from the assumption of purely linear thought implicit in the traditional division between octave and sestet and in the discrete units of cognitive structure imaged by true rhyme. Instead, he worked directly for his particularized insights, using the created metaphor of the poem in a unique way—as a structure built in time but held as a whole in the mind, with a complex interweaving of relationships established and modified by those progressive modulations of rhyme we have examined.

All this was a truly remarkable achievement. But, of course, Tuckerman did not manage it entirely by himself; the sonnet was a popular form with the Romantics and the American Sentimentalists, though they used it essentially without innovation. Very's innovations were not in the form as such, but in his own special diction and voice. W. E. Channing, whose sonnets Tuckerman read carefully and critically in 1853, used a perfectly regular pre-Miltonic Italian form (and the writing is bad). But Wordsworth was doing some experimenting, and he strongly influenced Hallam and Tennyson.

Tennyson wrote a fair number of sonnets—over fifty. One was written in 1851 as a formulary public sonnet, and eight were written much later in life—all perfectly regular Italian sonnets. But the remainder were written before he was twenty-five (the ones published were in the 1830 and 1832 *Poems,* and by nearly all of them Ricks in his edition writes, "An irregular sonnet, like most of T.'s early ones" and "Not reprinted" or "Not reprinted till restored in 1872 as 'Juvenilia' "). In a careful study of the sonnets, Dougald B. MacEachen tells us that in these early ones, "Tennyson employs twenty-seven different rime schemes." Though some readers thought that this showed Tennyson was "without any clear idea of how a sonnet should be written," MacEachen thinks it merely indicates that he was not yet craftsman enough to fit his material to this exigent form and also "was trying new patterns for the sonnet much as Wordsworth had done and was still to do."[18]

MacEachen, like Tennyson's contemporaries, assumes that the more conventional the better when it comes to the sonnet and that Tennyson eventually learned that lesson. He notes that in the 1832 *Poems,* Tennyson was moving somewhat toward orthodoxy and by 1851 "had evidently come to the conclusion that the best sonnet form was the regular Italian."[19] If that is true, we may be grateful again that Tuckerman did not continue to follow Tennyson's lead but took the early work's influence and moved out beyond it.

In his commonplace book, apparently compiled in the 1850s (the clippings are all from that period or later and the hand-writing is characteristic of that time), Tuckerman copied four of these early sonnets, with other poetry, under the heading "Tennyson—early poems."[20] They can be scanned as fairly regular if one ignores the imperfect rhymes; but if I use the conventions I outlined earlier, I get this (for "Mine be the strength of spirit fierce and free"):

a b b a a c a c a' a b a" a a'

How intently Tuckerman studied these unusually rhymed son-nets and used them as a basis for his experimentation we can only guess; certainly he quite rapidly went far beyond them.

-----

[18] Dougald B. MacEachen, "Tennyson and the Sonnet," *Victorian News-letter* 14 (Fall 1958): 2.

[19] Ibid., 3.

[20] MS. Am 1349 (10), Houghton. Tuckerman, probably during this same period, also copied another of the early sonnets, "Buonaparte," in the back of his copy of volume two of the 1842 (Boston) *Poems,* now at the Houghton Library.

But it is very likely that Tennyson's influence served Tuckerman in another way to establish the effective form of the sonnets. The beginning quatrain of each sonnet consistently imitates the rhyme scheme of *In Memoriam,* a poem which, as I have noted, Tuckerman much admired and which clearly influenced his own extended elegy—that is to say, the first two sonnet series. Ricks perceptively states that this stanza form, "though it permits convergence, does so on the strict condition that it be temporary—that it not be, in the strictest sense, final."[21] Tuckerman used this quality, but, characteristically, with an added freedom, to work out from the secure base at the beginning of each sonnet to richly complex structures of departure and return and of progressive, precise, but never final definition.

It seems clear that Tuckerman, even at this fairly early point in his mature work, had moved far past his contemporaries, both in his poetic theory such as we may infer it and in actual practice. Matthiessen is surely correct when he writes, "Emerson, Thoreau, and Whitman all conceived of themselves primarily as poets, though, judged strictly by form, none of them was."[22] No one should judge those writers strictly by form ("neither meaning nor sound can operate independently"—Gross), but neither can we call them very good poets when they misunderstand or neglect poetic form. Emerson had natural talent and the benefit of good reading, and he was able to write some good poems; but they were in an essential way accidental. As Matthiessen also reminds us, because Emerson "liked to call nature the 'metaphor of the divine mind,' he was always brushing it aside to come to the very source of truth . . . incapable of being restrained within the hard actuality of experience."[23] But that hard actuality is where the resources for poetic form exist.

---

21 Ricks, *Tennyson,* 229.

22 F. O. Matthiessen, *The American Renaissance: Art and Expression in the Age of Emerson and Whitman* (1941; reprint, Oxford Univ. Press, 1968), 55.

23 Ibid., 54.

Thoreau was afflicted with the same disabling, uninformed idealism about the poet's unique craft: "Poetry is the mysticism of mankind. . . . There are indeed no *words* quite worthy to be set to [the poet's] music. . . . It is not recoverable thought, but a hue caught from a vaster receding thought."[24] He seems not to have understood how a poem actually works, though he obviously did learn some important things about *prose*, probably from the long discipline of his journals.

Whitman, also attracted to Emerson's idealism and moved greatly by his experience with Italian opera, conceived of his poems essentially as songs. Without the benefit of good instruction or accurate intuition about the formal nature of music, he sought to develop purely imitative rhythms and such large-scale musical effects as recitative and aria, amplification and recapitulation, crescendo and diminuendo. He did not understand that most of these require subtle resources available only in music and that in pursuing them he was ignoring many of the subtle resources available only in poetry. He especially neglected the cognitive effects possible through using the tension between rhythm and meter. Meter was an "encumbrance" from which Whitman explicitly declared independence, not taking account of the possibility that his yearning to get the energy of the sea and the tempest and the force of his own grand emotions into poetry might actually require regular measures. He did not see that meter derives from what Coleridge called "the balance in the mind effected by that spontaneous effort which strives to hold in check the workings of passion." Thus Whitman disregarded the tools by which the poet can create a controlled metaphor for release of energy in the mind and then can image the mind's *response*, not merely the thing itself. Instead he endeavored "to let nature speak, without check, with original energy."[25]

---

[24] Henry David Thoreau, *A Week on the Concord and Merrimack Rivers* (Boston: Houghton Mifflin, 1893), 433.

[25] These quotations of Coleridge and Whitman are from Matthiessen, *American Renaissance*, 567.

Matthiessen is right to say that Thoreau and Melville and Whitman "would have agreed with Emerson's decree that 'it is not metres, but a metre-making argument that makes a poem'; for, with the release of energy in which they shared, they were sure that their content outran the boundaries of earlier conventions of expression." However, he is neglectful of Tuckerman (whose work he may well not have known) when he continues:

> But the writing of poetry becomes inordinately difficult without a living tradition to draw upon and modify. Thoreau and Melville both evolved richly modulated harmonies in their prose rhythms but were able to command far less music when they tried to borrow the more exacting medium of verse, which had hardly yet become acclimated in America.[26]

As we can see most clearly in the sonnets of the "elegy" under consideration here, Tuckerman had the patience and skill to develop new conventions of expression for the concerns he shared with the other Romantics and for the passions and insights of his own life when earlier conventions were not sufficient, rather than scorning conventions and trusting natural expression. For the help he needed he humbly apprenticed himself to the "living tradition" that *was* available—English poetry. He then developed his own gifts and responded to the unique influences of his New England life in such a way that he became one of the very first—at about the same time as Whitman but in quite a different way—to take the medium of verse and make it fully "acclimated in America." Whitman, of course, made an enormous contribution to creating an "American" poetry and has been the major influence on our central poetic and critical tradition since; Tuckerman's great value, I believe, lies in the alternative he creates, with Dickinson, of a poetry more true to the rational

---

[26] Ibid., 56.

and moral potential of language than Emerson and Whitman understood or achieved in their poetry.

I have already demonstrated how carefully and intelligently Tuckerman studied the techniques and experiments of others, especially Tennyson. I have also noted how he recognized the appropriateness of Tennyson's chant for adequately highlighting the effects of metered verse and that he adopted that chant for his own reading. His meticulous craftsmanship is particularly indicated in the many successive slight revisions that continue, even through the various printings of *Poems.* It is also clear in his working notebook,[27] where he fills pages with carefully wrought phrases and rhyme sets, sometimes blocking out whole poems with the rhyme words separated to the right margin so that the structure shows more distinctly.

Those rhyme structures for the sonnets are perhaps Tuckerman's most important single innovation in poetic form. Again, it must be emphasized that they were almost unique among his contemporaries, though they built on tentative experiments by Wordsworth and especially Tennyson. Emily Dickinson is the only other poet of the century to experiment effectively with partial rhymes,[28] and she seems to have used them for a very similar purpose. Both poets used combinations of full and partial rhymes to work meaningful variations on a conventional rhyme scheme; they made varying degrees of departure from and return to a basic pattern in order to build a complex but unified structure for felt meaning in the mind. The question of possible influence between them is unavoidable; but, if there is any, it most likely went from Tuckerman to Dickinson, because she seems to have done her experimenting with modulated rhyming in the early 1860s, after Tuckerman's *Poems* were published.[29] Connections be-

---

[27] MS. Am 1349 (3), Houghton.

[28] See Yvor Winters' analysis of "Farther in Summer than the Birds," in *In Defense of Reason*, 293.

[29] Though there is absolutely no direct evidence, it is tempting to believe they knew of each other and of each other's work, as Donald Stauffer recognizes in his *A Short History of American Poetry* (New York: E. P. Dutton and Co.,

tween their work are evident not only in their extraordinary formal artistry but in shared themes and images (notably that of insect voices, like the sea, suggesting nature's threatening presence) and similar use of the post-Symbolist method to deal with interior moral change and to comprehend their responses to death and mortality.

Whatever their exact relationship, both of these fine poets in their formal technique anticipated twentieth-century poets who have been wrongly credited with the innovations I have described. In "Stations of the Breath: End Rhyme in the Verse of Dylan Thomas," Russell Astley has made an important analysis of the use of various forms of partial rhyme by Thomas and his models, Yeats and Wilfred Owen.[30] He demonstrates how Yeats, after 1904, began to work with consonance of different kinds, essentially as a variety to complement true rhyme. Owen, and then Thomas in the 1930s, pursued these experiments much further, discriminating more variants of

---

1974), 122. Dickinson lived only eighteen miles from Greenfield, in Amherst, and was a close friend of Edward's wife and of Tuckerman's son Frederick and his wife, Alice Cooper. A letter of condolence from Emily to Edward's widow was written just two months before Emily's own death in 1886 (Samuel A. Golden, *Frederick Goddard Tuckerman: An American Sonnetteer* [Univ. of Maine Press, Bulletin 54, no. 12 (April 1952)], 5), and a note from Dickinson to Tuckerman's daughter-in-law, Alice Cooper Tuckerman, on the birth of one of her babies—probably the one who became Mrs. Orton Loring Clark (Margaret), since she inherited it—hangs framed on a wall in the Hugh Clark home in Amherst. It is not dated but must have been written between 1881, when Alice married Tuckerman's son Frederick, and 1886, when Dickinson died:

> Dear friend, with the trust that the Madonna and Child are as
> safe as sacred, accept this happy [undecipherable word].
>   E. Dickinson

> Let me commend to Baby's attention the only commandment
> I ever obeyed. Consider the Lilies.
>   E. Dickinson

[30] Russell Astley, "Stations of the Breath: End Rhyme in the Verse of Dylan Thomas," *Publications of the Modern Language Association* 84 (October 1969): 1595–1605.

consonance and building whole poems with them. Thomas even developed a hierarchy within the various types as a structure from which he could work progressive variations with degrees of difference between syllables and then return to a kind of resolution. This hierarchy changed as Thomas turned increasingly to assonance and its parallel variations in the 1940s—and the experimentation itself circled back as Thomas in his last work returned to true rhyme and simple stanzas.

Astley has refined and carefully illustrated a helpful terminology for describing varieties of end rhyme, one that I have used in part in my discussion of Tuckerman's work above. Astley's essay is essentially descriptive; it does not explain what these experiments have to do with the meaning and quality of the poetry. But it does give us a definite picture of Thomas doing what Thomas himself praised in Owen, "experimenting technically, deeper and deeper driving towards the final intensity of language."[31] Astley does qualitatively describe one nice effect—one, in fact, quite similar to Tuckerman's achievement in his earlier experiments: He says of Thomas's "Once it was the colour of saying" (a thirteen-line sonnet beginning with a traditional quatrain, rhyming *a b b a*), "[The last two] lines are coupled in sense only: they do not rhyme with each other but are in consonance with the two first lines of the poem, thereby establishing a more subtle, though definite, feeling of completion."[32]

But Astley was surely wrong, in the light of what I have shown in Tuckerman (and can in Dickinson), in his sweeping claims for the originality of Yeats's and Thomas's experiments. Statements he made about Thomas are much more true of Tuckerman:

> He early developed a system of consonant correspondence unique with him or, at the very least, never before

---

[31] Ibid., 1605, quoted from Dylan Thomas's *Quite Early One Morning* (New York: New Directions, 1954), 125–26.

[32] Ibid., 1596.

exploited with so full an awareness of its potentialities. . . . This controlled use of true rhyme to raise into relief certain fixed points in a design otherwise marked by consonances is something new in English verse. Masculine and feminine endings had been set in contrast by others, but [Thomas] seems to have been the first English poet to realize that consonance and true rhyme might be regarded as two things rather than as two kinds of one thing.[33]

W E C A N R E T U R N now perhaps better prepared to appreciate fully the finest section of Tuckerman's "elegy," what is indeed probably his greatest single sonnet:

And change with hurried hand has swept these scenes:
The woods have fallen, across the meadow-lot
The hunter's trail and trap-path is forgot,
And fire has drunk the swamps of evergreens;
Yet for a moment let my fancy plant   [5]
These autumn hills again: the wild dove's haunt,
The wild deer's walk. In golden umbrage shut,
The Indian river runs, Quonecktacut!
Here, but a lifetime back, where falls tonight
Behind the curtained pane a sheltered light   [10]
On buds of rose or vase of violet
Aloft upon the marble mantel set,
Here in the forest-heart, hung blackening
The wolfbait on the bush beside the spring.

(Sonnet II: 18, p.27)

The writing is strong and clear throughout, with no hint of the softness of syntax or the facile diction that slightly mars even the best of the other sonnets. The general mystery of change is given a local habitation in an image and rhythmi-

---

[33] Ibid., 1595, 1596.

cally created feeling that permanently haunts the mind but makes absolutely no gesture toward obscurity or excess of any kind. Tuckerman is again using the device later employed with great effectiveness by Dickinson in poems like "There's a certain Slant of light." He reduces the astronomical scale of the catalogue of change in the previous sonnet, II: 17, and symbolizes interior, moral change through change in the landscape. The particular changing landscape he chooses provides an even more apt allegory than Dickinson's. It focuses our attentions on human impact on the natural environment and thus can be used not only to *image* moral change but *itself has moral implications* related to the central theme of the entire elegy—the struggle to understand the claims and responsibilities of mortality.

In the first four lines of the poem, Tuckerman gives a quick vignette of the successive changes that have been brought by what we call "civilizing" activity into the local New England landscape. These lines convey a sense of our habitual destructiveness and forgetfulness of the past; but the poet is one who does not forget, and he gives us, in the next four lines, a lovely remembrance of something he never actually saw, the Connecticut River valley at the end of the eighteenth century. The image of natural beauty is expressed in language that is precisely true to that beauty and yet hints at its passing: "Haunt" is one of those "keys" of the post-Symbolist method, a kind of pun that exploits the ability of words to act at the level of both vehicle and tenor, here giving both the place that the doves frequented and the sense that it is now haunted only by their memory. "Umbrage" is another such pun (meaning shadow, but also suspicion and displeasure); the former "golden *umbrage*," the autumn-colored shadows of the treelined river, is shadowed as well by the hint and pain of the future destruction. The use of the Indians' name (Quonecktacut) for what was once but is no longer *their* river (because they have been driven out of Connecticut by Tuckerman's ancestors) subtly communicates our destructive imposition on other humans as well in the process of "civilization."

As Tuckerman moves into the sestet, a complexity of reaction, prepared for by the images of beauty and destruction in the octave, is marvelously achieved and held. There is deep sense of loss; that precious natural beauty and the human value of another culture are gone forever. But then Tuckerman provides, posed against each other, both the image of a civilized home of the present, an achieved human island curtained off and sheltered, with inner warmth and light and human amenity, and also a context of enormous darkness imagined from the past—the threatening forest, with real wolves. In that last stunning image, he reminds us that the wolves were baited with poison so that humans could survive and create that vase and mantel—which are perhaps less appealing than the wild dove's haunt but are yet less appalling than the wolfbait and the need for it.

In some ways this is one of Tuckerman's most regular sonnets. There is the normal octave and sestet division in both theme and syntax. The main substitutions in the iambic metrical norm are few and are quite directly imitative:

The wŏods / hăve fál- / lĕn, ăcróss / thĕ méa- / dŏw·lót

gives a verbal stumble to "fallen" by dividing the word between two feet, the second of which is an anapest, which in turn is split by the caesura. One substitution in the meter is used for effective emphasis and parallelism in a fine syntactical construction: An emphatic trochee is used at the beginning of the sestet (line 9), which starts to tell of the primitive darkness that went with the former beauty and then holds off for four lines which further qualify the complexity with an image of the unnatural but secure, lighted present. The sestet's initial negative emphasis is then picked up with another trochee (which also repeats that initial "here") at the beginning of the powerful last couplet. But, of course, there are many subtle variations in rhythm that work with the syntax to create the balances and juxtapositions, the slowing and speeding, that give us the feel of the mind moving in a specific, complex insight. And that effect is brilliantly complemented by the rhymes.

Using the conventions for scanning partial rhymes, I get a structure which indicates the complex variations on two rhymes, some rhymes, such as those of lines 5 and 6, actually related to both the *a* and the *b* rhymes, and some, such as 9 through 12, departing from the *b* rhyme in various subtle stages:

$$a \quad b \quad b \quad a \quad a'b' \quad a'\underline{b}' \quad b'' \quad b'' \quad b''' \quad b''' \quad b'''' \quad b'''' \quad \underline{a}'' \quad \underline{a}''$$
$$1 \quad 2 \quad 3 \quad 4 \quad 5 \quad 6 \quad 7 \quad 8 \quad 9 \quad 10 \quad 11 \quad 12 \quad 13 \quad 14$$

The first quatrain is perfectly regular in rhyme and also in syntax, with a runover connecting the "b" lines but the "a" lines coming to full stops. Then Tuckerman begins to work his subtle antitheses and uses his rhymes as a metaphor for what is happening. There is a series of what might have seemed only like regular couplets, with a slight slip in rhyme in the fifth and sixth lines. But with the new conventions we can now see that 5 and 6 are progressive variations from the "a" rhyme (partial consonance) and also the "b" rhyme (partial consonance again) and are in full consonance with each other, with 6 then tied back in an extra way to "b" by assonance, to make a case of what is called close rhyme. Lines 7 and 8, 9 and 10, and then 11 and 12 have true rhyme in pairs, but each set is also in consonance with "b." Then the last rhyming couplet forms a close rhyme with lines 1 and 4 and partial consonance with 5 and 6, in perfect support of a conclusion that is not a simple linear answer to a problem, as in the Shakespearean sonnet. It is instead a paradox that is invested with a *precise* condition of ambiguity (the ambiguity is not an escape from careful thought but an honoring of irreducibility that will yield no more to the most careful thought). This is done by using the partial rhymes to create complex interconnections, in the metaphoric structure built in the mind, back to both the beauties of a dark and dangerous time and *also* to our dangerous destructiveness in fighting that danger.

The next sonnet reviews that dangerous and uncouth time of "a lifetime back" from the viewpoint of more specific political and religious history of Greenfield. Finally, the last poem of the elegy returns to the sister-twins, to Anna, and to Tuckerman's struggle to use these "dark shadings of the past" in coping with his grief. The writing in both concluding poems is consistently effective and they both successfully contribute to the general theme. In addition, there are some remarkable images and lines. Especially impressive are lines 4 and 10 of Sonnet II: 19 and lines 5 through 10 of Sonnet II: 20:

> And faces, forms and phantoms, numbered not,
> Gather and pass like mist upon the breeze,
> Jading the eye with uncouth images:
> Women with muskets, children dropping shot
> By fields half harvested or left in fear   [5]
> Of Indian inroad, or the Hessian near;
> Disaster, poverty, and dire disease.
> Or from the burning village, through the trees
> I see the smoke in reddening volumes rolls,
> The Indian file in shadowy silence pass   [10]
> While the last man sets up the trampled grass,
> The Tory priest declaiming, fierce and fat,
> The Shay's man with the green branch in his hat,
> Or silent sagamore, Shaug or Wassahoale.
>   (Sonnet II: 19, p. 28)

> O hard endeavor, to blend in with these
> Dark shadings of the past a darker grief
> Or blur with stranger woes a wound so chief,
> Though the great world turn slow with agonies.
> What though the forest windflowers fell and died   [5]
> And Gertrude sleeps at Gulielma's side?

> They have their tears, nor turn to us their eyes:
> But we pursue our dead with groans and cries
> And bitter reclamations to the term
> Of undiscerning darkness and the worm;   [10]
> Then sit in silence down and darkly dwell
> Through the slow years on all we loved, and tell
> Each tone, each look of love, each syllable,
> With lips that work, with eyes that overwell.
>
> (Sonnet II: 20, p. 28)

Tuckerman shows conclusively in this group of sonnets that he is not just a minor poet capable of an occasional good line or striking image or a few successful but isolated poems. Sonnets II: 15 through II: 20 are fashioned into a fully integrated set of six stanzas that make a completed pastoral elegy within the larger elegy of the first two sonnet series. The unified group confirms the achievements of Sonnet I: 10 and Sonnet I: 28, but it also goes far beyond them.

I have digressed somewhat in order to show how the elegy demonstrates Tuckerman's mature technical mastery, particularly his use of complex structures of partial rhyme, to image the complex turns of concept and feeling inherent in his themes of praise and grief—a use which is apparently both original with Tuckerman and, until the twentieth century, unique to him and Dickinson. But what is most important is that this technical brilliance, including other forms of "rhythmic cognition," well serves Tuckerman's metaphoric structure that both unifies the six stanzas and also moves through various levels of intensity (reaching peaks in Sonnets II: 16 and II: 18, which I have analyzed in detail) and through a complex series of thematic developments.

Tuckerman begins with an unusual use of an elegaic convention in which his subject, his wife Anna, is transformed into mythic "sister-twins" who once dwelt in a pastoral landscape that is now decayed. He builds to a powerful evocation of the subtle, incomprehensible finality of all change and loss, focusing on a perfectly realized and representative detail of

that decay—the sudden falling in quiet moments of wind-
loosened glass panes from the sisters' deserted farmhouse.
Tuckerman expands his vision of change—of "variance"—to
include the whole solar system and then returns to a different
form of pastoral decay—the slow, destructive encroachment
of civilized man on the wilderness and on its primitive human
inhabitants—reaching another climax in a precise and moving apprehension of the ambiguity of change. He creates a
complex image of man's moral accountability—involving both
gain and loss—in his "evolution" from a past time of unutter-
able darkness and danger but also of unique natural beauty
and innocence to the safe and rationalized but sheltered and
artificial present. He modulates from this intense perception
through a description of other, more positive elements of the
change from that dangerous past and then closes his elegy
with a direct look at the difficulty of relating these metaphoric
images of change and loss to his own "darker grief." He concludes that—useless as it may seem, because despite his
Romantic yearning there is no actual response of the dead or
of the past or of the natural world to his need—he must continue in the task (of which this elegy is a supreme part) of dealing with his grief as best he can with the resources of his mind
and art.

This elegy is a poetic achievement of the highest order, but
Tuckerman continued to reach that level in individual sonnets
and groups throughout the five series. And, at least once, he
surpassed it, in his great statement of mature reconciliation to
mortality, "The Cricket," which I examine next.

Graves of Hannah and Frederick Tuckerman, Greenfield, Massachusetts.

VI

MATURITY: AN ODE

Yet even mid merry boyhood's tricks and scapes,
Early my heart a deeper lesson learnt:
Wandering alone by many a mile of burnt
Black woodside, that but the snowflake decks and drapes;
And I have stood beneath Canadian sky
In utter solitudes, where the cricket's cry
Appals the heart, and fear takes visible shapes;
And on Long Island's void and isolate capes
Heard the sea break like iron bars. And still
In all I seemed to hear the same deep dirge
Borne in the wind, the insect's tiny trill,
And crash and jangle of the shaking surge,
And knew not what they meant, prophetic woe?
Dim bodings wherefore? Now indeed I know.

Sonnet II: 30

T UCKERMAN was, from his youth, fearfully fascinated by the sounds of the cricket and of the sea, and evidently quite early they began to work together in his mind toward a powerful significance. Both sounds, of course, have the natural potential, which has long been felt and exploited in the case of the sea, to symbolize the vast, inscrutable nonhuman world and the primitive or unconscious mind. Thus these sounds also evoke the conscious mind's premonitory dread of death or loss of identity. Partly because of his Romantic inclinations Tuckerman was extraordinarily sensitive to the "dim bodings" brought by the "deep dirge" of such sounds; and some time after they had turned out to be prophetic indeed of great personal woe, he was able to articulate that premonition in one of his finest metaphoric creations, "The Cricket."

The sound of the cricket is heard often in the early poems: "the innumerable clink and chime / Of the night crickets," their "tinkle" and "tick." By the time of Sonnet I: 10, written shortly after Anna's death, the more ominous implications begin to intrude. In that autumn landscape moving toward death, "the cricket chides" (early manuscripts have "cheeps" and "creaks"). Later, but before the 1860 *Poems* were published, Tuckerman wrote the fine sonnet quoted at the beginning of this chapter.

At about the same time, he also produced the following (rather embarrassingly ill-written) lines, in a stanza of "The Old Beggar" that is concerned with impinging mortality, the time "when the heart is old and the head is gray / And Grief cometh home like a child to stay":

> Alas! when the daylight is weary to see
> When the grasshopper's song shall a burthen be,
> When the jar of the cricket is bitter to hear,
> And the hum of the harvest fly stings the ear. (p. 161)

The reference is to Ecclesiastes 12:5–7:

> Also when they shall be afraid of that which is high, and fears shall be in the way, and the almond tree shall flourish, and the grasshopper shall be a burden, and desire shall fail: because man goeth to his long home, and the mourners go about the streets: Or ever the silver cord be loosed, or the golden bowl be broken, or the pitcher be broken at the fountain, or the wheel broken at the cistern. Then shall the dust return to the earth as it was: and the spirit shall return unto God who gave it.

Tuckerman develops the full weight—the prophetic woe—of that "burden" in the form of a long ode, "The Cricket," written sometime after 1860. It is an "irregular" ode (varying line lengths and stanzas) of the kind developed by Cowley from the Pindaric form and used by Dryden, Gray, Wordsworth, and others for an increasing variety of subjects, though they retained the defining seriousness of subject and elevation of style. The Romantics well known to Tuckerman (such as Keats and Shelley, whose influence on this poem is obvious) further developed more personal forms. According to Abrams the Romantic odes used "description and passionate meditation, which is stimulated by an aspect of the outer scene and turns on the attempt to solve either a private problem or a generally human one."[1]

Tuckerman's success in resolving, in general human terms, the great private problem of his life, his grief and its attendant despair, has met with quite universal acclaim from those who have read "The Cricket." Winters, with characteristic penetration and concision, provided, in a short review of the first edition in 1950, the main outlines of an interpretation and appreciation of the poem, which have not been effectively challenged or greatly improved upon since, though his student, N. Scott Momaday, further developed Winters's basic insights and Mordecai Marcus strengthened them with an independent but quite similar reading of the poem.[2]

---

[1] M. H. Abrams, *A Glossary of Literary Terms,* 4th ed. (New York: Holt, Rinehart and Winston, 1981), 124–25.

[2] The first edition was a limited one of 290 copies by the Cummington Press, Cummington, Mass. Yvor Winters' review appeared in *Hudson Review* 3 (Autumn 1950): 453–58; Winters develops essentially the same ideas in his foreword to the N. Scott Momaday edition ("An Edition of the Complete Poems of Frederick Goddard Tuckerman" [Ph.D. diss., Stanford Univ., 1963]; published, with a shortened introduction and a foreword by Yvor Winters, by Oxford Univ. Press in 1965) and in Winters, *Forms of Discovery: Critical and Historical Essays on the Forms of the Short Poem in English* (Denver: Alan Swallow, 1967), 259–63. Janet A. Mueller's discussion of the poem is in her "Frederick Goddard Tuckerman: A Critical Study" (Master's thesis, Stanford Univ., 1960), 51–61; Momaday's discussion appears in the introduction to his dissertation, "An Edition of the Complete Poems," 36–43, and is developed further as part of a critical discussion of Transcendentalism in "The Heretical Cricket," *Southern Review,* n.s., 3 (Winter 1967): 43–50. Mordecai Marcus's analysis—apparently little, if at all, influenced by Winters—appeared in *Discourse* 5 (Winter 1961–62): 69–82. Donald B. Stauffer, in his *A Short History of*

I do not intend to engage here in a comprehensive analysis of "The Cricket," which could itself be the subject of a substantial book. Instead I will focus on certain achievements in the poem that reveal Tuckerman's mature skills and preoccupations and that demonstrate his success in providing certain resolutions to major Romantic dilemmas—particularly what might be called "the tragedy of language." But first I will give a brief summary, slanted toward my special concerns here, and offer a reedited version of the poem.

THE POET, on a summer afternoon, invokes the cricket—as muse and also as subject—in a gentle, pastoral manner, one that is effectively ironic in view of what follows. In the second stanza the poet establishes the cricket's pervasive presence throughout the landscape. The total effect is a drowsiness charged with foreboding—a Romantic, languishing, pantheistic trance, which lulls yet gives a growing sense of danger. This effect is increased as the sound of the multitudinous crickets explicitly calls to mind the sea, that primordial symbol of the physical universe from which our human consciousness was born (or separated) and into which it will die (or merge again). The sound thus evokes the unconscious and sometimes thrillingly suggestive, but irrational and perhaps destructive, elements that remain in us. This is made certain in the third stanza as the cricket is associated with "the burthen of the unresting Sea," as a "bringer of all things dark," and nostalgia for childhood and death is explicitly developed.

The fourth stanza extends the cricket's ubiquity to time as well as space, through association with certain mythological figures of Greece. As Momaday writes:

American Poetry (New York: E. P. Dutton and Co., 1974), 120–23, has a brief but excellent treatment of "The Cricket," which compares it perceptively and favorably to "Thanatopsis," "When Lilacs Last in the Dooryard Bloom'd," and "Further in Summer than the Birds."

> Mythology is outside the scope of historical experience
> in the same way that the realization of death is outside the
> scope of rational experience.... What [the cricket]
> symbolizes is beyond the capacity of the rational mind
> to understand, but it is nonetheless real. Unlike man, who
> has severed his existence from primitive nature, the
> cricket is an integral part of nature. And, like death, it
> has absolute existence in a dimension incomprehensible
> to man.[3]

Tuckerman thus follows his most direct model for the poem, Keats's "Ode to a Nightingale," in extending a captivating natural sound (that he has already established as part of the subrational world) into the prerational world as it increasingly embodies all forms of release from the pains of rational human existence, including death.

The fifth stanza unifies this complex theme. Tuckerman develops the myth of an enchanter who took dangerous drugs in order to understand the speech of nonhuman creatures. This is one of Tuckerman's symbols for his own yearning to *know*, and thus perhaps control and reveal, the nonrational, the subhuman. The fascination with loss of identity, the yearning to leave behind grief and despair, the hope to bridge the frustrating remoteness of nature's *meaning* that comes with human alienation from the nonhuman, and the desire to return, to merge with nature—all are fully felt and fully sustained. But the poet makes a deliberate choice to resist these temptations. He recognizes that the price for loss of self-consciousness is some form of death, which takes with it the very values for which he is yearning. The choice is self-defeating, though some of Tuckerman's more famous contemporaries, such as Emerson and Whitman, seem never to have realized it. With a kind of somber common sense Tuckerman accepts his human nature—with its tragic urges and limitations—and the responsibility to live fully at the human level until his life comes to its end.

---

[3] Momaday, Introduction to "An Edition of the Complete Poems," 38, 41.

It is fairly obvious that Tuckerman uses the devices, developed by pre-Romantics and Romantics, of emotionally charged perception of natural details and associational development. However, a careful reading shows that he does so with a total control that prevents destructive excesses and allows him to reject (both explicitly and in practice) certain Romantic tendencies affecting both form and idea. Particularly in stanzas II, III, and V, Tuckerman progressively integrates the imagery, using a controlled crescendo of carefully modulated combinations of details, images, and rhythms, integrated with an increasingly clear and powerfully felt theme: Nature is fascinatingly beautiful and temptingly mysterious; and death and the primitive, which are part of nature, constantly encroach upon us unless consciously resisted. To yield to them—to renounce human language and rational thought—in the hope of perfect understanding and unity, in the desire to escape our painful self-awareness and experience of loss and change, is a delusion. That merging will cost everything, including the yearning itself, the hoped-for understanding, and any ability to express those things. Nature will eventually have her way with us; but we must live now as human beings, retaining the means to see nature's beauty and to find what understanding is possible.

I now present the entire text, because I believe it is important to read the poem as a whole before analyzing and comparing it. A copy of an additional, probably later, manuscript has been recovered that Momaday did not have available, on the basis of which (and through comparison with the other manuscripts) I have made a few changes, in addition to a correction in spelling.[4]

---

[4] See Appendix II for an extended discussion of the special problems of editing "The Cricket" and my justifications for departures from Momaday's text, based on my own research and also that of T. Patrick Lynch, reported in his "Still Needed: A Tuckerman Text," in *Papers of the Bibliographical Society of America* 69 (1975): 255–65.

I

The humming bee purrs softly o'er his flower;
  From lawn and thicket
The dogday locust singeth in the sun
  From hour to hour:
Each has his bard, and thou, ere day be done,   [5]
  Shalt have no wrong.
So bright that murmur mid the insect crowd
Muffled and lost in bottom-grass, or loud
  By pale and picket:
Shall I not take to help me in my song   [10]
  A little cooing cricket?

II

The afternoon is sleepy; let us lie
Beneath these branches whilst the burdened brook,
Muttering and moaning to himself, goes by;
And mark our minstrel's carol whilst we look   [15]
Toward the faint horizon swooning blue.
  Or in a garden bower,
Trellised and trammeled with deep drapery
  Of hanging green,
  Light glimmering through—   [20]
There let the dull hop be
Let bloom, with poppy's dark refreshing flower:
Let the dead fragrance round our temples beat,
Stunning the sense to slumber, whilst between
The falling water and fluttering wind   [25]
  Mingle and meet,
  Murmur and mix,
No few faint pipings from the glades behind,
  Or alder-thicks:
But louder as the day declines,   [30]
From tingling tassel, blade, and sheath,
Rising from nets of river vines,
  Winrows and ricks,

Above, beneath,
  At every breath,   [35]
At hand, around, illimitably
Rising and falling like the sea,
  Acres of cricks!

III

Dear to the child who hears thy rustling voice
Cease at his footstep, though he hears thee still,   [40]
Cease and resume with vibrance crisp and shrill,
Thou sittest in the sunshine to rejoice.
Night lover too; bringer of all things dark
And rest and silence; yet thou bringest to me
Always that burthen of the unresting Sea,   [45]
The moaning cliffs, the low rocks blackly stark;
These upland inland fields no more I view,
But the long flat seaside beach, the wild seamew,
  And the overturning wave!
Thou bringest too, dim accents from the grave   [50]
To him who walketh when the day is dim,
Dreaming of those who dream no more of him,
With edged remembrances of joy and pain;
And heyday looks and laughter come again:
Forms that in happy sunshine lie and leap,   [55]
With faces where but now a gap must be,
Renunciations, and partitions deep
And perfect tears, and crowning vacancy!
And to thy poet at the twilight's hush,
No chirping touch of lips with laugh and blush,   [60]
But wringing arms, hearts wild with love and woe,
Closed eyes, and kisses that would not let go!

IV

So wert thou loved in that old graceful time
  When Greece was fair,
While god and hero hearkened to thy chime;   [65]
  Softly astir

Where the long grasses fringed Caÿster's lip;
Long-drawn, with shimmering sails of swan and ship,
   And ship and swan;
    Or where   [70]
    Reedy Eurotas ran.
Did that low warble teach thy tender flute
   Xenaphyle?
Its breathings mild? say! did the grasshopper
Sit golden in thy purple hair   [75]
    O Psammathe?
    Or wert thou mute,
Grieving for Pan amid the alders there?
And by the water and along the hill
That thirsty tinkle in the herbage still,   [80]
Though the lost forest wailed to horns of Arcady?

V

Like the Enchanter old—
Who sought mid the dead water's weeds and scum
For evil growths beneath the moonbeam cold,
   Or mandrake or dorycnium;   [85]
And touched the leaf that opened both his ears,
So that articulate voices now he hears
In cry of beast, or bird, or insect's hum,—
Might I but find thy knowledge in thy song!
   That twittering tongue,   [90]
Ancient as light, returning like the years.
   So might I be,
Unwise to sing, thy true interpreter
Through denser stillness and in sounder dark,
Than ere thy notes have pierced to harrow me.
   So might I stir
   The world to hark
   To thee my lord and lawgiver,
   And cease my quest:
Content to bring thy wisdom to the world;   [100]
Content to gain at last some low applause,

              Now low, now lost
Like thine from mossy stone, amid the stems and straws,
      Or garden gravemound tricked and dressed—
      Powdered and pearled   [105]
      By stealing frost—
In dusky rainbow beauty of euphorbias!
For larger would be less indeed, and like
The ceaseless simmer in the summer grass
To him who toileth in the windy field,   [110]
      Or where the sunbeams strike,
Naught in innumerable numerousness.
      So might I much possess,
      So much must yield;
But failing this, the dell and grassy dike,   [115]
The water and the waste shall still be dear,
And all the pleasant plots and places
      Where thou has sung, and I have hung
      To ignorantly hear.
Then Cricket, sing thy song! or answer mine!   [120]
Thine whispers blame, but mine has naught but praises.
It matters not. Behold! the autumn goes,
      The shadow grows,
The moments take hold of eternity;
Even while we stop to wrangle or repine   [125]
      Our lives are gone—
      Like thinnest mist,
Like yon escaping color in the tree;
Rejoice! rejoice! whilst yet the hours exist
Rejoice or mourn, and let the world swing on   [130]
Unmoved by cricket song of thee or me.

That final section, particularly in those lines near the end
that attempt to confront us with our mortality, is to me extremely moving. But its power is dependent on what Tuckerman has built from the beginning: In the second stanza the
theme and an effect of intoxication are united in what also
serves as straightforward description of an afternoon's reverie.

"Burdened brook" flirts with pathetic fallacy; but in the context of the whole poem the brook's burden is a real one, because water in various forms becomes a source and symbol of progressively more threatening, overwhelming forces. Moreover, there is a near pun on the other sense of "burden," as when we speak of the burden, or "burthen," of a song.[5] This is merely a transition from the quiet opening, as the single cooing cricket is multiplied throughout the landscape, on the way to the full sense in the third stanza (where there is an explicit tie-in with "burthen of the unresting sea") of water multiplied in the same way as is the cricket—to become a symbol of that physical universe from which we literally come, from which we now feel self-consciously apart, and into which we will return in death. As Tuckerman builds the intensity of his meaning and means, he takes us from "faint horizon, swooning-blue" to the brewer's *"dull* hop" and the opiate poppy, tempting us to *"dark"* refreshment with its *"dead"* fragrance (italics added). The formerly insignificant little cricket hypnotically fills our awareness and helps move us toward a trance-like revery (often directly *sought* in Romantic experience) and beyond. It is described here in rhythms and sounds that achieve increasingly powerful metaphoric identity with the rising and falling sea—and thus also evoke the sea's tempting fearsomeness.

Our awareness that the sense can be tempted and stunned to more than restful slumber is reinforced by the rhythmic effects that Tuckerman creates. The second stanza begins with a rather calm five-line introduction, with all the lines in regular iambic pentameter except for the trochee at the beginning of the third line, where the energy of the brook's "burden" starts to build. But then there is one complex twenty-one-line

---

[5] It is interesting that in MS. Am 1349 (2), Houghton (a complete draft in ink of *Poems,* apparently prepared for the printer), next to the last line of Sonnet I: 3, where he describes a moment of irrational succumbing to grief (caused, I believe, by Anna's death), Tuckerman at some time pencilled "burthened brook."

sentence which slowly gathers in excitement through a combination of subject matter and images and variations in rhythm, length of line, and sound. This begins to be particularly noticeable in lines 25–27:

> The falling water and fluttering wind
> Mingle and meet,
> Murmur and mix.

(In one manuscript Tuckerman shows his clear intention, though I think he there overdoes it, by adding another anapest to line 25 for imitative effect: "The faltering water and fluttering wind.") The intended hypnotic effect is assisted by those short lines, with their parallel nasals and rocking rhythms. This effect is greatly increased when Tuckerman interrupts the syntax of the next clause (between "but" in line 30 and "Acres of cricks!" in line 38) with a long series of enveloping expressions of the cricket's presence, in phrases that are made progressively more intense through the way he uses variety in length of line and position of caesura (and other pauses) in relation to the sustained syntax. The result, among other things, is literally breathlessness.

Meanwhile, the rhythmic metaphor for the cricket's growing power in the mind is complemented by the end rhymes. They are increased in number through the use of frequent short lines and are all tied to each other by various forms of true and partial rhyme, and they are all united as rhymes on the imitative words Tuckerman used for the hypnotic sound of the cricket: "chide," "tick," "tingle," "cheep," "creak," "clink," "chime." Energy is also built through the progressively audacious though perfectly apt diction ("tingling tassel," "illimitably / Rising") which culminates in an almost jovial colloquialism: "Acres of cricks!"

The third stanza transfers this accumulated energy into a long, meditative passage that consolidates and expands the meaning of the symbolic structure. It reminds us first that the cricket is dear to the child, who is, of course, in the eyes of the

Romantic superior to the man because still close to the primitive. Then the sea and cricket are further identified as symbolic of those things which remain primitive in us and delight us. But that identification reminds us that those things also elude our understanding and control. In fact, they include the death that will ultimately claim us through our mortality, after slowly stripping us of the dear mortal things and people around us.

Tuckerman uses in stanza III an interesting development from the sonnet form. It is essentially an integrated double sonnet of twenty-four lines. Tuckerman employs two syntactically self-contained quatrains, rhymed *a b b a* and *c d d c*, to introduce his contrasting themes of the cricket's primitivistic attractiveness and its increasing suggestion of death. He then continues with a series of couplets, many of which are tied by various forms of rhyme back into the original quatrains, as he develops the complex interrelationships of those themes. Two lines, in the long series telling what the cricket brings, achieve with special force a unified complexity of theme, image, and rhythmic effect:

> Forms that in happy sunshine lie and leap,
> With faces where but now a gap must be.

The horrifying pervasiveness of the foreboding which the cricket brings, in contrast to the bucolic repose which it also signifies, appears in the last lines of the stanza. Tuckerman tells us that the cricket no longer evokes the light sensuality of his *first* knowledge of Anna in their courtship. That particular point is clearly intended, because it is insisted upon too overtly in one of the five manuscripts of "The Cricket" (see Appendix II). There Tuckerman writes, "No chirping touch of lips with *tittering* blush" instead of "with *laugh and* blush" (italics added), thus not only doubling the imitative suggestion of the cricket already present in "chirping" but also carrying the imitation into the sound and movement of "tittering."

In the speaker's present, "now," the cricket, operating

mainly in its contrasting darker suggestiveness developed in this stanza, brings back again Tuckerman's *last* knowledge of Anna, at her death. At that time he wildly held and kissed her as she moved—in the "upper chamber in a darkened house" of Sonnet: I: 10—into that impenetrable dimension of death that now tempts him:

> No chirping touch of lips with laugh and blush,
> But wringing arms, hearts wild with love and woe,
> Closed eyes, and kisses that would not let go.

As Winters writes, "To establish the cricket as a symbol, and temporarily almost as a deity, of nature and of death is no simple feat."[6] Tuckerman's cricket becomes, in its way, as powerful a symbol as Melville's whale. But—and this, we may suspect, is the chief reason why the poem tends to be neglected—that very achievement makes "The Cricket," in Momaday's phrase, "a testament of heresy."[7] It is heresy from a certain Romantic viewpoint, but much more from a Transcendentalist viewpoint. The Romantic yearning for primal unity led to various forms of preoccupation with nature and the temptation to merge with it in revery, sleep, intoxication, mindlessness— even death. But it was Emerson and his explicit pantheism, preached with Calvinistic fervor, that gave the notion of achieving union with nature through death the emotional force of an unmitigated religious good. This notion has been an obsession for American poets ever since, and the seriousness of Tuckerman's struggle in "The Cricket" is one result.

Tuckerman's Anglican orthodoxy and his scientific naturalism kept him clear of the Emersonian error, and the result is better poetry than Emerson's (for instance, compare Emerson's "Threnody" on his own most bitter loss—that of his son). Matthiessen helps explain why this should be so:

---

[6] Yvor Winters, "A Discovery," *Hudson Review* 3 (Autumn 1950): 457.
[7] Momaday, "Heretical Cricket," 51.

Yeats came to feel, in spite of a youthful devotion, that Whitman as well as Emerson "have begun to seem superficial, because they lack the Vision of Evil."[8]

> ... What Goethe said of himself, that he was incapable of writing tragedies because he could not tolerate discords unresolved, was far truer of Emerson.... He was confident that no such thing as "pure malignity" can exist.... How an age in which Emerson's was the most articulate voice could also have given birth to *Moby-Dick* can be accounted for only through reaction.[9]

Reaction is also what accounts for "The Cricket." Emerson, with remarkable honesty, confessed, "I grieve that grief can teach me nothing."[10] However, Tuckerman's grief, deeply felt and intelligently encountered with patiently developed skill and with the full resources of language, had, in the course of perhaps eight years, taught him much. And he was able to make an uncompromising moral judgment, a clear rejection of Emersonian doctrine. Tuckerman did not try to do this with some ungrounded didactic assertion such as occurs as the end of Bryant's "Thanatopsis," but through direct confrontation with the tempting mystery of nature and death, fully realized in the poetry. "The Cricket" conveys both the seductive evil of surrender to that dark, dissolving realm and also the poet's rejection—somewhat melancholy but firm—of such an ultimate betrayal of his humanity.

IT MUST SEEM an injustice in the ideal world of Emerson's disciples, but it appears true that union with nature not only brings with it the ultimate cost of what Keats called "easeful death" in his "Ode to a Nightingale" but also exacts the

---

8 F. O. Matthiessen, *American Renaissance: Art and Expression in the Age of Emerson and Whitman* (1941; reprint, New York: Oxford Univ. Press, 1968), 181.

9 Ibid., 184.

10 Quoted by Matthiessen, p. 181, from Emerson's "Lecture on the Times" (1841).

Holograph of Tuckerman's poem "The Cricket" from Houghton MS. Am 1349(7). Used by permission of Houghton Library, Harvard University.

proximate penalty of loss of language. The attempt to know and speak like dumb beasts is too often nearly successful. Tuckerman deals with this dimension of the temptation even more fully than Keats does in the great poem which most influenced "The Cricket." He explicitly rejects the temptation toward nonhuman speech and shows his rejection in the quality of his own thought and language. At the beginning of the fifth stanza, the poet fantasizes, as many Romantics have, about such meaningful communication at a nonrational level. He imagines that he thereby might convert the world to the cricket's wisdom and gain the "low applause" of the subhuman world. But he gradually recognizes the impossibility of this choice—how delusory it is. The applause is indeed "low," in all sorts of ways, and Tuckerman shows a somber wit in his use of the word. The very hope for communication—even perception itself—is a product of our rational nature and cannot be satisfied by denying that nature. Whatever we might possess by a surrender to the subhuman world, we would "yield" much more. If we lost identity—merged completely with all nature—"larger would be less indeed." The poet-narrator accepts full awareness of what this decision costs: the necessity of living and communicating at the human level, with all the human limitations, until the end of our lives.

The Romantics generally felt, with intense power and anguish, the alienation from nature that is imposed by the self-consciousness of the rational mind. They realized the inadequacy of language, given its basically conceptual, generalizing foundation, to provide full access to the infinitely detailed complexity and flow of "real" experience. As we noted earlier, some of the Romantics, especially the French Symbolists and nominalist philosophers, pushed this anxiety to the point of conviction that any image, any formulation, any expression, immediately became dead because it fixed something of a reality that is essentially flowing and changing. They felt that man, in moving away from his primitive nature, moved away from nature itself. There remained much that had absolute reality in a dimension not fully accessible to man—

things like nightingales, crickets, and death itself. They realized that part of their own nature, part of their own feelings,
remained in that dimension which the rational mind could
not completely comprehend. The temptation was to solve this
dichotomy by escaping into primitivism, even into death
itself—sometimes in the delusion that it was the way to lose
the insistent self-consciousness of reason and that it was worth
the price, sometimes merely in the hope for the rest and
silence of oblivion ("Nothing is lost by this sublimation except
all"—Geoffrey Hartmann).

"The Cricket" gives ample evidence that Tuckerman felt this
temptation as deeply as any of the Romantics, and yet he firmly
rejected both death and primitivism—while neither underestimating the difficulty of the choice nor implying that the
alternative is other than painful. Tuckerman realized the
world can be known most fully through using most fully the
resources of language, even though language itself alienates us
from the world. Like the other Romantics he knew that to talk
is to suffer—and to lie—but he expressed better, I think, than
even the greatest of them his conviction that not to talk is to
be alone, to die. He felt with Romantics the mind-matter
separation, the sense that full communion with nature is possible only through repudiation of the confronting, alienating
mind, through resorting to pantheistic mysticism. He also
came to know the truth expressed later in Dickinson's little
rhyme about nature (the conclusion of "What mystery pervades a well!"):

> But nature is a stranger yet;
> The ones that cite her most
> Have never passed her haunted house,
> Nor simplified her ghost.
>
> To pity those that know her not
> Is helped by the regret
> That those who know her, know her less
> The nearer her they get.

As we progressively yield ourselves to nature, in the hope of direct knowledge, we gradually depart from the fulness of human life; and if we entirely join nature we entirely leave human life—and the ability to know anything. For Tuckerman the only solution is to accept our limited (but uniquely valuable) *human* knowledge, the product of experience, feeling, and thought. "The Cricket" is his specific refutation of the temptation to desert human language and the fundamentally rational structure that undergirds it. He knew that both of these human gifts are immitigably part of our alienation from perfect identification with nonhuman reality but that both of them also immeasurably increase our perceptions and powers compared to the nonhuman.

The last stanza of "The Cricket" is both an impressive defense and an excellent example of the use of the perceptions and powers that language provides. The temptation to surrender to intuition, to move toward primitivism, to renounce language, to embrace the premonitions of death is fully felt and realized. But the final subordination of intuition to reason—the acceptance of life in human terms—is clear, honest, undeluded. There is a conscious judgment, a relinquishing that is deliberate. There is no optimistic reprieve, no tacked-on moral sentiment to relieve our sense of mortality's painful claims. The affirmation is a human one: "The water and the waste shall still be dear." But those dear things of mortality themselves reveal to the poet their own passing, and his own eventual death, without being able to give him understanding of the meaning of death. The poet returns, without solace but without despair, to a life of which death is an ultimate part.

There is in this poem a particularly clear recognition, not common to some other Romantics, especially the American Transcendentalists, of the difference between the poet's human song and the cricket's seductive chirp. Tuckerman chooses the former because he knows that the Romantic quest for an absolute cosmic integrity, for identification with the Oversoul, for merging into a pantheistic whole (a quest symbolized here by the yearning to become subhuman, to know the cricket's song), is ultimately dehumanizing. It is destructive of the very tools that poets must use in their craft, some of which tools all humans in fact must use to remain human. Tuckerman knows that language is part of the inevitable barrier between humans and the nonhuman: We can feel and express the temptations toward perfect unity with nature, can even praise the natural world, *only* because we remain consciously, painfully apart from that which we praise, finally and inescapably alienated. Language, with all of its limitations, is part of the price we must pay for literature—and for humanity.

The Romantic nominalists were exceedingly sensitive to the tragic paradox in the very fact of language. Silence is the only condition proper to extreme skepticism about the efficacy of language to transcend the irreducible otherness of things outside the mind; but silence is hardly a *solution* for human beings, least of all for poets. Compromises must be made, and their nature and degree will determine poetic style; but to the degree that those compromises are specious, untrue either to a proper epistemological skepticism or to the nature of language, they will produce bad poetry. Tuckerman recognized (it is in fact part of the subject of this poem) the tragic necessity of compromise, and in his poetry he holds a steady course, true both to his nominalistic skepticism and also to his understanding of language and his faith in its ability to do *some* things.

Emerson and many of his disciples have wanted language to do too much and have thus used it to do less than it could. They have tried to make language serve for direct transmission of nonmental reality, which because of its inescapably conceptual nature it cannot do; and they have thus neglected its capacity to treat mental reality, which it is able to do by means of that conceptual nature—the only means of access to the reader's understanding. To attempt to move words onto the other side of the subject-object void and treat them as if they could be purified of denotation, like music—or like the speech of nonhuman creatures existing in the realm of nature—leaves them in a condition described by A. J. Ayer:

"They point to something that is going on, but they do not tell us what it is."[11]

We must accept a measure of looseness in the fit between words and things, a bit of "falsehood," if we are to get at the possible truths of conceptual meaning. If our aim is to make language simply *reproduce* raw experience, we will lose the control necessary for language to form various kinds of metaphors that get close to the essence of experience and thus give us the ability to *understand* experience.

Wallace Stevens once said, "A poet's words are of things that do not exist without the words."[12] Words cannot be things— or, in themselves, experiences. We cannot speak the language of the beasts, nor retreat from consciousness and the need to speak as humans—unless we accept the ultimate unity of death, with all its losses. But we can, through skillful bringing of words to bear on things and experiences, create a new thing, human thought in language in the poem, neither Kant's *"ding an sich"* nor a mental concoction, but a real and valuable— created—world. It is a limited world, with pains and anxieties, but the only one we can have for development and communication of what is uniquely human. How ultimately satisfying it is may depend on whether one's faith is that it is merely an ephemeral human creation, a game to occupy us until final doom, or whether it is rooted ontologically and shared by God. Either way it is all we have and we had better respect it.

I CLAIMED earlier that Tuckerman's respect for language, despite his full sensitivity to its limitations and to the Romantic yearning to transcend it, is *demonstrated* as well as reaffirmed in the fifth stanza of "The Cricket." He describes the action of the old Enchanter, who, in order to gain power to understand directly the nonhuman world, searched for evil herbs in

<hr>

[11] A. J. Ayer, *The Problem of Knowledge* (London: Macmillan, 1956).

[12] Wallace Stevens, *The Necessary Angel: Essays on Reality and the Imagination* (New York: Alfred A. Knopf, 1965), 32.

moonlit swamps—"and touched the leaf that opened both his ears." Using fully the cognitive resources of language, Tuckerman develops rhetoric that gives us in that one line both a complex scene of action, the intended result, and also the feel of the poet's thought as he reconstructs that scene as an image of his own temptation. Later, as the speaker rejects the parallel temptation to escape the alienation from nature which even rational *consciousness* inevitably brings—the temptation to merge with nature's lovely forms and share the cricket's wisdom, including comprehension of death—he gives us the exact texture of a nominalistic universe of discrete, meaningless particulars ("Naught in innumerable numerousness"). But at the same time he gives us that non-human world's possible human significance and the feeling appropriate to his rejection of the temptation to merge with it—and thus to lose the power to apprehend it in human terms:

> For larger would be less indeed, and like
> The ceaseless simmer in the summer grass
> To him who toileth in the windy field,
>   Or where the sunbeams strike,
> Naught in innumerable numerousness.
>   So might I much possess
>   So much must yield.

One who could not resist the temptation as Tuckerman did was Whitman. Despite his exaltation of the "self," Whitman felt deeply the painfulness of personal identity, the estrangement from the All that rational consciousness brings. He had a solution: "I weave all things into myself." And D. H. Lawrence, who, like many, had profited from Whitman's opening of horizons, was ungratefully furious: "His poems . . . are long sums in addition and multiplication, of which the answer is invariably MYSELF. He reaches the state of ALLNESS. And what then? It's all empty.

Just an empty Allness."[13] Lawrence saw clearly where this had led—to a loss of the concern and the power to make distinctions:

> Anything, so long as he could merge himself.
> Just a horror. A sort of white flux. . . .
> Death!
> Death is now his chant! Death!
> Merging! And Death! Which is the final merge. . . .
> . . . when Whitman embraces an evil prostitute: that is not sympathy. The evil prostitute has no desire to be embraced with love; so if you sympathize with her, you won't try to embrace her with love. The leper loathes his leprosy, so if you sympathize with him, you'll loathe it too.

With the power to make distinctions goes the power to value properly what must be valued above other things—and thus to make moral choices. The exaltation of all things to a single level of pantheistic ALLNESS paradoxically *reduces* their worth, because worth is only meaningful by comparison. The goodness, truth, and beauty that Whitman admired can only be defined, and thus valued, on a scale that includes evil, falsity, and ugliness. Whitman's exaltation tends to reduce the writing of poetry to an endless cataloguing of indistinguishable and undistinguished particulars, with even their particularity slighted, because the discriminating power inherent in the nature of language is not respected.

Perhaps in the same year that "The Cricket" was written—1865—Whitman wrote "When lilacs last in the dooryard bloom'd," which has similarly been called an elegaic ode on the subject of the poet's greatest grief. But the horrors of war and the assassination of Lincoln could not move Whitman beyond Emersonian orthodoxy: "I say there is in fact no evil." The perennial, tragic human quest to come to terms with the fact of death, to understand the claims of mortality and pre-

---

[13] D. H. Lawrence, *Studies in Classic American Literature* (1923; reprint, New York: Viking Press, 1961), 166–67; the following quotations from Lawrence are from pages 168, 169, and 176 in this edition.

pare to put them by—a quest Tuckerman participates in passionately and profoundly—is swept away in one stroke. The symbolic hermit thrush can support none of the realistic ambiguity of Tuckerman's cricket (or Keats's nightingale). While Tuckerman resists the temptation to "find [the cricket's] knowledge in [its] song," Whitman tells us that "the voice of [his] spirit tallied the song of the bird." And that song is a carol to death, the "strong delivress" which leads the dead to be "lost in the loving floating ocean of thee."

Tuckerman's poetry reveals a lifelong set of painfully self-educative journeys out into increasingly mature questions and back to more comprehensive resolutions—concerning his poetic vocation, language itself, the nature and goodness of God, his own griefs and those of others, his mortality. "The Cricket" is a supreme example. Whitman's elegy, in contrast, even though it too is a kind of theodicy, is a simple, antirational claim for the triumph of unity in death ("I glorify thee above all"). The result is an inability to move us, except through sentimental association and thus to sentimental acceptance, with those images of human suffering in war that close the poem, or to claim our serious attention to his call for individuality after he celebrates the individual's dissolution.

As Robert Pinsky observes in his study of Landor to which I have referred earlier, "To find the right way to say a thing is to feel the right way about it." For Tuckerman, as for Landor, "serious ethical questions were problems of tone and definition and every stylistic problem was an ethical trial of the man."[14] In contrast Whitman eschewed meter and rhythm and sought to make language do impossible tricks (such as directly copy the sea or music). But he sought to do so without serious prosodic effort, by merely letting things flow naturally, in a rhythm of sorts built from syntactical parallels, a prosody of grammar that gave no ability to control precisely either feeling or meaning. Thus for Whitman there are no serious ethical

---

[14]Robert Pinsky, *Landor's Poetry* (Chicago: Univ. of Chicago Press, 1968), 154.

questions and no stylistic problems; the giving in to the temptations of Transcendental pantheism removes the need, and the human benefits, of both. Tuckerman saw and did things quite another way:

> God lends the light we use, the strength we keep.
> So let us use that light, . . .
> So daily use it, that the mystery
> Of life we touch: in cloud and wind and tree,
> In human faces that about us dwell,
> And the deep soul that knoweth heaven and hell.
>
> (Sonnet IV: 3, p. 52)

I WILL BRIEFLY discuss three other nineteenth-century poems which are similar in theme and quality to "The Cricket." At least two of them probably influenced the writing of Tuckerman's poem: Keats's "Ode to a Nightingale" (1819) and Tennyson's "Tithonus" (1832; revised 1860). The third, Dickinson's "Further in Summer than the Birds" (1866?), may very well have been influenced by "The Cricket," or at least by Tuckerman.

The development and rejection of the Romantic death wish in Keats's "Ode" is quite similar to that in "The Cricket" and was most certainly well known to Tuckerman. There is a similar opening, in which the poet is tempted toward a hypnotic trance. However, the nightingale is not developed as a powerful symbol of that temptation through being given any intrinsic part in the process, nor is the bird itself associated directly with nature and death as Tuckerman's cricket is (the nightingale's sound is not itself hypnotic or foreboding—nor does it evoke something that is, such as the sea). Keats merely compares his own mortal and conscious state with "what thou among the leaves has never known." Then he *states* the temptation to join the nightingale in her realm and in the "forest dim," the "embalmed darkness" that has encroached upon him in his revery.

Finally the poet confesses that he has been "half in love with easeful Death" and that "now more than ever seems it rich to die." In Momaday's brief comparison of Keats's "Ode" to "The Cricket," he is quite hard on this prevailing irresolution:

> In Keats the idea of death is cherished as an aspect of im-mortality. The wish for death is paramount, and it takes precedence over the function of the mind to recognize reality. At the end of the poem we are left with equal alternatives: "do I wake or sleep?" The question would seem to preclude the possibility of conscious moral judgment.[15]

But I think Momaday is too critical. In the midst of being *half* in love with death, it only *seeming* rich to die, Keats explicitly recognizes that in death the continuing song and life of the nightingale would be lost to him. He would lose the very pre-monition and suggestion of the temptation of death that made possible the pain and beauty of the poem, if he were to suc-cumb to the temptation:

> Still wouldst thou sing, and I have ears in vain—
> To thy high requiem become a sod.

Walter Jackson Bate is right in his claim that Keats is here working out one of the first examples of "a form of lyric debate that moves actively toward drama."[16] In the first four stanzas, Keats is tempted by and works toward identification with the nonhuman bird (with its freedom from man's "fever" and "fret"), but in the last four stanzas his separateness is clearly

---

[15] Momaday, Introduction to "An Edition of the Complete Poems," 42.

[16] Walter Jackson Bate, *John Keats* (1963; reprint, New York: Oxford Univ. Press, 1967), 500; "The Cricket" is of course one such example, too—an interior dramatic monologue that becomes a debate in the mind.

presupposed. His quest for liberation from human mortality is "resolved," not when he seeks to leave the world of actual process, but when he accepts that world, though such an acceptance involves also a qualified understanding and acceptance of eventual death.[17] Bate quotes a letter written by Keats a year after writing "Ode to a Nightingale" that directly states his insight developed in the poem: "I wish for death every day and night . . . and then I wish death away, for death would destroy even those pains which are better than nothing. Land and Sea, weakness and decline, are great separators, but death is the great divorcer for ever."[18]

In a passage that the fourth stanza of "The Cricket" is quite obviously modeled on, Keats extends the sound of the nightingale back into prehistory and the primitive in man. The passage ends with an explicit reminder that those realms ("faery lands forlorn") are, like death, no longer real alternatives to man: "Forlorn! the very word is like a bell / To toll me back from thee to my sole self." Then there is a claimed return to integrity of the kind demonstrated at the end of "The Cricket," and Momaday is right that the ending seems irresolute. But that ending does not destroy the poem or the judgments that have preceded its final vagueness, and that irresoluteness seems to me to embody Keats's own integrity to his epistemological uncertainty—an uncertainty that Tuckerman had moved beyond but which remains valid and even, for many, preferable. That irresoluteness may thus be a reason to value Keats's poem more than Tuckerman's.

However, it is still appropriate to ask what Keats *does* with his remarkably similar *theme* that might compare with Tuckerman's mastery, in "The Cricket," of the elements of poetry that give "rhythmic cognition." Keats was, indeed, in the spring of 1819, working to improve his formal skill, to write with more care. He was in particular, as he put it, "endeavouring to discover a better sonnet stanza than we have. The

---

[17] Ibid., 506.
[18] Ibid., 508.

legitimate [Petrarchan] does not suit the language over-well from the pouncing rhymes—the other kind [Shakespearean] appears too elegaic—and the couplet at the end of it has seldom a pleasing effect."[19] The desire to experiment and improve is certainly commendable; but, though Bate offers the quotation above in praise, it is certainly naive about what the prosodic effects are that can work in a poem.

Keats's sonnets written just before the odes are "experimental" in their rhyme schemes—combining elements of the two traditional kinds and employing some imperfect rhyming. But there is no evidence (internal or external) that Keats had any sense of doing something that was more than ornamental, anything that significantly related sound to sense; and the same is true of the stanza forms that he developed for the odes from this melding of sonnet rhyme schemes.

Bate does not even venture onto this terrain, leaving the explication of the complex (but certainly not uniquely profound) theme as supposed justification enough for the reputation of the poem. "O for a life of Sensations rather than of Thoughts!" Keats wrote Benjamin Bailey in November 1817. The *sensations* are there in this poem written two years later and are powerfully engaging in their isolated appearance ("No hungry generations tread thee down"); but the Romantic temptation to desert consciousness, to distrust the careful working out of thoughts with the tools of language, is deeply felt, and Keats's uncertainty about what he is learning is the theme of the odes: "Was it a vision, or a waking dream?"

Though it seems highly likely that Keats's "Ode to a Nightingale" most influenced the overall theme and large-scale structure of "The Cricket," a new work by Tuckerman's more influential mentor, Tennyson, may well have provided the direct impetus for writing the poem and a more specific basis for its tone and rhythmic effectiveness. In 1833 Tennyson wrote a poem he called "Tithon," which he spoke of as a

---

[19] Ibid., 496.

"pendant" to "Ulysses" and which continued his struggle with the meaning of Hallam's death by evoking a situation in which immortality might be a curse. He uses the myth of that ever-withering lover of the goddess of the dawn, who had been granted eternal life without eternal youth. "Tithon" was never published; but in 1860 Tennyson rewrote it as "Tithonus," lengthening and improving it, and published it in the *Cornhill* magazine. Tuckerman may have seen a pirated copy in America or, more likely, first read it when it was published in the 1864 *Enoch Arden and Other Poems*—which would, if I am right in the following analysis, place the writing of "The Cricket" after that date.

"Tithonus" is certainly one of Tennyson's finest poems. It is thus fortunate that this particular instance (perhaps the final one) of the major poetic influence on Tuckerman's work came at a time (at the height of his mature powers) when he was perhaps best prepared to value and use it.[20] Tennyson's poem certainly conveys—more powerfully than Keats's, I think—a sense of the mingled fear and fascination of death that is also the theme of "The Cricket"; it is, as Ricks says, "Tennyson's subtlest and most beautiful exploration of the impulse to

---

[20] Other influences from Tennyson's work, as we might expect after such a long and intense apprenticeship, can be seen in various details of "The Cricket." For instance, the theme and tone and some specific phrasing from Tennyson's song "Tears, Idle Tears" are echoed in Stanza III; compare Tennyson's

> Dear as remembered kisses after death,
> And sweet as those by hopeless fancy feigned
> On lips that are for others; deep as love,
> Deep as first love, and wild with all regret;
> O Death in Life, the days that are no more.

and Tuckerman's

> Renunciations, and partitions deep
> And perfect tears, and crowning vacancy!
> . . . .
> But wringing arms, hearts wild with love and woe,
> Closed eyes, and kisses that would not let go!

suicide."[21] And it has fine achievements in its rhythmic effects
that allow, for instance, the following analysis by Ricks of just
the first few lines (which I quote first):

> The woods decay, the woods decay and fall,
> The vapours weep their burthen to the ground,
> Man comes and tills the field and lies beneath,
> And after many a summer dies the swan.
> Me only cruel immortality
> Consumes: I wither slowly in thine arms . . .

> The first four lines breathe peace and equanim-
> ity; such a death is breath-less, not breathless. But
> the fifth line disturbs all this, first by its immediate
> inversion ("Me only . . . "), unlike anything in the
> previous lines; next with the epithet "cruel," which
> springs with further force because the previous lines
> had not contained a single adjective; and disturbs it
> finally by its predatory enjambment (Me only cruel
> immortality / Consumes).[22]

The energy of that runover, the first in the poem, reflects back
on the first four lines, which thus become a moving statement
both of the usually saddening transitoriness of mortality and
of unusual envy for it. The nonhuman world that had tempted
Tithonus was superhuman rather than subhuman, but its gain
is as much a loss—here, too, in Tuckerman's words, "larger
would be less indeed." Tithonus will go on forever in impotent
embrace of his goddess ("Yet hold me not for ever in thine
East"). But in the myth, of course, we know (in a way that
invests the poem with another dimension) that neither the fear
of consuming immortality nor the hope of death will be realized for the speaker of this poem. Instead, he will be turned
into a grasshopper, whose song, in Romantic mythology, is

---

[21] Christopher Ricks, *Tennyson* (New York: Macmillan, 1972), 129.
[22] Ibid.

carried into winter by the cricket as a symbol of hope for nature's perpetuation (e.g., Keats's "On the Grasshopper and the Cricket"). As Ricks writes, "With a profound circularity of return, both 'Ulysses'—which yearns to have a future—and 'Tithonus'—which yearns to have no future—can find no room for the future tense of hope."[23]

But this praise suggests a limitation in the poem, if it is compared to "The Cricket." The myth gives, as does "The Cricket," some insight into the need to accept *human* life, with death as an ultimate part of life; but "Tithonus," because it is limited to the cognitive perspective of the protagonist, is essentially confined to his dramatic situation (i.e., speaking to his goddess-lover). It thus can only give us magnificent *hints* of the mingled hope and fear reflected in the protagonist's voice; it cannot give us what Tuckerman achieves: the precise definition of and basis for a qualified hope that is communicated directly to us from the poet's own mature understanding and in his own voice.

A similarly successful, though perhaps less ambitious, poem than the two just discussed is one of Emily Dickinson's:

> Further in Summer than the Birds
> Pathetic from the Grass
> A minor Nation celebrates
> Its unobtrusive Mass.
>
> No Ordinance be seen
> So gradual the Grace
> A pensive Custom it becomes
> Enlarging Loneliness.
>
> Antiquest felt at Noon
> When August burning low

---

[23] Ibid., 134.

> Arise this spectral Canticle
> Repose to typify.
>
> Remit as yet no Grace
> No Furrow on the Glow
> Yet a Druidic Difference
> Enhances Nature now.

This poem was written about 1866, and there is some reason to think that it was influenced by (or possibly influenced) "The Cricket." Dickinson once referred to her poem in a letter as "My Cricket." Her theme is precisely that clearly felt, regretted, but accepted separation from the nonhuman found in Tuckerman's poem, as she creates a subtle allegory between the humanly imperceptible but irrevocable change of seasons and the changes of states of being that lead up to and include death. In addition, the haunting strangeness of the poem is achieved, not only by the powerfully but economically embodied theme but by a masterful modulation of partial rhymes away from and back to true rhymes.

The comprehensive power of the poems by Tuckerman and Dickinson, when compared to the others on quite similar themes which I have discussed in this chapter, seems to be a product of the successful use of the post-Symbolist imagery I have defined earlier and a closely related skillful attention to rhythmic cognition. Certain themes seem to benefit particularly from the integrated embodiment of a poem's theme in the details of nature's basic processes that is characteristic of the post-Symbolist ideal.

Hallam, in his early essay on Tennyson's "picturesque" quality, suggests this in discussing the last lines of "Oriana" ("Thou liest beneath the greenwood tree; / I dare not die, and come to thee, / Oriana—/ I hear the roaring of the sea,"): He says the merit of applying that last natural image to the "leading sentiment" is in "resigning it to the accordance of inanimate Nature, who, like man, has her tempests, and occasions of horror, but august in their largeness of operation, awful in their dependence on a fixed and perpetual necessity."[24] By the same token, it may be that the post-Symbolist method tends to be most effective with, or even is best limited to, certain themes—themes which can take full advantage of the inherent potential in natural forms, that can best realize the Romantic desire to directly relate nature to the mind. Those themes include, for instance, the mystery and inevitability of death; the irrational, absolute cleavage between the human and nonhuman; the tendency of nature to absorb all being in mindless union and the human temptation to succumb to that tendency. But if this seems a limitation, it is important to remember that these are not only the great Romantic preoccupations but perennially central human themes.

---

[24] A. H. Hallam, "On Some of the Characteristics of Modern Poetry, and on the Lyrical Poems of Alfred Tennyson," *The Englishman's Magazine* (August 1831): 625–26.

VII

REPUTATION

> I have read the volume of poems, and think it a remarkable one. . . . I question whether the poems will obtain a very early or wide acceptance from the public either in England or America because their merit does not lie upon the surface, but must be looked for with faith and sympathy. . . . The second reading does more for them than the first; and I have no doubt many of them will glow brighter and brighter on repeated perusal. . . . The great difficulty with you will be to get yourself read at all; if you could be read twice, the book might be a success.
>
> Nathaniel Hawthorne, 1861

TUCKERMAN'S reputation seems to be the object of a rather perverse fate. The negative of Hawthorne's prophecy quoted above (that a single or careless reading of the poems would not reveal their value) seems continually to be fulfilled by the more widely influential critics like Hyatt Waggoner who, on the evidence of his few pages on Tuckerman in *American Poets from the Puritans to the Present,* at best skimmed him only once when he published the book in 1968 and did not reread or reconsider him when he revised that history in 1984. Those critics thus make their own self-fulfilling prophecies, like this one of Waggoner's: "Tuckerman seems likely to remain, what he has been for the past century, a poet overpraised by those with special biases, unjustly ignored by most, continually 'rediscovered' and then forgotten again."[1] On the other hand, the positive of Hawthorne's prophecy—

---

[1] Hyatt H. Waggoner, *American Poets from the Puritans to the Present,* rev. ed. (1968; reprint, Boston: Houghton Mifflin, 1984), 255.

that repeated reading would make the poems "glow brighter and brighter"—has tended to be fulfilled most often by less prominent critics or Europeans like Samuel Golden, Mordecai Marcus, and Roland Hagenbüchle, who read carefully and seriously but who for various reasons only partially perceive Tuckerman's virtues and even for their good insights do not have wide readership; or by influential pundits such as Edmund Wilson and Irving Howe and Lawrence Buell, whose main interests are not in poetry and who come close to damning with faint praise; or by well-known but severely judgmental critics like Winters and his student, Momaday, whose "special biases" provide too many an excuse to ignore them.

It is a particularly painful turn of fate, a kind of tragedy, that Yvor Winters became Tuckerman's chief champion—and at the same time his greatest stumbling block. Winters was the critic in our time most able, by virtue of his qualities of mind and temperament, to understand and analyze and appreciate Tuckerman's mind and work—who, indeed, went through a Romantic exaltation and then despondency very similar to Tuckerman's own and came out to a similar view of the world and a similar way of writing poetry, one that retained a similar combination of the best of Romantic insight and sensitivity and of Classical comprehensiveness and control. The critical response since Momaday's edition in 1965 is, as I will show, almost universally obsessed with response to Winters's heretical, obdurate foreword, rather than attentive to the poetry. If critics read the poetry even once it is clear that too many do it furiously, with Winters' words rankling ("the less said about Poe and Whitman the better"; "the greatest poem in English of the century") and thus further obscuring what Hawthorne called Tuckerman's "hidden fire." It would seem now that it was a mistake for Momaday to include that foreword by Winters, even though the choice was perfectly just, in every sense.

However, Winters was not responsible for Tuckerman's neglect in the nineteenth century nor the timid and short-lived response to Bynner's rediscovery in the thirties. A review of the criticism of Tuckerman's work—now that I have explored the qualities of his mind and poetry, the special nature of his genius—will provide some useful insight into American criticism itself and, more importantly, will perhaps help modern critics and teachers go about making a more adequate response to Tuckerman's achievement.

TUCKERMAN sent copies of the privately printed 1860 *Poems* to about thirty people—noted men of letters, critics, relatives, and friends.[2] Perhaps no more than about fifty copies were printed, since James Fields, in a letter asking for permission to print "two more" poems from the volume in the *Atlantic* (besides "Rhotruda," which he reports was "liked exceedingly"), says, "I do not consider your book *published,* as it has only been sent to a few friends."[3] At any rate it is quite clear that Tuckerman was trying to get some external perspective, from some whose judgment he valued, on the worth of what had become his vocation, before submitting his work to a prestigious printing house.

As I have demonstrated, the poems show a continual anxiety about their own worth, and one form of Tuckerman's despair and grief is the temptation to discontinue writing. But the struggle to make the poems was also part of the antidote to those problems. Sonnet 37 of the Second Series (the last poem in the 1860 edition) is obviously a kind of postscript, giving a classical frame to the two series and indeed the whole volume. After promising Anna in the previous poem to continue to "the full completion of this worldly day" and not to "cease to hold a hope and aim," Tuckerman brings before his "Maker" "these offspring of my sorrow, hidden long / And scarcely able

---

[2] A list of these, written by Tuckerman, is in MS. Am 1349 (4), Houghton, and is reproduced in Samuel A. Golden, *Frederick Goddard Tuckerman* (New York: Twayne, 1966), on pages 18 and 153; in addition, there is evidence that copies were seen by Harriet Beecher Stowe (this was the copy that Eaton finally obtained), William Ellery Channing, James T. Fields, W. E. Gladstone, Edward Moxon and another publisher in England, and James Russell Lowell.

[3] Dated at Boston, June 25, 1861, Houghton Autograph File.

to abide the light." There is no coy pretense here, I believe; he had written and would continue to write, as Bynner says, "straightly to himself," with no need for publication to give meaning to his task. But there is good evidence that he wanted to reach a broader audience: he continually submitted individual poems to prominent magazines, from 1849 to not long before his death in 1873, and Jeffrey D. Groves has discovered and commented on an 1864 letter from Tuckerman to James T. Fields (an editor of both *The Atlantic Monthly*, which had published individual Tuckerman poems, and of Ticknor and Fields, which was about to publish Tuckerman's book) that shows "for a while, at least, [he] actively pursued an association with the leading publisher of his day in order to promote the successful public reception of his work."[4] Nevertheless, Tuckerman reveals himself as an extraordinarily gentle and reticent man, though fully self-contained, when he writes Hawthorne asking permission to send him a copy of the poems, and, after receiving it, writes again, asserting:

> For the book, which I offer with a certain tremor to yourself, I claim little, but that it is New Englandy (I hope), was not written to please anybody, and is addressed to those only who understand it. . . . My hope is to have the book published in England (if it seem worthy), as here I fancy it would be but coldly received, even with that proviso.[5]

Tuckerman was quite perceptive about the comparative worth of different parts of his work. He certainly seemed to know, on the evidence of the numerous and carefully made manuscript copies, that "The Cricket" was his best poem. In 1861, before "The Cricket" was written, he seemed to value the sonnets most. In a letter to James Russell Lowell, Emerson asked Lowell to return his copy of Tuckerman's *Poems* if he had it, because "the poet, in sending me his book, requested

---

[4] "A Letter from Frederick Goddard Tuckerman to James T. Fields," *The Huntington Library Quarterly* 52.3 (Summer 1989): 403–8.

[5] Dated at Greenfield, April 10, 1861, Houghton Autograph File.

my attention to the Sonnets, which I have not yet read."[6] It is likely that Tuckerman was very conscious that he was doing new things with his rhyming structure and themes, and he must have been disappointed in the response. Not only is there no evidence that Emerson ever read the sonnets, though he praised the other poems, but only a few of those who responded to the 1860 *Poems* even mention the sonnets; and the reviewers in England of the 1863 edition and in America of the 1864 edition could not understand his innovations in the sonnet form and dismissed them as ignorance or mere waywardness.

In addition to Hawthorne, only Jones Very (who used the sonnet form extensively but in an extremely traditional manner) and an old family friend, John Seely Stone, were attentive to the sonnets. Very was most drawn to the content of the two series included. In a letter to Tuckerman he praises the somewhat didactically affirmative Sonnet I: 28, which I have discussed earlier, and writes that the concluding sonnets of the Second Series, which describe Tuckerman's determination to live out his life courageously despite his continuing grief, "are beautifully expressed and call forth my deepest sympathy with your loss and with the faith which sustains us."[7] Stone is perceptive about the overall burden of the sonnets: "I know not whether the Sonnets, in particular, may be regarded as a sort of partial autobiography of their author, breathing out the broken utterances of a heart, crushed and sorrowing over the early death of a loved one."[8]

Tuckerman must have been particularly interested in the judgment of the more renowned men of letters whom he respected. Besides Hawthorne, he sent copies to Tennyson,

---

[6] Quoted in Samuel A. Golden, *Frederick Goddard Tuckerman: An American Sonnetteer* (Univ. of Maine, Bulletin 54, no. 12 [April 1952]), 30, from Ralph Waldo Emerson, *The Letters of Ralph Waldo Emerson,* ed. Ralph L. Rusk, 6 vols. (New York: Columbia Univ. Press, 1939), 5:248.

[7] Dated at Salem, April 24, 1861, Houghton Autograph File.

[8] Dated at Brookline, March 19, 1861, Houghton Autograph File.

Emerson, Longfellow, and Bryant. There is no record of Tennyson's response (though Bynner, perhaps on the basis of family tradition related to him by Tuckerman's granddaughter, ventures that the 1863 London edition "may have been the result of Tennyson's interest" and that Tennyson seemed "to have been impressed with a more than casual and passing quality in Tuckerman's poetry").[9] Emerson's letter shows that the two poets were not strangers ("I have much to say about this book, and when we ride again in a train together, I hope you will give me a chance to say it"), but it also indicates rather superficial taste. His favorite poem was "Rhotruda," a merely competent narrative of a medieval legend (Emerson is right in saying to Tuckerman that "it should be bound up as a fifth in your friend Tennyson's 'Idyls' ").[10] Emerson further suggests his limited understanding of what is going on in a poem by mentioning, as Tuckerman's chief qualities, "love of native flowers, the skill to name them and delight in words that are melodies." The evidence of Emerson's essay, "The Poet," indicates that he also probably agreed with the judgment of W. E. Channing, which Emerson recorded in his journal:

> Yesterday wrote to F. G. Tuckerman to thank him for his book, and praise "Rhotruda." Ellery Channing finds two or three good lines and metres in the book thinks it refined and delicate but says young poets run on a notion that they must name the flowers, talk about an orchis, and say something about Indians; but he says, "I prefer passion and sense and genius to botany."[11]

---

[9] Witter Bynner, ed., *The Sonnets of Frederick Goddard Tuckerman* (New York: Alfred A. Knopf, 1931), 3.

[10] Dated at Concord, March 28, 1861, Houghton Autograph File; Emerson made the suggestion to Fields which led to the publication of "Rhotruda" in the *Atlantic* in 1861 and then included it in his own anthology, *Parnassus*, in 1874.

[11] Golden, *Tuckerman: An American Sonnetteer*, 30, quoted from Ralph Waldo Emerson, *Journals of Ralph Waldo Emerson*, ed. Edward Waldo Emerson and Waldo Emerson Forbes, 10 vols. (Boston: Houghton Mifflin, 1909–14), 9:318–19.

Tuckerman would have found this amusing, because, back in 1853—during that long apprenticeship which, as we have seen, included extremely close attention to the details of poetic form and of the natural world—he had noted, in his copy of Channing's *Poems,* the utter banality of some of the lines resulting from that "passion and sense and genius" which Channing preferred (e.g., "The Bible is a book worthy to read").[12]

Longfellow, in writing to Tuckerman, gives his opinion of the poems as "very favorable," calling them "thoughtful and full of feeling." He adds: "Best wishes for the success of your volume. I mean its external success with the world, which is something quite apart from its internal success, as an expression of your own thought and feelings."[13] This distinction between kinds of "success" (which Hawthorne was also to make, a week later) is central to the responses of the three men, among the recipients of the *Poems,* who had been most involved in practical criticism—William Cullen Bryant, George Ripley, and Henry T. Tuckerman, the poet's cousin. Though Tuckerman was evidently somewhat interested in eventual popular success, he cared most about careful assessment, hoping for verification of his own sense of the worth of his life's work. In that regard most of the responses of these men were probably not very helpful, but they are revealing of the criticism of the time.

H. T. Tuckerman was also a poet (his work was anthologized in the late nineteenth century when Frederick's was not), but he was mainly a critic of some note and an extremely popular personal essayist.[14] Henry, as "H. T." was known to his cousin,

---

12 W. E. Channing, *Poems* (Boston: Little, Brown and Co., 1843), 36. Copy, with Tuckerman comment, in Tuckerman papers, Hugh Clark home, Amherst.

13 Dated at Cambridge, April 5, 1861, Houghton Autograph File.

14 Carl Bode, *An Anatomy of American Popular Culture, 1840–1860* (Berkeley and Los Angeles: Univ. of California Press, 1960), 208–11. It is an amusing coincidence that, as Max J. Harzberg in *The Readers Encyclopedia of American Literature* informs us, this Tuckerman, Henry T., "was valued more highly by his American contemporaries than his writings justify" and that, as *Webster's*

was part of the Knickerbocker circle in New York and was able
to arrange for responses to Frederick's poems from Bryant
(which Frederick requested him to do) and George Ripley
(arranged by Henry as a substitute for Charles F. Briggs, the
editor of *Putnam's Monthly,* whom Frederick had also requested
he contact).[15] Henry wrote Tuckerman on June 28, 1861, refer-
ring to "general impressions" of the *Poems* that he had written
earlier (the letter is lost) and adding that upon reflection those
first reactions "are confirmed."

> I think critics would be apt to consider you too exclusive a
> disciple of a class of poets—than which none are more
> dear [undecipherable word] but who still represent a spe-
> cial phase and form of the poetic Sympathies and of
> which class Wordsworth, Keats and Tennyson, different in
> some respects, as they are, may be deemed the first great
> representatives. Somewhat of the directness and clear,
> emphatic style of Pope, Gray and Campbell would par-
> tially promote the *recognition* of your merits. So much for
> the *objective* estimate—to which, I dare say, you are in-
> different: Considered as compositions of personal sen-
> timent—the poems seem to me often graceful and
> genuine—but somewhat limited in scope inasmuch as the
> details of natural beauty and the moods of a special sor-
> row form the staple, but, while a wider range would pro-
> pitiate a larger audience, those whose lives and feelings
> are in relation with yours would respond the more ear-
> nestly on account of the individual Sentiment which un-
> derlies and permeates the poems. I perceive many pecu-
> liarities of expression which strike me as defects; but this
> is so entirely a matter of taste, that I do not venture to
> specify. . . . My opinion is based upon what I believe to be

---

Biographical Dictionary notes, "The conventionality of his sonnets gave rise to
[the] word 'tuckermanity.'"

[15]Charles Frederick Briggs is the author of the earliest surviving
"criticism" of Tuckerman's work, having sent him a letter on June 13 of what
must have been 1854 apologizing for the delay in publishing "Picomegan,"
promising it would appear (as it did) in July, and tactfully adding, "Of course,
so delicious a piece of verse could not be denied a place in the pages of a
magazine that is always ready for good things" (Houghton Autograph File).

> the average standard of sympathy among lovers of poetry;
> personally I find much more to enjoy and commend in
> the book.[16]

H. T. Tuckerman was a figure the likes of which we will see again, a polite Sentimentalist who thought that feelings are merely sympathies and details of expression in a poem are merely matters of taste.

But another respondent whom Henry chose, George Ripley, was capable of something better, though Henry recommended him for the slightly dubious reasons that Ripley "has been 'reader' to our leading publishers here for several years" and "is a scholar and an aesthetic as well as technical critic: knows public taste and the laws of literature" (he was literary critic for Horace Greeley's *New York Tribune*). F. O. Matthiessen claims that Ripley "possessed solid critical gifts that have not yet received their due assessment," being, as a founding editor of *Harper's,* "one of the first to gauge the importance of both *A Week on the Concord and Merrimack Rivers* and *The Scarlet Letter*" and the writer (in his review of *Moby-Dick* in the December, 1851, *Harper's*) of "the best piece of criticism that Melville was accorded during his life-time."[17] Ripley's understanding of the special possibilities of poetry was not complete, but the intelligently laudatory letter he wrote to Frederick's cousin was certainly one with which, as Henry said in passing it along, the poet could not "but be gratified"; it contains some of the best specific criticisms and distinctions made before Bynner's work in 1930.

> I do not hesitate to advise the author to venture on [the
> poems'] publication. They have more than ordinary merit,
> in my opinion, especially for a first appearance in print.
> I am struck with the fidelity and skill with which they seize
> upon those aspects of nature that appeal to the imagina-

---

[16] Houghton Autograph File.

[17] F. O. Matthiessen, *American Renaissance: Art and Expression in the Age of Emerson and Whitman* (1941; reprint, New York: Oxford Univ. Press, 1968), 251n.

tion. If not a disciple of Wordsworth, the author is at least imbued with his spirit. He seems to be almost as familiar with the details of New England scenery as Bryant himself and easily transmits them into golden materials for his thoughtful, suggestive verse. In the sphere of emotions he betrays genuine feeling. There is nothing inflated, forced or artificial in his expression of sentiment. Where the subject admits of pathos and tenderness, he moves freely and with natural grace and vigor. I should judge that he writes from his own experience and not from his studies or recollections.

His versification is often in excellent harmony with his theme; but it is certainly too harsh and rugged for the popular taste—perhaps for any taste. He delights in unnecessary inversions, in the use of unheard of and unattractive words and phrases, and often accumulates epithets and illustrations with a burdensome prodigality. I do not admire his attempts at humor. They are diffuse, which is fatal, and scarcely ever show the concentrated and sparkling point, which humorous poetry demands.

The "Hymn for the Dedication of a Cemetery" is beautiful and touching in its quiet simplicity. So are many of the Sonnets. . . . I think the author has a true poetic view and a richness of thought and sentiment; but the execution needs much toning down and pruning of eccentric turns and phrases.[18]

Tuckerman's cousin also used his good offices to get a response from Bryant, despite "the important demands, just now, upon his time" in relation to the developing Civil War; he sent a copy to Bryant's country home and got a "frank" response that he felt it was no breach of trust to convey to Tuckerman if it would "go no further":

---

[18] Dated at Brooklyn, June 27, 1861, and enclosed with the letter from H. T. Tuckerman, dated at New York, June 28, 1861, both Houghton Autograph File. Part of the Ripley letter is reproduced, but with an extremely misleading error in transcription (pages 2 and 3 are omitted and 1 and 4 run together), in Golden, *Tuckerman: An American Sonnetteer*, 34.

> It seems to me that Mr. T. has a strong love of Nature and
> a remarkable perception of her beauties. In this consists
> the charm of his work and its claim to originality. What
> many facilities of expression and verification—but it
> seems to me that the thought is too often [undecipherable
> word] and mystical and that he too often allows the reader
> to perceive that he has been a diligent student and is an
> intense admirer of Tennyson.[19]

H. T. Tuckerman then writes, "This is very like the opinion
I originally expressed to you and, in substance, accords with
that of Mr. Ripley. I think it would be the judgment of nine-
tenths of your readers who are acquainted with English
poetry." Bryant had written some fine criticism, theoretical
and practical, in the 1830s, and earlier than that had written
"Thanatopsis," perhaps the one American poem written
before "The Cricket" that bears comparison with it (despite
the sharp break in Bryant's poem between the impressively
written evocation of the earth as a great charnel house and the
merely asserted "unfaltering trust" in an afterlife). But in his
comment on Tuckerman, perhaps because he was too busy, he
merely generalizes about the obvious—or, in using the term
"mystical," is just wrong.

Of as much help to Tuckerman as these noted critics was
probably the friend of Hawthorne, George S. Hillard, who
writes to the poet as follows:

> I have read [the poems] with much interest, and certainly
> I recognize in them the power and genius of a true poet.
> They show a very fine perception of natural beauty,
> tenderness and delicacy of feeling, and no common skill
> in wielding the resources of our language.... You are
> really a poet, a maker; you have originality in poetical
> construction and combination: but your style wants light-
> ening and bracing, and sometimes clearness.

---

[19] Dated at New York, July 8, 1861, Houghton Autograph File. Golden has
reprinted this in *Tuckerman: An American Sonnetteer*, 33–34, but with errors in
transcription.

Hillard also expresses that same lack of understanding of what Tuckerman was doing with his intense new use of natural detail which (along with misunderstanding, if not simple rejection, of his technical experiments) is universal in the criticism during his lifetime. He continues:

> Your observation of nature is too minute, and there is too much of individual detail in your delineations. Bonaparte once said, "What is Nature? The thing is vague and unmeaning. Men and passions are the things to write about..." Our poets, it seems to me, are in danger of carrying the descriptive element too far.... In this busy age men will not read what takes them any trouble to comprehend—I mean of poetry. Look at our two most popular poets, Bryant and Longfellow—how much they owe to their style, and how little of originality there is in either. You have plenty of the ore of poetry, but you seem to me not quite patient enough in elaboration.[20]

In these early letters, then, we find the main outlines of Tuckerman's fate: He is criticized for those poems which emulate the then *too* modern Romantics like Wordsworth (in print then over sixty years), Keats, and especially Tennyson, even though the work he values most, in the sonnets, has already become more modern than theirs. And that best work, especially in its integrated use of natural detail and rhythmic cognition to form powerful metaphors of his understanding and feeling, is rejected as ignorantly or willfully excessive, or (if the critic wants to imply his own superior understanding of both the poetry and the benighted public) as good but not saleable.

TUCKERMAN was sufficiently satisfied with the critical response he had sought that he published "Rhotruda" in the

---

[20] Dated at Boston, January 17, 1864, Houghton Autograph File. Hillard was sent a copy of the 1860 *Poems* three years earlier and read it then but, as he apologetically admits, was delinquent about responding.

July 1861 *Atlantic* and then a sonnet, "The Starry Flower," in June 1862, and "Coralie" in April 1863. In 1863 he had the *Poems* republished in London by Smith, Elder and Co., with only a few changes from the 1860 edition; and in 1864 Ticknor and Fields did him the compliment of bringing out the *Poems* in Boston in their Standard Author series, using the Smith, Elder plates (which were used again in 1869 for a second reprinting by Little, Brown and Co.). Tuckerman's interest in the public's response was great enough (at least through 1864) that he sent out copies for review to over thirty publications in the United States and England and then collected in a scrapbook the reviews and advertisements of the 1863 and 1864 editions, as well as those of the poems published in the *Atlantic Monthly.*[21]

"Rhotruda" was greeted in the *Boston Transcript* as "the production of a new poet, but one whose exquisite genius must soon make him famous." However, none of the poet's critics could find the space or the insight for criticism that might have helped that happen; the praise is generally faint and unspecific, the dispraise equally superficial. Many London reviewers were taken with the details of a distant and exotic landscape, some with Tuckerman's "true poetic taste"; but most of them objected to his reliance on Tennyson and his "obscurity," "barbarous and inappropriate terms and phrases," and "inelegant expressions." Though possessing "the faculty of picturesque word-painting," he was to them "rather a rustical poet."

American critics greeted the 1864 edition of Tuckerman's

---

[21] The list of publications that were sent copies is on a separate sheet in the scrapbook (MS. Am 1349–9, Houghton), with crosses by eight which subsequently gave reviews and an indication by the side of some of whether the review was "favourable" or "spiteful." The scrapbook contains about six different reviews of the issue of the *Atlantic* that contained "Rhotruda," one of the issue which contained "Coralie," copies of "A Starry Flower," two parodies of it ("The cloudy style, the verbal mist that floats"), and a response to the parodies by one "Julia" ("O noble Sonnet, ringing, peal on peal"); then there are about ten reviews and notices each of the 1863 London and 1864 Boston editions, from which my quotations in the following paragraphs are taken (see Appendix I for a complete listing).

Poems with more care and, paradoxically, less provinciality than the English, but they were limited in much the same way in that they praised his faults or minor virtues and missed his strengths. The review in the *Atlantic Monthly* is perceptive about some of the general matters:

> These poems show by internal evidence that they are the productions of a man of refined organization and delicate sensibility to beauty, who has lived much in solitude and tasted of the cup of sorrow. . . . [The poetry] has one quality to a high degree,—and that is, a minute knowledge of the peculiarities of the natural world as it appears in New England.

But that review in effect dismisses Tuckerman as too derivative, too involved with the emotions of sorrow, too full of "description" and yet in need of "more prose": "One must almost be a poet himself to enter into full communion with him."

Precisely. Tuckerman has needed, and rarely received, readers willing to listen to his work *as poetry,* willing to understand (or intuit) that he is working with specifically *poetic* means, willing even to try to become somewhat like the poet himself in concern for sound—willing, in short, to give that second, repeated reading that Hawthorne called for. The New York weekly *Round Table* put its finger (actually, its fist) squarely on the problem: "The portion of the volume which evinces the most poetical talent, and which appears the most like an expression of genuine feeling on Mr. Tuckerman's part . . . is christened 'Sonnets,' though most of them violate all the known laws of that artificial species of verse." Other reviewers, as had the critics in London earlier, call attention to "a certain vagueness and dreaminess," an overuse of "descriptive powers," "more imperfect rhymes than correct ones," only a "faint sense of rhythmical melody" (meaning regularity). The *New York Times* review praises Tuckerman's descriptive precision, without seeing its significance beyond mere ornament, and resigns him to the "inexorable fate of all our young poets": "his poems are somewhat Tennysonian."

With no one available to call attention to Tuckerman's post-Symbolist journey far beyond Tennyson's picturesque mellifluousness, or to explain his experiments in building structures of rhyme and in relating image to idea, he was bound to be misunderstood and urged to change—in many of the same ways as his Harvard classmate, T. W. Higginson, was just then in the process of urging Emily Dickinson to change. But Tuckerman was no more willing than Dickinson to change, and he quickly faded from public notice and apparently in turn took no notice of the 1869 reprinting of *Poems.*

There is one final indication of the general assessment of Tuckerman in his own time. In 1871, S. Austin Allibone took a few lines in his *Critical Dictionary of English Literature* to give the basic facts of Tuckerman's life and publications and chose to quote the following from the 1863 review in the London *Athenaeum*: "This volume is rich in the materials of poetry, though they are by no means turned to the best account.... When Mr. Tuckerman writes plainly he ceases to be imaginative, and when he attains to imagination he becomes obscure." [22]

TUCKERMAN was included in Emerson's anthology, *Parnassus,* in 1874, a year after his death, and then he was essentially forgotten for thirty years. But after Walter Prichard Eaton had seen two of Tuckerman's sonnets in a manuscript of Louis How's unpublished anthology, he got a copy of the 1864 *Poems* through Goodspeed's (it took them a year) and read it with growing appreciation. Eaton then wrote an essay for the *Forum,* which appeared in 1909 and stimulated Witter Bynner to get permission from the Tuckerman family to examine the Tuckerman papers—and that eventually led to Bynner's pub-

------

[22] S. Austin Allibone, *A Critical Dictionary of English Literature and British and American Authors,* 3 vols. (1871; reprint, Detroit: Gale Research Co., 1965), 3:2466; this entry appears between very favorable ones, each about fifty times as long, for Edward Tuckerman and Henry T. Tuckerman.

lication of the complete *Sonnets*. But Eaton, and Bynner to a lesser degree, tended to fall into the same kind of mistake that Eaton attributed to Tuckerman's contemporaries—that of reading *only* through their own strong prejudices, without much second thought, and thus missing or mistaking his qualities:

> The poetry . . . lacking narrative interest, palatable plati-tudes, lyric lilt, but being rather, contemplative, aloof, delicately minor and in many ways curiously modern, must have fallen on ears not attuned to it. . . . He was, in a sense a modern before his time, but without sufficient consciousness of his modernity to fight. He was a mute, inglorious Robert Frost.[23]

No doubt readers today (including myself, of course) are as conditioned by our own times as Eaton was by his (or George Ripley by his), though we can hope to learn from their errors and consciously try to broaden our perspective. How-ever that may be, Eaton was unable to understand Tuckerman's use of the sonnet, accusing him, in the first version of his essay, of scorning or not knowing the rules and calling his com-binations of various devices an "unfortunate trick."[24] By the time he revised his essay in 1922, Eaton had reconsidered this and merely claims Tuckerman had "a greater interest in his mood than in the 'rules' of poetry." He even speculates about how much closer, if Tuckerman had continued to write, he might have come to the "modern note in poetry." But it is clear that Eaton means a particular kind of modernity— imagistic free verse. After in effect dismissing some of the more traditional, but skillful, non-sonnets, he notes Tucker-man's "progress from the old metres to freer forms" and quotes, as his best example of Tuckerman's excellence, all

---

[23] Walter Prichard Eaton, "A Forgotten American Poet," in *Penguin Persons and Peppermints* (Boston: W. A. Wilde, 1922), 55; this is an improved and slightly enlarged revision of the essay published in *Forum* 41 (January 1909): 62–70.

[24] Eaton, "Forgotten American Poet," 64.

four stanzas of "I took from its glass," a poem that is indeed unique in Tuckerman for its freedom. Eaton wishes "that some of our vers libre practitioners could equal it." But of course the poem he quotes is not free verse, nor, as he claims, is it unrhymed; it uses a very high number of anapestic variations from the stanzaic norm of one iambic trimeter line followed by three lines of iambic pentameter, and it employs, in each stanza's second and third line, some of the subtle forms of partial rhyme I discussed earlier. But it is indeed one of Tuckerman's finest poems, particularly elegant and moving in its combinations of stately repetitions with direct emotional appeal.

> I took from its glass a flower
> To lay on her grave with dull accusing tears;
> But the heart of the flower fell out as I handled
>   the rose,
> And my heart is shattered, and soon will wither away.
>
> I watch the changing shadows,
> And the patch of windy sunshine upon the hill,
> And the long blue woods; and a grief no tongue
>   can tell
> Breaks at my eyes in drops of bitter rain.
>
> I hear her baby wagon,
> And the little wheels go over my heart:
> O when will the light of the darkened house return?
> O when will she come who made the hills so fair?
>
> I sit by the parlor window
> When twilight darkens, and winds get cold without;
> But the blessed feet no more come up the walk,
> And my little girl and I cry softly together.

In his introduction to the extremely important edition of Tuckerman's sonnets that Eaton's essay stimulated, Bynner quotes these same lines (though he mistakenly thinks they are part of "Coralie"[25]) and notes that the phrasing is "interestingly akin to the phrasing of the great Chinese poets concerning nature, concentrated, simple and accurate," and that "Tuckerman, moreover, often deals as directly as they do with emotion between persons." But Bynner could not appreciate the poem he joined with this one, "Coralie," any more than Eaton could and thought Eaton was right to dismiss it. They were to a degree right (the five stanzas of "Coralie" are indeed not very good), but I suspect the reasons they would have given were bad. To judge by their other choices, they simply could not appreciate Tuckerman's classicism, his ability to work small variations on a norm for larger effect.

The challenge, with Tuckerman, is not merely to pick what fits our contemporary prejudices and thus dismiss whole sections of his work, but to understand him on his terms and to make careful distinctions of quality throughout. Otherwise we perpetuate a cycle of mild rediscoveries wherein former blemishes are made out to be virtues and former virtues turned into blemishes. It is for this reason that Bynner could completely ignore a fine poem like "Inspiration" and could dismiss a great one like "The Cricket" as "attic" poetry.[26] He was able, in fact, to reduce his discussion of the non-sonnets to a page of quoted lines and passages—essentially images—divorced from their all-important context.

However, Bynner, following Eaton's valuable precedent, gave ample and effective quotations of whole sonnets; and, de-

---

[25] N. Scott Momaday, ed., *The Complete Poems of Fredrick Goddard Tuckerman* (New York: Oxford Univ. Press, 1965), 142. In his persuasive catalogue of problems in the Momaday edition, T. Patrick Lynch points out that Tuckerman's manuscript, table of contents, and first edition all show that "Coralie" and "I took from its glass" are two separate poems, rather than one poem, as Momaday, following Bynner's lead, published them ("Still Needed: A Tuckerman Text," *Papers of the Bibliographical Society of America* 69 [1975]: 261). The mistake was apparently made because "I took from its glass" is untitled and follows the titled "Coralie."

[26] Golden (*Frederick Goddard Tuckerman,* 161) reports this from a letter from Bynner.

spite an overemphasis on Tuckerman as a recluse (which, of course, the poems alone do tend to invite), he made some penetrating formulations of the poet's qualities of mind and artistic skill:

> Not only are the sonnets the fine thoughts of a devout stoic, they are the subtly fine craft of a devout poet. (p. 17)

> The austere melancholy which dominates the sonnets is tempered throughout, let me stress, with his sense of natural beauty, which heals even while it wounds. (p. 34)

> All in all, if my judgment is in any way sound, Tuckerman's sonnets rank with the noblest in the language and dignify America with poems not bettered in their kind by anyone of his time or since. (p. 36)

Bynner's own fine reputation as a poet attracted a good deal of attention to his edition. Only one reviewer, Eda Lou Walton in the *Nation,* agreed fully with his ranking of Tuckerman, but her status as a prominent poet and scholar gave great weight to her unreserved praise of the sonnets and her placing of Tuckerman in the select company of Dickinson and Whitman. She shows, through her general understanding of what is going on in the sonnets and good choice of examples (II: 14 and V: 3), that she knew what she was talking about:

> Tuckerman's sonnets have to do with a deep personal grief,—the loss of his wife—with the first violent shock to the very foundations of his sensitive mind and with the slow rebuilding of his life through the twenty years that followed; they are introspective, analytical, concrete, and emotional. Tuckerman was a serious-minded man concerned always with his own relationship to the life he must live through and this concern is the philosophical undercurrent of his thought. But better than this, he was a poet and had a poet's eye and sensibility. He saw the natural scene as it actually existed, not, as did some of his contemporaries, in romantic guise; he felt emotion in terms of homely experience, and here he is allied with Emily

> Dickinson; he groped toward truth which would be no
> false message to a people but a personal truth valuable to
> his own soul. He withdrew more and more into himself,
> and his sonnets grew more and more introspective and
> thoughtful—their form more original and abrupt. And
> always they had that swift certainty of image, that clarifi-
> cation of intense thought which is poetry. They are not, of
> course, all equally great sonnets, but in almost every one
> there is something which is convincing, which indicates
> that Tuckerman was indeed a poet of attainment, and that
> we should do well to list him with his contemporaries,
> and perhaps above them, although he wrote so little.[27]

Though we can assume she might well have been able to do so,
Walton does not attempt to show how Tuckerman's "clarifica-
tion of intense thought" was achieved through his "more
original" form. The other reviewers seem to be in no position
to try.

William Rose Benét agrees with Bynner that the "irregu-
larities" in the sonnets may have been intentional but confesses he cannot see what the intentions were and thus is
unable to agree with Bynner's high estimation; his choice of
two comparatively mediocre sonnets (III: 8 and IV: 10) does
not inspire my trust.[28] In the *New York Herald Tribune*'s review,
which begins with a sweeping attack on the then-current
"experimental itch," Ben Ray Redman goes further than
Benét: "The insensitivity of Tuckerman's ear is important.
Granting him all the freedom he claimed, what use did he
make of it?" I have provided an answer to that question in
preceding chapters. Redman's lack of position to begin to answer this question is revealed in his comment on Tuckerman's
unusual rhyming, which shows that he thought mere *variety*

---

[27] Eda Lou Walton, "A Neglected Poet," *Nation* 133.3452 (September 2, 1931): 234–35.

[28] William Rose Benét, "Round About Parnassus," *Saturday Review of Literature* 7 (February 7, 1931): 584. Benét continued to think of Tuckerman; he was
the first to anthologize him since Emerson (*Oxford Anthology of American Literature*, 1938) and also included a short note on him in *The Readers' Encyclopedia*
that he compiled in 1948.

of regular rhymes the highest goal of rhyming and mere decoration its purpose:

> Often his rhymes are horrible examples of the monotony
> produced by successions of similar vowel sounds. The
> following sequence of rhyming words is typical: mark,
> play, day, char, say, way, appal, stark, responsibility, all,
> dark, spark, fall, die. And such a sequence, I submit, is
> bad, whether or not we call the poem in which we find it a
> sonnet.[29]

The anonymous reviewer in the *New York Times* is reduced to
the level of the 1864 reviewer in the New York *Round Table:* "His
rhyme schemes generally present such grotesqueness of
pattern that there is no pattern at all. Therefore, it is just as
well to forget that these poems . . . are named after the magic
weave of Petrarch and Shakespeare . . . and to take them solely
as lyric poems."[30] On the other hand, the reviewers in the
Boston Transcript[31] and the *New Republic* praise Tuckerman's
work in the sonnets highly, the latter writing, "Its orientation
is subjective. Its tone is sad, but with a relieving dignity. It is
extraordinarily sensitive to the spectacles and events of
Nature; and its verbal music is of a very high order."[32] And
Theodore Morrison, in the *Bookman,* makes some perceptive
comments ("The movement of his lines has a fine breadth,
vigor, and dignity which make the reader prick up his ears at
once with the sense that something important is being said").
But Morrison is not quite sure what to make of the unusual
form ("It is of no importance that he rhymed his sonnets irreg-
ularly; rather it testifies to his natural strength and his honestly
personal use of the form that he could make free with its

-----

29 Ben Ray Redman, "Old Wine in New Bottles," *New York Herald Tribune
Books* 7 (June 7, 1931): 12.

30 "A Contemporary of Lowell and Whittier," *New York Times Book Review,*
May 24, 1931, 12.

31 F. E. W., "The Sonnets of an American Poet," *Boston Transcript,* June 13,
1931, 1.

32 "Book Notes," *New Republic* 69 (November 18, 1931): 26–27.

conventions without destroying its essential character").
Perhaps because of the limitation of prosodic understanding
which lies behind such a comment (generously intended
though it is), he concludes that "some ultimate hindrance prevents [the sonnets'] full success" and that Tuckerman is "better in parts than in the whole."[33]

Bynner also invited some of his friends among contemporary American poets to respond to his discovery. According
to Golden, Edwin Arlington Robinson's copy (which Golden
examined at Colby College, Waterville, Maine) shows little
evidence of thorough reading; but Robinson had written to
Bynner that he "enjoyed and admired" the sonnets and,
though he could not "rate them quite as high" as Bynner did,
they did have "astonishing good lines." Robert Frost
responded, "They have high lines that a blind man could feel
with his fingers."[34]

The obsession with Tuckerman's irregular use of the sonnet
and his impressive lines, without explanation of what makes
them impressive or what their relationship is to the full
purpose of the poem, has continued to plague Tuckerman's
reputation. Yvor Winters's footnote to his essay on Jones Very
in 1936 (published in the *American Review* and then in 1938 in
Maule's Curse) is a lone early exception. In it Winters calls
Tuckerman "unquestionably a distinguished poet," claims
that Sonnet I: 10 is "beautifully executed," and begins to explore Tuckerman's unique relationship to the Romantic and
Symbolist movements, an exploration that Winters continued
in his teaching and in his important essay on "The Cricket" in
1950.

Another poet, Stanley Kunitz, who was acquainted with both
Bynner and Winters, included a substantial and generally fair
entry on Tuckerman in his 1938 edition (with Howard Hay-

---

[33] Theodore Morrison, untitled review in "Poetry" section, *Bookman* 73
(April 1931): 205–6.

[34] These comments were reported to Golden in a letter from Bynner in
1963, quoted in Golden's *Frederick Goddard Tuckerman*, 143.

craft) of *American Authors 1600–1900*. In this article he, like others, points out that "Tuckerman took liberties with the sonnet form which were not always understood, and the substance of his poetry was ill-suited to the prevailing Romantic taste." He also reports that, because of Bynner's edition, "in the last few years Tuckerman has been widely and sympathetically read."[35] In that same year William Rose Benét, who had done the lukewarm review of Bynner's edition in the *Saturday Review*, published the two sonnets he had included in that review, plus four others, in the first twentieth-century anthology to contain Tuckerman's work, the *Oxford Anthology of American Literature*.[36]

Louis Untermeyer made a much better choice of sonnets when he included a completely different six in his *Anthology of the New England Poets from Colonial Times to the Present Day* in 1948. He chose, among others, the excellent sonnets I: 10 and II: 17 and thus was able to demonstrate his claim that "the sonnets have genuine distinction" and that "Tuckerman shifted the traditional rhyme-scheme to fit his shifting moods,"[37] though he did not analyze in detail the relationships implied in that accurate statement. George Whicher went a step further in 1950 by including the entire twenty-eight sonnets of the first series in *Poetry of the New England Renaissance (1790–1890)*. He perceptively allies Tuckerman with Dickinson as the two poets "who exploited to the limits of nineteenth century capacity the possibilities of a poetry of the inner life." He notes the "highly unorthodox handling of rhyme schemes and brilliantly original imagery with which Tuckerman

---

[35] Stanley Kunitz and Howard Haycraft, eds., *American Authors 1600–1900* (New York: H. W. Wilson, 1938), 763.

[36] *Oxford Anthology of American Literature*, ed. William Rose Benét and Norman Holmes Pearson, 2 vols. (New York: Oxford Univ. Press, 1938); Benét also included a short note on Tuckerman when he wrote *The Readers' Encyclopedia*, 2d ed. (New York: Thomas Y. Crowell, 1965), 1029, in 1948, but again emphasized the same narrow distinctiveness: "Since [Bynner's edition] modern poets have admired Tuckerman's free use of the sonnet form in his melancholy verse."

[37] Louis Untermeyer, ed., *An Anthology of the New England Poets from Colonial Times to the Present Day* (New York: Random House, 1948), 477–78.

attempted to analyze and objectify his grief" and relates this process of building metaphors into symbols to Eliot's objective correlative. However, he does not explain in detail what he means and thus does not show whether he could see the important differences between Eliot's work and what Tuckerman was doing. And a closing comment by Whicher reveals a narrowness in his perspective which by now is familiar: "Tuckerman strikes us today as a strange exotic in the Connecticut Valley."[38]

A welcome relief to this improved but still narrow-gauged criticism was the publication of "The Cricket" in a beautiful limited edition by the Cummington Press in 1950 and Winters's response in the *Hudson Review*. Continuing this improvement in Tuckerman's fortunes was the publication by Mordecai Marcus of a corrected edition of "The Cricket" in the *Massachusetts Review* in 1960 and then of Marcus's fine essay, "The Poetry of Frederick Goddard Tuckerman: A Reconsideration," in *Discourse* the following year. In the meantime, Samuel Golden had done a master's thesis on Tuckerman and published it in 1952 as a University of Maine monograph. In it he provides useful biographical information that had been unavailable to that point, quotes from the correspondence with Tennyson and the responses to the 1860 *Poems*, and includes some of the previously unpublished works.[39]

It is unfortunate that Marcus's essay in *Discourse*, a publication of Concordia College in Moorhead, Minnesota, could not have had a wider audience. Marcus provides independent support for Winters's analysis of "The Cricket" and his overall estimation of Tuckerman's quality, yet he is somewhat more temperate and gives himself room to demonstrate specific evidence for his position. He provides the first detailed attention to the achievements in rhythmic cognition in Tuckerman's work, although in this respect he remains somewhat vague and

---

[38] George F. Whicher, ed., *Poetry of the New England Renaissance (1790–1890)* (New York: Rinehart, 1950), xvii.

[39] Golden, *Tuckerman: An American Sonnetteer.*

tends toward the imitative fallacy, a common feature of criticism since the 1950s. On Sonnet V: 16 he writes, "The slow accentual crowding of 'give not me' creates a beautiful lingering emphasis; the alliteration, accentual crowding, and harsh consonants in the fifth and sixth lines are also effective correlates to the sense."[40] Marcus is in general convincingly sympathetic, and his estimate of Tuckerman's limitations is apt, though, in my opinion, somewhat overstated: "Many of Tuckerman's sonnets are pervaded by weaknesses like those occasionally visible in the better ones: discursiveness; trite phrasing, uncontrolled self-pity, and lack of dramatic or symbolic unity." However, Marcus, too, is unable to resist using expressions like "languid exoticism," "recluse," and "archaic phrasing," and the impulse to assume there must be good reasons for Tuckerman's neglect leads him to assert faults without demonstration and to dismiss everything but the sonnets and "The Cricket."

The same problems seem to mar the substantial consideration given Tuckerman in *Patriotic Gore* (1962) by Edmund Wilson, perhaps the most widely read and respected critic to praise him. Wilson makes a remark that illuminates all of the criticism of Tuckerman to date: "It is easier to give an idea of Frederick Tuckerman's little grotesqueries than to illustrate his peculiar excellence."[41] And he proceeds mainly to do that easier thing: he focuses on what Bynner had wrongly supposed, in his introduction to the *Sonnets,* was Tuckerman's "delight in the invention or resyllabling of words [and] references . . . to persons and events that seem to have existed only in his own imagination."[42] He thus lumps Tuckerman with Irving and Poe and James Branch Cabell as typically American inventors of mythologies. He cites a number of "outrageous" examples that leave the innocent reader with an indelible

---

[40] Ibid., 73.

[41] Edmund Wilson, *Patriotic Gore* (New York: Oxford Univ. Press, 1962), 494.

[42] Ibid., 18.

sense of an exotic recluse whose "unrecorded characters had really come to live with him in the solitude of Greenfield," a "dissociated poet [who] also invented words, very much in the manner of Joyce."[43] However, as Momaday notes in his edition of the *Complete Poems,* published in 1965, "since the publication of Wilson's book, and in some measure because of it, most of the obscure names in Tuckerman's sonnets have been identified."[44] Momaday himself proceeds to explicate and show the purposeful relevance of many allusions that Wilson finds "outrageous"; and in his 1966 work Golden, as one of his many fine services to Tuckerman scholarship, is able to show in detail that *all* of the "invented" references and names have been identified as real and were effectively used.[45]

This is, of course, an example of what has occurred often in the criticism of Tuckerman. The poet is accused of some limitation—"rough" meters, "ignorance" of the sonnet forms, a "private" mythology, willful "obscurity"—but a limitation which is later found by others to reflect only a limitation in the critic, a lack of understanding or perspective or independent judgment.

Wilson is perceptive enough about some things: "One has really to read his poems in sequence . . . . He is able to accept and ennoble the incidents that make up his own life in a style that never lapses, like Wordsworth's, though it cannot sustain the level of Yeats."[46] And he quotes in full the three fine sonnets at the end of the Fifth Series. However, Wilson manifests—as does most American criticism, not least in the past forty years when it could have known better because the insights were available—ignorance of or disregard for the place of rhythmic cognition and of strong syntax and pure diction in the achievement of good poetry's special quality and meaning. Nevertheless, much gratitude is finally due

---

[43] Ibid., 493.

[44] Momaday, *Complete Poems,* xvii.

[45] Golden, *Frederick Goddard Tuckerman,* 79–92.

[46] Wilson, *Patriotic Gore,* 494–95.

Wilson. In addition to his significant notice of Tuckerman in *Patriotic Gore,* he encouraged and assisted in the publication by Oxford University Press in 1965 of Momaday's edition and wrote a statement for the book jacket that praised Tuckerman as "one of the few fine original poets of the later nineteenth century in the United States."

Momaday's introduction to his edition, a reduced version of the introductory essay written for his dissertation, is especially important because, as Allen Tate says in another book jacket statement, to his scholarship Momaday "adds a superior critical sense which enables him to relate Tuckerman not only to his New England contemporaries, but to the wider horizon of romanticism in England and France." I have tried in my own work to be true to Momaday's admirable statement in the preface to his edition:

> If the poems of Frederick Goddard Tuckerman are to be considered a real and legitimate part of American literature, we must be willing to search out their historical as well as their literary meaning. I refer, not so much to the explicit, but the *consequent* historical meaning. It seems to me that historical analysis is an indispensable step in the critical process. The critics of Tuckerman's poems will have always to keep before them the poems themselves as the central concern; yet they will have also to look at the intellectual age against which the poems assume so crucial an individuality. It will be necessary to carry on the investigation implied in the foreword and introduction.

But the juxtaposition of the foreword by Winters with Momaday's own introduction has tended to detract quite seriously, I suspect, from the effect of the edition. As a student of Winters (like myself, and I must face the same danger), Momaday seems somewhat hedged in by some of Winters's categories and judgments. Thus, even though his introduction is more temperately phrased and extends to independent insights, since it comes immediately after Winters's essay (which in a book jacket understatement Norman Holmes

Pearson says "challenges and stimulates"), it appears more unreasonably anti-Romantic and obsessively anti-Emersonian than Momaday may have intended—or at least more than seems to have been helpful to Tuckerman's cause. Most critics who since then have written on Tuckerman have seemed unable to "keep before them the poems themselves as the central concern," because they could not ignore the gauntlet thrown down in that foreword and introduction.

Even Irving Howe, who recognized that criticism of Tuckerman had been sparse and unsatisfactory and from whom one might have expected better, wrote a review for the *New York Review of Books* that is largely derivative of Wilson and Winters and Momaday. At the same time, despite acknowledged "respect" for Winters, Howe indulges in some shadowboxing with him over "The Cricket." But, with a somewhat more acceptable grace and politeness than Winters would adopt, Howe expresses the uniqueness of Tuckerman in the Emersonian milieu (showing that despite Waggoner's later inarticulate disgust with them, Winters and Momaday did understand Emerson in terms that more "respectable" critics could also accept). According to Howe, Tuckerman

> had no taste for the soaring line, the vatic pronouncement, the inflammation of selfhood which Emerson was drawn to and Whitman practised; . . . [he] wrote from a sharper endowment of common-sense realism. . . . In the sonnets and "The Cricket" [he] writes out of a hard awareness of human limitation: he does not confuse himself with the cosmos, the trees, or the spiritual aether. . . . In the nineteenth-century American context, where poets too often are straining to inflate the self into a universal presence or to roll it into a neat capsule of wisdom, this even-voiced meditation—it is by no means conversational speech—comes as something of a relief.[47]

Howe also usefully spots a characteristic problem in

---

[47] Irving Howe, "An American Poet," *New York Review of Books,* March 25, 1965, 18.

Winters's criticism: "It does not seem an unavoidable duty for the critic to name 'the greatest poem of the century.' " And it would certainly be difficult for me to think Howe's insight entirely lacking when he quotes the entire Sonnet I: 10 ("An upper chamber in a darkened house") and praises it as "one of the lovelier sonnets," illustrative of Tuckerman's "high meditative eloquence."

The reviewer of Momaday's edition in the *Times Literary Supplement* was so mesmerized by Winters's foreword that he entitled his piece "Tuckerman the Great" and indulged in a full *Times* page of retributive parody, ending with the hope that Winters's work was also parody, "a deft illustration of what happens when the critic forgets his standing in relation to any particular text." When this reviewer does try to be straightforward he reveals profound unsteadiness in his own standing in relation to the particular text:

> When it came to the expression of deep personal feeling, the real stuff of poetry, Tuckerman is most impersonal. . . . Hardly one of the sonnets is entirely satisfactory; a rhyme misses or the metre falters or—the worst of his faults—the meaning fades into obscurity. . . .
>
> [He] was a very minor romantic poet who had no hope of surviving the surge of reaction against the nineteenth century that nearly swamped Tennyson.[48]

The *New York Times Book Review* had probably the most widely read commentary on Momaday's edition. In it Richard Eberhart, though he avoids jousting with Winters, displays other counterproductive characteristics of Tuckerman criticism (such as faint praise and formulary rehearsals of minor virtues or faults) that he might have been expected to be perceptive enough, as a poet himself, to avoid:

---

48 "Tuckerman the Great," *Times Literary Supplement* 64 (December 2, 1965): 1102.

> From Tuckerman we learn of the menace of the Indians and of tragic situations of the heart. He has a 19th century feeling for New England woods and streams. . . . Tuckerman has little technical invention, writing mainly in set forms. He is old-fashioned in style and tone, but can sprinkle a sprightly rhyme sense on "Lines Written in the Blue Ridge" ("drown ten" / "mountain" and "moss sips" / "gosslips").[49]

Those rhymes (actually more humorous than "sprightly"), though they are Eberhart's only quotation from the poetry, are unrepresentative; and although Eberhart seems to like them they come from one of Tuckerman's lesser poems.

In a book on a select group of American poets published just before the *Complete Poems* (and therefore without benefit of that first complete edition and Momaday's introduction), Denis Donoghue paid Tuckerman the tribute of one full chapter (of eight) and some perceptive praise of his unique integrity and anti-Transcendentalist scruples (e.g., "The poet is invariably alone, and whether he finds intimations of ease or pain in the landscape, he is never tempted to blur the line of demarcation between himself and nature, the one and the Not-me, subject and object"[50]). But, though Donoghue quotes liberally, and intelligently, from Bynner's edition of the sonnets and from the Cummington edition of "The Cricket" ("the third stanza is Tuckerman's greatest achievement and one of the finest in modern poetry"), he fails to discuss the poetry in terms other than its themes. Thus he does not do justice to Tuckerman's full achievement nor does he accurately perceive the themes themselves because, especially in "The Cricket," he misses the ironic qualifications on the stated content conveyed by the form.

Only a few published critics, since Momaday's edition, have

----

49 Richard Eberhart, "A Quiet Tone from a Rich Interior," *New York Times Book Review,* June 20, 1965, 5.

50 Denis Donoghue, *Connoisseurs of Chaos: Ideas of Order in Modern American Poetry* (1965); reprint, New York: Columbia Univ. Press, 1984, with the Tuckerman essay unchanged.

been able to avoid the characteristic limitations I have indicated above. A short note by Robert Regan in *The Library Journal*,[51] with remarkably concise comprehension, finds Momaday's complete edition of comparable importance to the editions that had then rather recently been made of Edward Taylor and Emily Dickinson:

> Hardly unknown up to now but sorely neglected, F. G. Tuckerman . . . was influenced by Emerson, but his poems are denser, more difficult, and poetically far more rewarding than Emerson's. . . . Few English sonnets after Milton's can rival Tuckerman's, and if Winters's estimate of "The Cricket" . . . is excessive, careful and repeated readings of this great ode will demonstrate that the excess is at most slight.

And a fine, balanced discussion in a review of the 1965 edition (and other volumes of poetry) by George Lensing in the *Southern Review* calls Momaday's edition "a major contribution to the canon of nineteenth century American poetry." Lensing efficiently gives his readers a sense of Tuckerman's qualities and some of the reasons for them ("Tuckerman was a scientist, . . . an avid and authoritative student of astronomy, botany, and geology. As a result, he was able to bring to the mainstream of American romanticism a precision and freshness in nature description as well as an abundance of resources for metaphorical identities").[52]

Lensing is particularly accurate, I believe, in his evaluation of and his comments on the sonnets: "It is within the discipline of the sonnet that Tuckerman's precision of image is sharpest and force of statement is greatest." He selects Sonnet I: 10 as "one of the best," and it is the only poem he quotes entirely. His comment is both accurate and expansive:

---

[51] Robert Regan, Untitled review, *Library Journal* 90 (June 15, 1965): 2861.
[52] George Lensing, "The Lyric Plenitude: A Time of Rediscovery," *Southern Review*, n.s., 1 (Winter 1967): 199.

> The enigmatic "he" is given only the most shadowy per-
> sonal outline, but his dominance over the poet's emotions
> accumulates until the climactic power of the final qua-
> train. The quatrain itself eludes grammatical translation,
> but is dramatically appropriate to the undertones of
> terror in the poem.[53]

Lensing merely mentioned "The Cricket" (as a poem in which "Tuckerman as craftsman, as polished commander of diction and rhyme, is distinguished"), possibly because that same issue of the *Southern Review* contained Momaday's essay on that poem.

Those complementary essays by Lensing and Momaday, plus a short piece by Edwin Cady in a festschrift for Jay B. Hubbell, made 1967 a high point in Tuckerman criticism. The essay by Cady, who the year before had included eleven of Tuckerman's sonnets in his anthology, *The American Poets, 1800–1900,* makes a useful point that the preoccupation of literary criticism with "the great" has compounded the accidents of literary history which have obscured Tuckerman. Critics have been unwilling to engage in the humble task of elucidation of the powers of his work, which "are narrow in scope, but . . . intense, distinctive, and at many points perfect of realization." Cady praises the "virtuosity" with which Tuckerman used the Petrarchan sonnet in ways both true to international Romanticism and yet "decidedly American" and quotes ten of the best sonnets from the first two series, with spare but perceptive commentary, to support his judgment. He is especially insightful about the unique ways Tuckerman uses "the supreme lyric of Romantic egotism— the death of a beautiful woman" to establish himself as a "figure of rebellion against Romantic conventions," and he is effective in analyzing the range and power of Tuckerman's diction:

---

[53] Ibid., 201. I have removed, I trust, the perplexity about grammar in my earlier chapter on Sonnet I: 10.

> ... Learned and homely, international and regional at
> will, Tuckerman's diction at its best has the essential
> poetic qualities of fitness which becomes inevitability
> while it preserves strangeness. It exacts of the reader
> that astonishment which recognizes unpredictability
> in precise use.[54]

Hyatt Waggoner's book, published the next year, provides what is still one of the most widely read and influential appraisals of Tuckerman in the overall context of American poetry, at least in the English language.[55] It is also the most inadequate. In the preface to his *American Poets from the Puritans to the Present* (1968—revised 1984, with this passage unchanged) Waggoner writes that, despite his original intention to avoid a "thesis" book, in the course of the five years of writing he had

---

[54] Edwin H. Cady, "Frederick Goddard Tuckerman," in *Essays on American Literature in Honor of Jay B. Hubbell,* ed. Clarence Gohdes (Durham, N.C.: Duke Univ. Press, 1967), 149.

[55] *American Poets from the Puritans to the Present,* published by Houghton Mifflin in 1968 (rev. ed., 1984). The only criticism I have been able to find in languages other than English are a 1970 essay in Japanese and part of a chapter in a 1985 German book. "Frederick Goddard Tuckerman no Shi," by Shunsuke Kamei, published in *Eigo Seinen* (The Rising Generation) 116 (1970): 568–70, sets out to introduce Tuckerman's work to Japan (where it had not been anthologized) by conveying "as accurately as possible the power of his poetry." This purpose is admirably served by a summary of the author's gradual discovery of Tuckerman's parity with Whitman and Dickinson (through Wilson's *Patriotic Gore* and Edwin Cady's anthology). Kamei is especially impressed by the similar way in all three in which "through description of nature there is expressed a probing of human existence." Kamei reprints the English texts of Sonnets I: 22, II: 37, and V: 15, giving paraphrases and commentary in Japanese to assist readers in understanding the meaning of the poems. Kamei concludes, "While avoiding Whitman's poetical ambition and his desire for absolute affirmation of life, he shared Dickinson's severe self-awareness and humbly and at the same time magnificently expressed the majesty of life." (I am grateful to Professor Barry Jackman, of Carleton College, for a translation of this Japanese essay; a copy of the essay was graciously provided me by the University of Tokyo.) In *Die amerikanische Literatur bis zum Ende des 19. Jahrhunderts,* ed. Helmbrecht Breinig and Ulrich Halfmann (Tübingen, W. Ger.: Francke, 1985) Tuckerman is included in a chapter by Ludwig Deringer and Roland Hagenbüchle, "Amerikanische Lyrik des 19. Jahrhunderts," 213–14.

come to discover "that Emerson is the central figure in American poetry, essential both as spokesman and as catalyst" and that Emerson's essay "The Poet" is "the single most important critical document for anyone whose aim was to understand the development of our poetry."[56] These statements might well pass if they were merely *descriptive* of Emerson's undoubted influence, but it is soon clear that they are normative and even, in an amazing Emersonian leap of teleological faith, deterministically proscriptive; Waggoner believes we are beginning, rightly and irrevocably, a new Emersonian age that will rescue us from the dark, pessimistic realism of existentialism and religious neo-orthodoxy. It is hardly any wonder, then, that Winters's foreword and Momaday's introduction to the Tuckerman edition leave Waggoner with only patience enough for a perfunctory single reading of the poems, if that, and only speech enough to pronounce anathema on those critics rather than to discuss the poetry. But his allegiance to Emerson would make that discussion difficult in any case, because he gives in entirely to Emerson's claim for the poet as sayer, not maker—as properly engaged in discovering through prophetic impression rather than through what Winters has called the "forms of discovery":

> Thinking of the poet as a "namer" and a "sayer"—to use Emerson's terms—American poets have generally taken a rather top-lofty attitude toward the traditions, conventions, and "rules" that supposedly govern the practice of their craft. They have turned inherited poetic forms and traditional genres to their own purposes or abandoned them entirely.... From the beginning, the most representative American poets have anticipated the characteristic that more than anything else distinguishes the American poetry of our own day from that of the past and of other societies: in it *nothing* is known, nothing given, everything is discovered or created, or else remains in doubt.[57]

---

[56] Waggoner, *American Poets,* xi-xii.
[57] Ibid., xvi-xvii.

With such know-nothing top-loftiness, Waggoner feels quite free to join his poet-prophets and abandon any attention whatsoever to what might govern the practice of their *craft*. He was able to produce a book of seven hundred pages, discussing fifty-two of America's finest poets, including at least two extremely conscious masters of metrical artistry, Emily Dickinson and Wallace Stevens, without once betraying any understanding of rhythmic cognition or of the unique and precise instruments of discovery and communication it makes possible. He appears to see poetry as nothing more than a species of condensed and enigmatic prose, demeaning it to a mere forum for discovering parallels to his own philosophical predilections and a playground for his ability to make abstruse associations.

Aaron Kramer, also in 1968, published a book that more forthrightly and yet more modestly than Waggoner (and thus more usefully) deals with poetry as mere ideas. In *The Prophetic Tradition in American Poetry, 1835–1900,* he sets out to "test the vaunted courage and ethical sensitivity of our poets"[58] concerning such major issues of the nineteenth century as war with Mexico, slavery, mobocracy against minorities, and the like. Since he has no proscriptive agenda he is able to place Tuckerman equally among the other poets and judge him quite fairly—although, like Waggoner, along a narrow range that neglects form in favor of content. For instance, he sees the paralyzing Transcendentalist relativism that completely undermines Emerson's poetry on the slave issues, and he is willing to recognize the blind jingoism and deep-seated hatred of Mexicans of Whitman's blustery prose in support of the war with Mexico. He points out how those ethical failures carry over into the famous poems written later, the ones Waggoner praises unstintingly and holds up as the proper foundation for all American poetry.

Kramer quotes Tuckerman generously and approvingly on

---

[58]Aaron Kramer, *The Prophetic Tradition in American Poetry, 1835–1900* (Cranbury, N.J.: Associated Univ. Presses, 1968), 42.

the major issues, but this keeps his focus on the minor poetry
and away from the poet's formal strengths. He notes Tuckerman's objection to America's expansionism in "Margites"
and his sense of disgrace about the destruction of Indian civi-
lizations in "Mark Atherton." However, he fails to see a much
more powerful evocation of the loss of the New England past
in the "elegy" (Sonnets II: 15 through II: 20, that I discuss in
chapter 5) where, with great formal subtlety, Tuckerman relates that loss to the loss of his wife and to human loss in general. And because, like Donoghue, he neglects formal subtlety
that achieves shades of satire and regret, Kramer misreads as
anti-Mormon "The Latter-day Saint," a poem that he claims
"reflects and encourages the bigotries of [Tuckerman's] generation instead of deploring them."[59] But the poem actually uses
some very innovative rhyming and characteristically obscure
but meaningful references to describe an itinerant Mormon
missionary's visit to Greenfield and the failure of the jeering,
violent mob that forms to see his possible similarity to
the prophets that had been stoned by the villagers' biblical
predecessors.

In sharp contrast to Waggoner and with a broader purpose
than Kramer, Donald Barlow Stauffer, in his *A Short History of
American Poetry*, published in 1974, sees the strains of American
poetry as properly diverse. He also understands poetry as a
craft. These qualities enable him to describe and place
Tuckerman, as well as other poets, much more accurately than
Waggoner and more usefully than Kramer, I believe. He perceives Tuckerman's traditional mastery which places him
among the nineteenth century's great sonnetteers but also recognizes that his sonnets are highly "unorthodox in structure
and technique, his precision and clarity of language rival Emily Dickinson's, and his accurate and effective use of natural
imagery goes far beyond anything by Bryant or Thoreau."[60]

----

[59] Ibid., 179.

[60] Donald Barlow Stauffer, *A Short History of American Poetry* (New York:
E. P. Dutton and Co., 1974), 115.

Stauffer provides an excellent summary of Tuckerman's life and works, quoting generously from his own favorite poems, including Sonnet II: 16 (from what I have called the "elegy") and part of "The Cricket." Though he recognizes that Winters overpraised the latter poem, he sees that its quality and theme are similar to Dickinson's "Further in Summer than the Birds" and places it among the great nineteenth-century long poems that confront death. He perceptively suggests that "The Cricket" is perhaps unique in letting death "remain a mystery that both defines and intensifies life."[61]

The most important recent history of Tuckerman's period and place, Lawrence Buell's *New England Literary Culture from Revolution through Renaissance,* 1986, takes an important step toward breaking down the preconceptions that have tended to hide the poet's worth. Buell effectively undermines the traditional dichotomy between Calvinist and Unitarian literary cultures and demonstrates the effects on both cultures of European Romanticism and the erosion of Puritan theology. He thus makes room for literary historians and critics to see Tuckerman, like Dickinson, as one who combined conservative and liberal, Romantic and anti-Romantic, and religious and skeptical tendencies and influences in his own unique ways. Buell specifically recognizes that Tuckerman, "whose sonnets are far better than Jones Very's," has not even received the limited attention given Very, because he "lacks not only Very's striking oddity but his obvious link with the period's main religious currents."[62] And though he quotes and comments on only one of Tuckerman's sonnets (Sonnet II: 7, certainly not among his very best), he praises it as one of the most interesting exemplars of "the romance of repression," one of the four main "strategies" which he describes in New England poetics, and concludes:

---

[61] Ibid., 121.

[62] Lawrence Buell, *New England Literary Culture from Revolution through Renaissance* (Cambridge, Eng.: Cambridge Univ. Press, 1986), 52.

> Tuckerman is less easy to integrate into generalizations about the "New England mind" than Dickinson, whose poetry is more doctrinal and whose withdrawal into reclusiveness less easily reducible to the theory of a particular life trauma; but the Tuckerman pattern of passion repressed by the dual constraints of prosodic austerity and some internalized code of values, yet at the same time expressing itself all the more poignantly through that act of repression, puts him decisively in the regional mainstream.[63]

But Buell then neglects the opportunity he has created to use Tuckerman as evidence for his own central theme of important quality independent of the traditional categories or subsequent influences. He retreats, in a footnote, to the old tendency to dismiss Tuckerman as merely a New England curiosity by quoting Stauffer's phrase, "strangely modern," and Golden's inconsequent admission that Tuckerman "is still eluding categorization." Like many of the critics I have reviewed, Buell leaves his readers without evidence to support the faint praise or to pursue Tuckerman on their own.[64]

However, despite Buell's ultimate relapse, there is some evidence that this situation finally began changing in the 1980s, though mainly among European critics. In 1982 the West German scholar, Roland Hagenbüchle, gave a paper on Tuckerman at the European Association for American Studies biennial conference in Paris, which he published in 1984 in a collection of papers from the poetry sessions of the conference (*American Poetry between Tradition and Modernism 1865–1914*). In his paper Hagenbüchle simply announces that "Frederick Goddard Tuckerman has enjoyed a steadily growing audience of perceptive readers, and there is no need anymore at this stage to insist on the quality and originality of his work."[65] He

---

[63] Ibid., 123.

[64] Ibid., 431.

[65] Roland Hagenbüchle, "Abstraction and Desire: Dissolving Contours in the Poetry of Frederick Goddard Tuckerman," in *American Poetry between Tradition and Modernism, 1865–1914,* ed. Roland Hagenbüchle (Regensburg, W.

goes on to analyze, with respectful attention to qualities of both form and content, some of the better sonnets. He makes useful, but never disparaging, comparisons of Tuckerman's work to that of his contemporaries, seeing his voice as original and ahead of its time, like Whitman's and Dickinson's, but "clearly antagonistic to the Transcendentalist spirit" of Whitman and of more limited creative power than Dickinson's "bold 'modern idiom.'" And he concludes that "Tuckerman is more than just another minor poet"; his limited but excellent work is "a representative expression of the ideological and epistemological crisis of mid-19th century American culture."[66]

In a collection of essays by English critics, *Nineteenth-Century American Poetry,* published in London in 1985, David Seed compares the poetry of Very and Tuckerman ("the work of the one seems at times a throw-back to the seventeenth century, while the other's can sound surprisingly modern"[67]), with a focus on their isolated integrity and religious preoccupations. He explores the very different but effective uses they make of the sonnet form, analyzes with helpful subtlety the formal innovations Tuckerman develops in rhyme scheme, relation of octave to sestet, and connections between the sonnets; he sees these as expressions of Tuckerman's interest in process and sequence in his own spiritual odyssey. And he argues effectively for Tennyson's *In Memoriam* as the chief model for both form and content in Tuckerman's sonnets. Seed properly recognizes that Winters has done Very and Tuckerman "a

---

Ger.: Pustet, 1984), 70. As mentioned previously, the perspective of Hagenbüchle is included in Breinig and Halfmann, *Die amerikanische Literatur,* where, in a chapter on American lyric poetry of the nineteenth century, written by Hagenbüchle with Ludwig Deringer, Tuckerman is discussed with Melville, Crane, and Edgar Arlington Robinson under the subheading, "Die Desillusionerung der Jahrhundertwende" ["Turn-of-the-Century Disillusionment"].

[66] Ibid., 81.

[67] David Seed, "Alone with God and Nature: The Poetry of Jones Very and Frederick Goddard Tuckerman," in *Nineteenth-Century American Poetry,* ed. A. Robert Lee (London: Vision Press, 1985), 166.

disservice in exaggerating their good qualities" and that Tuckerman's perennial "hesitancy and melancholy" injure his work, but he concludes that both poets "embody important directions taken by the New England poetic mind in the period 1830 to 1870."[68]

T U C K E R M A N , then, has been until recently, perhaps more than any other American poet, the victim of the limitations of his critics. This has been in large part the result of his own special qualities: his precocious modernity, which went beyond the understanding of his contemporaries; and his broad comprehensiveness, which will not fit into nor be fairly revealed by the narrow, strongly normative categories of most of his modern critics. Even those who have appreciated Tuckerman have tended to praise only a few of his abilities or have emphasized the trivial ones, so that others have been inclined to disagree or to be unimpressed. For instance, Golden—unintentionally, I am sure—subtly undercuts the poet's worth by calling "The Cricket" his best poem and then giving it a cheery, banal reading (apparently in opposition to what he calls Winters's "lugubriousness") that reduces that subtle masterpiece to the level of the schoolroom poets and its highest achievement in technique to alleged forms of the imitative fallacy:

> When it is read as an afterpiece, as an epilogue or as a coda to the sonnets, the non-restrictive form inherent in the ode is ideal because, by its very use, Tuckerman establishes his emancipation from formal and technical problems of composition and, more importantly, announces his freedom from any sort of restraint—the thought which controls the whole poem.[69]

---

[68] Ibid., 191.

[69] Golden, *Frederick Goddard Tuckerman*, 113.

Golden also restricts proper appreciation by devaluing everything but the sonnets (and "The Cricket") and then showing no real basis for preferring the sonnets. He in fact demonstrates serious misunderstanding of them, mainly as a result, it seems, of his inability to conceive of them as an integrated series responding to Tuckerman's grief over Anna's death. For instance, he dismisses I: 10, that terrific self-reproach, one of the most perplexing and yet moving of nineteenth-century sonnets, as merely an interruption of Tuckerman's musings "to tell of a youth who had met an untimely death."[70] And he completely misreads I: 23, which is Tuckerman's painful attempt to understand the mystery of death through assessing an account—given him by one of the dead Anna's friends—of a visit to her by Anna's spirit. Golden, confusing both the characters and the experience, says the poem is "distinguished by the quiet dignity [it gives] to Anna . . . as she brings solace to a dying 'fair young mother.' "[71]

Winters was sometimes guilty of reducing Tuckerman to fit the outlines of a particular theory of the development of poetry, and his student Momaday perhaps learned too effectively and exclusively how to explicate Tuckerman's anti-Romanticism. Momaday has done best by Tuckerman, but since 1967 he has turned his interests elsewhere; others, who have done comparable work, like Mordecai Marcus and Edwin Cady, have been hampered by a limited audience. Perhaps the most hopeful and (we can hope) prophetic note in this rather gloomy litany was struck by Marcus, when in 1962 he suggested that further consideration of the reasons for the superiority of the sonnets and "The Cricket" to the other work be deferred until they "have received a fuller hearing through generous representation in anthologies of American

---

[70] Ibid., 52. For a quite different view, see my essay on "Tuckerman's Sonnet I:10: The First Post-Symbolist Poem," *Southern Review*, n.s., 12 (Spring 1976): 323–47, chapter 4 of this book, and the comments by Cady, "Frederick Goddard Tuckerman," 150–51.

[71] Ibid., 54.

literature."[72] This hope has been partially realized through the inclusion of "The Cricket" and good samples of the sonnets in most of the anthologies of general poetry and of American literature published since then, particularly after Momaday's edition appeared (see Appendix I: A Tuckerman Bibliography, section II.C, for a complete listing.) And it has borne some modest fruit in five very complimentary doctoral dissertations followed by some helpful articles by their authors, as well as the excellent essays, reviewed above, that have been starting to appear in the last few years.[73]

---

[72] Mordecai Marcus, "The Poetry of Frederick Goddard Tuckerman: A Reconsideration," *Discourse* 5 (Winter 1961–62): 82.

[73] See the entries under Eugene England, Oliver Houston Evans, John Raymond Getz, Jeffrey Groves, and T. Patrick Lynch in Appendix I: A Tuckerman Bibliography, Section IV.B. Besides his dissertation, which focuses on the sonnets, Lynch has published a substantial bibliographic essay, which severely and persuasively criticizes Momaday's edition, calling for a new edition on the assumption, developed in the dissertation but not the essay, that "the value of Tuckerman's poetry is high, a good deal higher, in fact, than the little attention given Tuckerman in American literature courses would lead one to suspect." I have published two essays of close analysis designed to help users of the anthologies teach Tuckerman, the one on "Sonnet I: 10" (1976) and one on the "elegy" comprising Sonnets II:15–20 (1982), and also a comprehensive examination of Tuckerman's relationship with Tennyson (1984). The two recent excellent essays by Hagenbüchle and Seed, cited in notes 64 and 66, bode well for the future.

VIII

CONCLUSION

FINALLY, then, let me summarize the present meaning and continuing challenge of Tuckerman's life and poetry. What he needs now is continued criticism, discussion, explication, and research into his life and intellectual context, all of which must begin with the poetry (all of it) and try to be fully responsive to his comprehensiveness. He needs critics who can understand and illumine all his strengths, especially his ability to use those resources unique to poetry, like the cognitive and affective powers of the various forms of rhythm. He is not merely a Romantic, nor yet exclusively an anti-Romantic; not just influenced by Emerson or simply reacting against Emerson's excesses; not to be confined by labels (even though they all fit some part of his work) such as classicism, modernism, Symbolism, imagism, or post-Symbolism. Tuckerman is most anti-Romantic precisely because, though he has as full a sense of the temptation as the great Romantics had, he refused, painfully, to see things on the basis of large-scale polarities. He refused, before careful analysis of other possibilities, to choose and embrace simplistically.

At the heart of Romanticism lie false dichotomies that Tuckerman healed, in himself and in the poetry he left us. His Anglican tendencies and training; his understanding of Coleridge from that perspective; his training in careful and realistic analysis by Justice Story and in careful and realistic observation by his brother Edward; his long apprenticeship in the English poetic tradition, aided by a particularly retentive mind and a strong immersion in Tennyson which he launched himself far beyond—all these prepared him for some unique and still extremely helpful resolutions to tragic dilemmas.

With the Romantics, Tuckerman yearned to be at home in the universe, to feel himself deeply related to its central reality, and he understood and participated in various efforts to bring that about—including the Emersonian temptation to assert a pantheism that would make everything divine and thus destroy all ethical distinctions and exalt simple merging, including the final merge of death. But Tuckerman also realized that alienation is part of the price we pay for our humanness, for conscious life and perceived feeling, that the void between the mind and the world remains, unless we destroy the mind in primitivism or death—or do away with the world in some form of subjectivism.

Tuckerman understood the related tragedy of language— that this resource of the conscious, rational mind also embodies our alienation from ultimately incomprehensible realms of being beyond our minds; that language is both made possible by and further increases such alienation, because in the cognitive dimensions of language we apprehend and feel our separateness; and that language is also what creates the very possibility and desire to know and feel as humans. He accepted the limitations of language and thus was able to exploit, in unique ways, its tremendous resources.

True to his nominalistic vision of the irreducible reality in constant flux outside the mind, Tuckerman wanted his poems to *be*. But equally as true to his faith in the ultimate rationality of creation and its Creator, in the image of whose rational mind man's was made, he also wanted them to *mean*. He struggled through to the skills that allowed him to embody his well-trained perceptions in language that could give us the natural details, but with ontological force. He learned particularly the control of precise effect that is possible through mastery of details of syntax and diction and rhythm and their adjustment in the poem into precisely varied harmonies that approach the particularity of real experience—that imitate its tang and flux—but that also imbue it with meaning. He understood that between the mind and external experience there is a third realm of being, a life *in* the mind, essentially in language—or at least one that language, used and carefully controlled as a set of fixed symbols agreed upon by humans, can be made to embody and communicate most fully. He knew that the processes of nature are meaningless, mere facts, but that our experiences of them are not meaningless. Those processes are the creations of a rational being who is genuinely related to us, by mind and language; thus, though those facts cannot be known directly, they can be made, in Thoreau's phrase, to "flower into truth."

Tuckerman shared the Romantic faith that his most delicate experiences were typified in nature, but he knew that this was possible not through easy identification of the internal and external but only through analogies that had to be discovered in their general potential in natural details and then shaped to precision of meaning by human language, a process that could thus create human meaning. The world of words served for him as a bridge across the skeptics' void; it was able to stand because its abutments were firmly fixed both in the mind and in reality.

Finally, Tuckerman refused, in the face of overwhelming grief, to justify his fate by either denying the world and its claims, including the reality of death, in the way of Neoplatonism or Whitman's pantheism, or by making the world everything and succumbing to despair or hedonism. In the sonnets he reaches a faith that explicitly faces the hope of a literal reunion after death with Anna ("This is the faith I bear; and look indeed / To hear her laugh again and feel her lips" [Sonnet II: 35]). But he recognizes that it is indeed mere faith and that he must continue to live the life given him with the knowledge and resources he has, including the full burden of his loss. "The Cricket" and the last three series of sonnets, most of which may well have been written after "The Cricket," show Tuckerman's continuing integrity to nature, to God, and to his own mind as his chosen life of accepted loss goes on. It is a life without despair or easy hope, with his knowledge of mortality's claims and the reality of its losses gradually clarified and increased in emotional exactness—and with his faith in continuing meaning for this life, and his hope for a future one, tempered by that growing knowledge and thus perhaps stronger. One of his last poems, probably written not long before the death this poem shows he anticipated, directly addresses us, the readers he could have only hoped the sonnets would eventually gain:

> And me my winter's task is drawing over,
> Though night and winter shake the drifted door.
> Critic or friend, dispraiser or approver,
> I come not now nor fain would offer more.
> But when buds break and round the fallen limb
> The wild weeds crowd in clusters and corymb,
> When twilight rings with the red robin's plaint,
> Let me give something—though my heart be faint—
> To thee, my more than friend!—believer! lover!
> The gust has fallen now, and all is mute—
> Save pricking on the pane the sleety showers,
> The clock that ticks like a belated foot,
> Time's hurrying step, the twanging of the hours:
> Wait for those days, my friend, or get thee fresher
>   flowers.
>
> (Sonnet V: 14, p. 65)

The poem is not unusual in any way—except that it is perfectly executed. The imminence of death, attractive though still resisted; the created sense of time passing (encroaching on the mind in the very process of the poem and its movement strangely slow but horribly hurried); yet that passage of time felt as continuing from the winter into a new spring where his poems, that survive him, might blossom as a gift— all these are communicated with clarity and control but moving completeness. Tuckerman retains fully, without some of the distracting softness of writing sometimes found there, the skills from the first sonnets, particularly the subtly modulated rhyming and bold but pure diction. And he leaves us with a characteristically austere sense of his desire to give himself to us, together with his recognition that he will not again be published in his lifetime, or perhaps ever be read by us. He leaves me grateful to be able to share my humanness with such a person.

WE KNOW VERY little of Tuckerman's life after 1861. His poems reveal no distraction, such as Thoreau suffered, into violent opposition to slavery or even into the passions of the Civil War, but a letter from a close friend refers to a speech that he made to the citizens of Greenfield as the storm was gathering.[1] He tells, in "An Incident," of a visit by an Englishman near the end of the conflict, in which they discuss some of the issues of the war and the hoped-for peace; he wrote a eulogy ("G. D. W.") for perhaps his closest friend, George D. Wells, who was killed in the war; and finally, a few years after the war, he was commissioned to do the "Ode: For the Greenfield Soldiers Monument." These poems are all imbued with a somber hope that some good may yet be built on the foundations of the civil conflict that exacted such a terrible cost.

In 1867 and 1868 Tuckerman had a correspondence with Hawthorne's widow concerning his wish (to which she eventually acquiesced) to buy Wayside, in Concord, as a residence.[2] He apparently planned to go abroad and then live near his son Edward, who would be attending Harvard (Frederick's two youngest children had gone to live with the Edward Tuckermans in Amherst, probably not long after Anna's death and, as that couple was childless, may well have been raised as their own children). But, though Mrs. Hawthorne's letter implies that a continuing and close relationship had developed

---

[1] This letter is loose inside Tuckerman's scrapbook of reviews, MS. Am 1349 (9), Houghton; the letter is dated at Boston, April 26, 1861, and is from Geo. B. [last name undecipherable].

[2] Sophie Hawthorne to Frederick Goddard Tuckerman, August 25, 1867, Houghton Autograph File.

between Tuckerman and Hawthorne and that she was therefore particularly anxious to have him buy Wayside, for some reason the sale fell through and in 1870 or early 1871 Tuckerman went to live in a boarding place, the American House, in Greenfield. In a letter from his son Edward to the younger son Frederick is a glimpse of Tuckerman at that time: "Your father and I have been busy getting the place in order and the garden being overrun with weeds has been ploughed and the greater part of it seeded down with oats and grass which will spoil its appearance."[3]

In 1869 Tuckerman wrote "The Shore" and was perhaps aware of the last edition of his *Poems.* In 1870 he performed the public duty, at the request of the citizens of Greenfield, of writing his "Ode" for their commemorative soldiers' monument (dedicated October 6), which still stands in the town square. Early in 1871, his son Edward died of an illness while at Harvard. The next year his brother Samuel, in a letter to Tuckerman's son Frederick (now 15 and at a boarding school) addressed the young man, perhaps only half-jokingly, as "the hope of the family."[4] In February 1873 Tuckerman sent three of his sonnets to the *Springfield Republican* (they were not published), and on May 9, at the age of 52, sixteen years almost to the day after Anna's death, he died of heart disease.

A somewhat dreary final chronicle? Perhaps. But Allen Tate's comment on Emily Dickinson[5] can be adapted well to Tuckerman: All pity for his starved life is misdirected; his life was one of the richest and deepest ever lived on this continent.

---

[3] This letter, dated at Greenfield, May 29, 1870, is in the Tuckerman Papers, Hugh Clark, Amherst; sale of the home was reported in the *Greenfield Gazette and Courier,* April 17, 1871.

[4] Samuel Tuckerman to Frederick Tuckerman, Jr., Houghton Autograph File.

[5] Allen Tate, "Emily Dickinson," in *Emily Dickinson: A Collection of Critical Essays,* ed. Richard B. Sewall (Englewood Cliffs, N.J.: Prentice-Hall, 1963), 19–20.

Appendix I: A Tuckerman Bibliography

I am grateful to Witter Bynner, Samuel Golden, and N. Scott Momaday for their pioneering work on Tuckerman materials and to Jeffrey D. Groves for reporting important new discoveries for the Tuckerman bibliography in his 1987 dissertation.

I.   MANUSCRIPTS AND OTHER PRIMARY SOURCES

A. All surviving primary manuscript materials, plus juvenilia, scrapbooks, herbariums, an astronomical and meteorological journal, letters, and other materials, are in the Houghton Library at Harvard University (herein referred to simply as Houghton), catalogued as follows:

MS. Am 1349:

(1) Small red journal that belonged to Tuckerman as a child. The latest entry is "Frederick G. Tuckerman came home to live in May 1843."

(2) Notebook: fair copy for 1860 *Poems*.

(3) Notebook: originally a fair copy, in pencil, for *Poems*, predating (2). Later, after erasure of the fair copy, used as a scratch book for various poems, rhyme schemes, etc., including probably the earliest surviving copy of "The Cricket."

(4) Notebook: fair copy of unpublished poems, including copy of "The Cricket," probably later than the one in (3).

(5) Notebook: fair copy of unpublished poems.

(6) Notebook: fair copy of sonnet sequences I and II.

(7) Box containing miscellaneous unbound poems, published and unpublished. Contains the only copy of "Nature

and Necessity" and two copies on single sheets of "The Cricket."

(8) Astronomical and meteorological journal for the years 1847–50.

(9) Notebook containing clippings of Tuckerman's poems and reviews of his book.

(10) Notebook containing miscellaneous clippings.

(11) Herbarium entitled "Wildflowers gathered in Scotland and England during the summer of 1851." Also contains entries from 1854, when Tuckerman visited England again.

MS. Am 1763:

(1) Herbarium entitled "Wild Flowers." Dated Greenfield 1850 but with entries as late as 1868.

B.   At the home of Tuckerman's great-grandson, Hugh Clark, in Amherst, Massachusetts, in addition to twenty-six of the thirty-three volumes surviving from the poet's library— many with important notes and markings—there are miscellaneous memorabilia, including a set of letters from Hannah Tuckerman to her mother from Europe (1854–55), Tuckerman's beautiful laptop writing desk, a framed letter from Emily Dickinson to the Edward Tuckermans on the birth of a child (1883), some fine original drawings of Frederick and Hannah, and a photograph of the three brothers. These materials are in the process of being donated to the Houghton Library and a local museum.

C.   Letters to and from Tuckerman (listed chronologically):

1831(?). "Cousin" to Tuckerman. MS. Am 1349 (1), Houghton.
April 29, 1833. Frederick to Edward Tuckerman. MS. Am 1349.1 (10), Houghton.
January 1, 1852. Frederick to Edward Tuckerman. MS. Am 1349.1 (11), Houghton. The poem and commentary on a separate sheet that was enclosed in this letter are now in MS. Am 1349 (7), Houghton.

June 13, 1854. Charles Frederick Briggs to Tuckerman. Houghton Autograph File.

January 26(?), 1855. Frederick to Edward Tuckerman. Houghton Autograph File. This is published in Cecil Y. Lang and Edgar F. Shannon, Jr., eds., *The Letters of Alfred Lord Tennyson*, 2 vols. (Oxford: Clarendon Press, 1987), as are the following letters, dated January 31, February 6, 8, and 22 (extract), July 8, and October 17, 1855, and January 25, 1860. This collection is hereafter cited as *Letters of Tennyson*.

January 31, 1855. Tuckerman to Alfred Tennyson. Houghton Autograph File. Typed copy. Original at Tennyson Research Centre, Lincoln, England. Published in *Letters of Tennyson*, 2:104.

February 6, 1855. Alfred Tennyson to Tuckerman. MS. Am 1349.1 (5), Houghton. Published in *Letters of Tennyson*, 2:106.

February 8, [1855]. Emily Tennyson to Tuckerman. Houghton Autograph File. Published in *Letters of Tennyson*, 2:107.

February 22, 1855. Tuckerman to Alfred Tennyson. MS. Am 1349.1 (9), Houghton. Typed copy. Published in *Letters of Tennyson*, 2:108–9.

July 8(?), 1855. Alfred Tennyson to Tuckerman. Houghton Autograph File. Slightly but significantly misquoted by Bynner (*Sonnets*, p. 29) and Samuel A. Golden, *Frederick Goddard Tuckerman: An American Sonneteer* (Univ. of Maine Press, Bulletin 54, no. 12 [April 1952]) 19–20. Published in *Letters of Tennyson*, 2:113–14.

October 2(?), 1855. Tuckerman to Alfred Tennyson. Quoted in Hallam Tennyson, 19–20. "Materials for a Life of A[lfred] T[ennyson]," 4 vols., unpublished [1894?], 2:152–53, Houghton Library Collection. Original apparently lost.

October 17, 1855. Emily and Alfred Tennyson to Tuckerman. Houghton Autograph File. Published in *Letters of Tennyson*, 2:132–33.

January 25, 1860. Emily and Alfred Tennyson to Tuckerman. Houghton Autograph File. Published in *Letters of Tennyson*, 2:250–51.

March 14, 1861. Tuckerman to Henry Wadsworth Longfellow. MS. Am 1340.2 (5635), Houghton.

March 18, 1861. Thomas William Parsons to Tuckerman. Houghton Autograph File.

March 19, 1861. John Seely Stone to Tuckerman. Houghton Autograph File.

March 22, 1861. W. D. Sohier to Tuckerman. Houghton Autograph File.

March 25, 1861. Jones Very to Tuckerman. Houghton Autograph File.

March 26, 1861. John Henry Hopkins to Tuckerman. Houghton Autograph File.

March 28, 1861. Ralph Waldo Emerson to Tuckerman. MS. Am 1189, Houghton.

April 2, 1861. Tuckerman to Henry Wadsworth Longfellow. MS. Am 1340.2 (5635), Houghton.

April 4, 1861. Tuckerman to Nathaniel Hawthorne. Quoted in Julian Hawthorne, *Nathaniel Hawthorne and His Wife*, 2 vols. Hamden, Conn.: Archon Books, 1968, 2:275 (this is a reprint of the 1884 edition by James R. Osgood and Co., Boston). Also in Golden, *Sonneteer*, p. 26.

April 5, 1861. Henry Wadsworth Longfellow to Tuckerman. Houghton Autograph File.

April 9, 1861. Nathaniel Hawthorne to Tuckerman. Houghton Autograph File.

April 10, 1861. Tuckerman to Nathaniel Hawthorne. Quoted in Julian Hawthorne, *Nathaniel Hawthorne and His Wife*, 2:274; Golden, *Sonneteer*, pp. 27–28.

April 14, 1861. Nathaniel Hawthorne to Tuckerman. Houghton Autograph File.

April 24, 1861. Jones Very to Tuckerman. Houghton Autograph File.

April 26, 1861. George B. Park(?) to Tuckerman. MS. Am 1349 (9), Houghton.

May 2, 1861. Sophia May Tuckerman Eckley to Tuckerman. MS. Am 1349.1 (2), Houghton.

May 3, 1861. Sophia May Tuckerman Eckley to Tuckerman. MS. Am 1349.1 (2), Houghton.

May 21, 1861. James T. Fields to Tuckerman. Houghton Autograph File.

June 25, 1861. James T. Fields to Tuckerman. Houghton Autograph File.

June 28, 1861. Henry T. Tuckerman to Tuckerman. Houghton Autograph File. Includes letter from George Ripley to Henry T. about Frederick's poetry, dated June 27, 1861.

July 8, 1861. Henry T. Tuckerman to Tuckerman. Houghton Autograph File. Includes quotation of comments by James Cullen Bryant about Tuckerman's poetry.

November 28, 1861. Tuckerman to James T. Fields. Case 7, Box 10, Gratz Collection, Historical Society of Pennsylvania.

April 6, 1863. Tuckerman to Ralph Waldo Emerson. MS. Am 1280 (3255), Houghton.

January 17, 1864. George Stillman Hillard to Tuckerman. Houghton Autograph File.

January 28, 1864. Tuckerman to James T. Fields. Huntington MS FI 5284, James T. Fields Collection, Huntington Library, San Marino, California. Published in Jeffrey D. Groves, "A Letter from Frederick Goddard Tuckerman to James T. Fields," *The Huntington Library Quarterly* 52.3 (Summer 1989), 405.

July 30, 1864. W. E. Gladstone to Tuckerman. Houghton Autograph File. Published in Bynner, *Sonnets*, 32.

August 25, 1867. Sophia Hawthorne to Tuckerman. MS. Am 1349.1 (3), Houghton.

April 5, 1868. Sophia Hawthorne to Tuckerman. MS. Am 1349.1 (3), Houghton. Published by Margaret Tuckerman Clark in *Yale Review* 23 (Sept. 1933): 214–15, and reprinted by Samuel A. Golden, *Frederick Goddard Tuckerman* (New York: Twayne, 1966), 44–45.

Also of importance for editorial purposes are copies of the 1860 edition of Tuckerman's *Poems* marked with corrections by him. The most important one is at the Houghton Library, marked "Imperfect Copy," and containing many revisions indicated in pencil and ink (almost all of single words). Others are at the Columbia University Library (dedicated to Charles H. Stedman), with ten substantive changes by Tuckerman (including a long emendation of "The Schoolgirl" that Momaday did not include in his edition) and three punctuation changes, all in pencil (cited by Thomas Patrick Lynch in "Still Needed: A Tuckerman Text," *Papers of the Bibliographical Society of America* 69 [1975]: 257); at the University of Chicago Library (dedicated to James T. Fields) with changes in pencil by Tuckerman (cited by Marcus in "The Text of Tuckerman's Poems," 406); and at the Greenfield Historical Society Library in Greenfield, Massachusetts, with forty-two numbered changes indicated in the margins in pencil and ink. (Momaday apparently did not examine any of these copies, except the Houghton, in preparing his edition.) In addition, in the letter dated November 28, 1861, Tuckerman asks James T. Fields to change "deepens" to "darkens" in "I took from its glass a flower," which was about to be published in the *Atlantic Monthly* (this is in the Historical Society of Pennsylvania, Philadelphia).

II. PUBLICATIONS

A. Individual poems, published in periodicals during Tuckerman's lifetime, chronologically listed:

"November" and "April." *Literary World* (New York), 5, no. 21
    (November 24, 1849): 444, and 6, no. 16 (April 20, 1850): 397.
"Mayflowers." *Living Age* 37 (Oct. 19, 1850): 118.
"Hymn. Written upon the Dedication of the Green River
    Cemetery," read at the dedication, October 7, 1851, clipping
    in MS. Am 1349 (10), Houghton Library, but published source
    not yet located.
"Inspiration," "Infatuation," and the sonnet "Again, again, ye
    part in stormy grief." *Living Age* 38 (May 22, 1852): 353.
"Picomegan." *Putnam's Monthly Magazine* 4 (July 1854): 36–37.

"Rhotruda." *Atlantic Monthly* 8 (July 1861): 72–75.

"Sonnet" ("The starry flowers, the flower-like stars that fade"). *Atlantic Monthly* 9 (June 1862): 731. This poem was then reprinted immediately in the *Boston Post* and the *Democrat*.

"Coralie" and "I took from its glass a flower." *Atlantic Monthly* 11 (April 1863): 472–73.

"Ode: For the Greenfield Soldiers Monument," read at the dedication, October 6, 1870, but published source not yet located. Clipping in MS. Am 1349 (3), Houghton Library, and dedication program, including poem, in MS. Am 1349 (10), Houghton Library.

In connection with reviews of the published *Poems*, "Pico-megan" was published in *John Bull* (London, 1863), "The starry flower, the flower-like stars that fade" in the *London Review* (March 7, 1863), "I took from its glass a flower," in *Parthenon* (London, 1863), and "Margites" in New York's *Round Table* 1 (March 5, 1864): 182.

B. Editions of printed texts:

Poems. Boston: John Wilson and Son, 1860. Private printing. This includes the first two sonnet sequences, preceded by thirty-four other poems, some quite long.

Poems. London: Smith, Elder and Co., 1863. The few slight differences from the 1860 edition are listed in N. Scott Momaday, ed., *The Complete Poems of Frederick Goddard Tuckerman* (New York: Oxford Univ. Press, 1965), 207.

Poems. Boston: Ticknor and Fields, 1864. Same plates as 1863 but with an "errata" list included, as follows:

> Page 53, line 15, for "poles" read "polls."
>
> Page 89, line 13, for "bog-hut" read "log-hut."
>
> Page 114, line 3, for "smiles" read "smile."
>
> Page 120, line 16, for "Rhotruda" read "Rhotrude."
>
> Page 141, line 15, for "plaint" read "paint."
>
> Page 152, line 17, for "Let" read "Yet."
>
> Page 162, line 17, for "raftsmen" read "raftsman."

> Page 178, line 12, for "splashed" read "plashed."
> Page 199, line 6, for "give" read "gave."
> Page 234, line 4, for "earthly" read "earthy."

Poems. Boston: Little, Brown and Co., 1869. Identical with 1864.

The Sonnets of Frederick Goddard Tuckerman. Edited, with an extensive introduction, by Witter Bynner. New York: Alfred A. Knopf, 1931. This is the first printing of all five sonnet sequences.

"The Cricket." Cummington, Mass.: Cummington Press, 1950. This is an edition of 290 copies, "printed from [Tuckerman's] Notebooks with permission of his granddaughter, Margaret Tuckerman Clark." Type was set from the penciled manuscript in MS. Am 1349 (3), Houghton Library, which Momaday designated "Cricket 1" (*Complete Poems,* 210); but then a list of changes was appended under "N. B.," using a copy of a manuscript now lost, which was provided to Cummington by Golden and which he has designated "Cricket 5" (*Tuckerman,* 1966, p. 161). The version of "The Cricket" published in *Massachusetts Review* 2 (Autumn 1960): 33–38, is the Cummington version with the appended changes from "Cricket 5" included in the text. See Appendix II for a discussion of editing problems with "The Cricket" and a suggested best version.

The Complete Poems of Frederick Goddard Tuckerman. Edited by N. Scott Momaday. New York: Oxford Univ. Press, 1965. (Published from "An Edition of the Complete Poems of Frederick Goddard Tuckerman," a doctoral dissertation at Stanford University, 1964, with Momaday's "Introduction" revised and shortened and the addition of a "Critical Foreword" by Yvor Winters.) The first complete edition, this includes the five sonnet series, "The Cricket," the other poems published in 1860, and, under "Unpublished Poems," eleven not included there (of which "Ode: For the Greenfield Soldiers Monument" was apparently actually published, though the location has not been found, and what Momaday prints separately as "Long Island" is actually a sequence of three sonnets that is exactly the same as Series III, nos. 11–13).

I have included in the present volume a few minor bits of Tuckerman's poetry Momaday did not publish: two slight verses from Tuckerman's youth (pp. 31–32) and an interesting part of the uncompleted "Poesy" (pp. 83–84), which became separated from the letter in which it was sent and was not seen by Momaday. Serious objections to Momaday's editorial procedures (particularly his reliance on manuscripts rather than the first printed edition) have been raised by Mordecai Marcus ("The Text of Tuckerman's Poems," *Massachusetts Review* 7 [1966]: 403–6), Edwin Cady ("Frederick Goddard Tuckerman," in *Essays on American Literature in Honor of Jay B. Hubbell*, edited by Clarence Gohdes [Durham, N. C.: Duke Univ. Press, 1967], 142n), and Lynch ("Still Needed: A Tuckerman Text"); and I argue for an improved version of "The Cricket," based on a manuscript Momaday did not see, in Appendix II. Clearly, given these objections and with Momaday's edition out of print, a new edition is needed, and I am at work on it.

C. Anthologies which include Tuckerman's work, listed chronologically:

Parnassus. Edited by Ralph Waldo Emerson. Boston: Houghton, Mifflin and Co., 1874. "Rhotruda." No commentary on poem or author by editor.

Unpublished and unnamed anthology. Edited by Louis How, working at the John Carter Brown Library in Providence, R.I. Collected about 1907. Two sonnets. (A letter from How to Eaton about his discovery of Tuckerman in the process of editing this anthology led directly to appreciation and eventual publication of Tuckerman in the twentieth century).

Oxford Anthology of American Literature. Edited by William Rose Benét and Norman Holmes Pearson. New York: Oxford Univ. Press, 1938. 2 vols. Six sonnets, III: 8, 11, 12, 13, and IV: 6, 10. Commentary at the end of vol. 2.

An Anthology of the New England Poets from Colonial Times to the Present Day. Edited by Louis Untermeyer. New York: Random House, 1948. Six sonnets, I: 1, 5, 10, 12, 19, and II: 17. Commentary at the beginning of the group of poems.

Poetry of the New England Renaissance (1790–1890). Edited by George F. Whicher. New York: Rinehart, 1950. Twenty-eight sonnets, I: 1–28. Commentary in introduction.

Poetry in English. Edited by Warren Taylor and Donald Hall. 1963. Reprint. New York: Macmillan, 1970. Four sonnets, I: 1, 4, 5, 17. No commentary.

American Poetry. Edited by Gay Wilson Allen, et al. New York: Harper and Row, 1965. "The Question," "Refrigerium," and seventeen sonnets, I: 22, 24, 25, 26, and II: 7, 8, 9, 10, 13, 14, 15, 16, 17, 21, 22, 23, 24. Short commentary with poems; bibliography at end of volume.

The American Poets, 1800–1900. Edited by Edwin H. Cady. Glenview, Ill.: Scott, Foresman, 1966. Eleven sonnets, I: 5, 9, 10, 13, 15, 22, 28, and II: 9, 16, 23, 37. No commentary.

Major American Poets to 1914. Edited by Francis Murphy. Lexington, Mass.: D. C. Heath, 1967. Twelve sonnets, I: 1, 10, 20, 24, 26, and II: 1, 2, 15, 16, 21, 29, 30, and "The Cricket." Notes with poems and short commentary at end of volume.

Poetry: An Introductory Anthology. Edited by Hazard Adams. Boston: Little, Brown and Co., 1968. One sonnet, II: 16. No commentary.

Quest for Reality: An Anthology of Short Poems in English. Edited by Yvor Winters and Kenneth Fields. Chicago: Swallow Press, 1969. Seven sonnets, II: 15–20 and V: 14, and "The Cricket." Short commentary in introduction.

American Literature: Tradition and Innovation. Edited by Harrison T. Meserole, et al. Lexington, Mass.: D. C. Heath, 1969. Six sonnets, I: 23, 24, 25, 26, 27, 28, "The Cricket," and "Under the Locust Blossoms." No commentary.

The Norton Anthology of Poetry. Edited by Arthur M. Eastman, et al. New York: Norton, 1970. Four sonnets, I: 10, 28, and II: 16, 18, and "The Cricket." No commentary.

The Literature of America: Nineteenth Century. Edited by Irving

Howe. New York: McGraw Hill, 1970. 3 vols. Six sonnets, I: 10, 28, II: 16, 18, III: 4, V: 2, and "The Cricket." Commentary and bibliography at beginning of poems.

The Poet in America: 1650 to the Present. Edited by Albert Gelpi. Lexington, Mass.: D. C. Heath, 1973. Nine sonnets, I: 10, 26, 28; II: 16, 17, 18, 33; III: 10; V: 4, and "The Cricket." Short commentary but also helpful informational notes on the poems.

Anthology of American Literature. Edited by George McMichael, et al. Riverside, N. J.: Macmillan, 1974 (3d ed., 1985). 2 vols. Nine sonnets, I: 7, 10, 19; II: 1, 6, 18; III: 8, 10, 16, and "The Cricket." Commentary and bibliography at beginning of poems and helpful footnotes.

America in Literature. Edited by Alan Trachtenberg. New York: John Wiley and Sons, 1978. 3 vols. Three sonnets, vol. 2., I: 10, and II: 18, 24, and "The Cricket." Commentary and bibliography at beginning, with informational notes on "The Cricket."

The Harper Anthology of Poetry. Edited by John Frederick Nims. New York: Harper and Row, 1981. Four sonnets, II: 3, 15, 16, 18, with a brief introduction and notes on the poems.

Survey of American Poetry. Edited by The Editorial Board, Granger Book Co. The Granger Anthology, Series 2, vol. 4. Great Neck, N.Y.: Granger Book, 1984. Five sonnets, I: 1, 5, 10, 12, 19, and "Rhotruda." Short biography at beginning.

The Harper American Literature. Edited by Donald McQuade et al. New York: Harper and Row, 1987. 2 vols. Seven sonnets, I: 10, 26; II: 16, 18, 22; IV: 10; V: 2, and "The Cricket" and "Under the Locust Blossoms." Commentary and bibliography at beginning.

III. TUCKERMAN'S READING

A. The surviving library, which includes Tuckerman's notes and markings, listed alphabetically, by author:

Akenside, Mark. *The Poetical Works of Mark Akenside.* Edited by Cooke. London; n.p., n.d.

Bigelow, Jacob. *A Collection of Plants of Boston and Its Vicinity.* 3d ed. Boston: Little, Brown and Co., 1840.

Browning, Robert. *Men and Women.* Boston: Ticknor and Fields, 1856.

Bulwer, Sir Henry. *The Rebel and Other Tales.* New York: Harper and Brothers, 1835.

Byron, Lord (George Gordon). *Lord Byron on Men, Manners, and Things.* London: n.p., 1834. No markings.

Channing, W. E. *Poems.* Boston: Little, Brown and Co., 1843.

Chaucer, Geoffrey. *The Poetical Works of Geoffrey Chaucer.* London: Moxon, 1843. No markings.

Congreve, William. *Congreve's Works.* Vol. 1. London: Loundes, 1774. Possibly only belonged to Edward; no markings.

Coleridge, Samuel Taylor. *Aids to Reflection.* Edited by James Marsh. Burlington, Vt.: Chauncey Goodrich, 1829. Edward's copy but a few notes and marks by Tuckerman.

Gay, John. *Gay's Poems on Several Occasions.* 2 vols. Glasgow: n.p., 1757.

Harris's Treatise on Insects. 2d ed. Boston: White and Porter, 1852. No markings.

Hawthorne, Nathaniel. *The Scarlet Letter.* Boston: Ticknor, Reed, and Fields, 1850. No markings.

Hunt, Leigh. *Wit and Humor.* New York: Wiley and Putnam, 1847.

Irving, Washington. *Beauties of Washington Irving.* Philadelphia: Carey, Lea, and Blanchard, 1835.

Lempriere, J. *Classical Dictionary.* London: T. Caldwell, 1820.

Longfellow, Henry Wadsworth. *The Golden Legend.* Boston: Ticknor, Reed, and Fields, 1852.

————. *Kavanagh.* Boston: Ticknor, Reed, and Fields, 1849.

————. *The Song of Hiawatha.* Boston: Ticknor and Fields, 1855.

Loomis, Elias. *An Introduction to Practical Astronomy.* New York: Harper, 1855. No markings.

Motherwell, William. *Poems, Narrative and Lyrical.* n.p., n.d. Hannah Tuckerman's book but marked by Frederick.

Smith, Asa. *Smith's Illustrated Astronomy.* New York: Cady and Burgess, 1849.

Southey, Robert. *Thalaba the Destroyer*. London: Longman and
Rees, 1801.

*Tennyson, Alfred, Lord. *Maud and Other Poems*. London:
Moxon, 1855.

*———. *Poems*. 2 vols. Boston: Ticknor and Fields, 1842.

*———. *Poems*. 2 vols. London: Moxon, 1842.

*———. *The Princess, A Medley*. Boston: Ticknor and Fields,
1848.

———. *The Princess, A Medley*. 4th ed. London: Moxon, 1851.

Tuckerman, Henry T. *The Optimist*. New York: Putnam, 1850.
No markings.

Tuckerman, Joseph. "Seven Discourses on Miscellaneous Subjects." *Christian Monitor* 18 (1811). No markings.

B. Notes in the volumes listed above give direct evidence of
Tuckerman's careful reading of these additional authors and
works: Armstrong; Browning; Burns; Butler; Byron; Carlyle;
Chaucer; Coleridge; Cornwall; Cowley; Denham; De Quincey;
Dickens; Donne; Dryden; Elton; Emerson; Hawes; Homer;
Hunt; Sir William Jones; James VI; Johnson; Keats; *Methodist
Hymnal;* Moore; Mitford; Ossian; Otway; Poe; Pope; Marlowe;
Milton; Scott; Shenstone; Shelley; Southey; Spenser; Swift;
Thomson; Whitman; *Wisdom of Solomon;* Wordsworth; Young.

IV.   SECONDARY SOURCES

A. Reviews:

1. Responses to the 1860 *Poems*.

Letters from the following, in response to presentation copies sent by Tuckerman in the spring of 1861, are now in the
Houghton Library Autograph File: Sophia May Eckley, the
poet's sister, containing also a report of comments by Byron's
granddaughter, Annabelle Noel; Ralph Waldo Emerson; W. E.

---

*These are located in the Houghton Library at Harvard University; the
other volumes listed are at Hugh Clark's home in Amherst, Mass., in process of being given to the Houghton Library.

Gladstone; Nathaniel Hawthorne; George S. Hillard; Bishop J. H. Hopkins; Henry Wadsworth Longfellow; J. S. Stone; Henry T. Tuckerman, the poet's cousin, containing also a report of the response of William Cullen Bryant and a letter of response from George Ripley; Jones Very.

In addition, Emerson reports the response of W. E. Channing: See *Journals of Ralph Waldo Emerson,* edited by E. W. Emerson and W. E. Forbes. 10 vols. (Boston: Houghton Mifflin, 1909–14), 9: 318–19.

2. Reviews of individual poems published in periodicals, of the first public edition (London, 1863) and of the first American edition (Boston, 1864), clippings of which are found in Houghton MS. Am 1349 (9); most substantial are the following: *Boston Transcript,* July, 1861; *Spectator* (London), 1863; *London Review,* March 7, 1863; *The Press* (London), March 14, 1863; *Athenaeum* (London), 1863; *London Reader,* 1863; *Observer* (London), 1863; *Parthenon* (London), 1863; *John Bull* (London), 1863; *Atlantic Monthly* 13 (January 1864): 777–78; *Boston Evening Transcript,* 1864; *Boston Post,* 1864; *Round Table* (New York), 1864; *Springfield Republican,* 1864; *New York Times,* 1864.

3. Reviews of Witter Bynner's 1931 edition, *The Sonnets of Frederick Goddard Tuckerman* (chronologically arranged):

Benét, William Rose. "Round about Parnassus." *Saturday Review of Literature* 7 (February 7, 1931): 584.

Morrison, Theodore. Untitled review in "Poetry" section. *Bookman* 73 (April 1931): 205–6.

"A Contemporary of Lowell and Whittier." *New York Times Book Review,* May 24, 1931.

Redman, Ben Ray. "Old Wine in New Bottles." *New York Herald Tribune Books* 7 (June 7, 1931): 12.

W., F. E. "The Sonnets of an American Poet." *Boston Transcript,* June 13, 1931, 1.

"Among Our Books." *Pittsburgh Monthly Bulletin* 36 (July 1931): 61.

Walton, Eda Lou. "A Neglected Poet." *Nation* 133.3452 (September 2, 1931): 234–35.

Short note in "Book Notes." *New Republic* 69 (November 18, 1931): 26–27.

In addition there are, in the papers of Witter Bynner, letters of response from Robert Frost and Edwin Arlington Robinson, which are quoted in part by Samuel A. Golden, *Frederick Goddard Tuckerman* (New York: Twayne, 1966), 143.

4. Review of the 1950 Cummington Press edition of "The Cricket": Yvor Winters. "A Discovery." *Hudson Review* 3 (Autumn 1950): 453–58.

This same edition, but with the Cummington errata list incorporated into the text and a useful introductory note by Mordecai Marcus, is in *Massachusetts Review* 2 (Autumn 1960): 33–38.

5. Reviews of N. Scott Momaday's 1965 edition, *The Complete Poems of Frederick Goddard Tuckerman* (chronologically arranged):

Howe, Irving. "An American Poet." *New York Review of Books,* March 25, 1965, 17–19.

Regan, Robert. Untitled short note. *Library Journal* 90 (June 15, 1965): 2861.

Eberhart, Richard. "A Quiet Tone from a Rich Interior." *New York Times Book Review,* June 20, 1965, 5.

Untitled short note in "Notes on Current Books." *Virginia Quarterly Review* 41 (Summer 1965): lxxxv.

Untitled short note in "Brief Mention." *American Literature* 37 (November 1965): 357.

"Tuckerman the Great." *Times Literary Supplement* 64 (December 2, 1965): 1102.

Donoghue, Denis. "The Store of the Human." *Hudson Review* 18 (Winter 1965–66): 601–7.

Ricks, Christopher. "The Age of Tuckerman." *New Statesman* 11 (April 8, 1966): 503–4.

Lensing, George. "The Lyric Plenitude: A Time of Rediscovery." *Southern Review,* n.s., 1 (Winter 1967): 197–228.

B. Books, essays, bibliographies, dissertations, and theses (listed alphabetically):

Boswell, Jeanetta. *Spokesmen for the Minority: A Bibliography of Sidney Lanier, William Vaughn Moody, Frederick Goddard Tuckerman, and Jones Very, with Selective Annotations.* Metuchen, N. J.: The Scarecrow Press, Inc., 1987.

Cady, Edwin. "Frederick Goddard Tuckerman." In *Essays on American Literature in Honor of Jay B. Hubbell,* edited by Clarence Gohdes. Durham, N.C.: Duke Univ. Press, 1967.

Clark, Margaret Tuckerman. "A Hawthorne Letter." *Yale Review* 23 (September 1933): 214–15.

Donoghue, Denis. *Connoisseurs of Chaos: Ideas of Order in Modern American Poetry.* 1965. Reprint. New York: Columbia Univ. Press, 1984.

Eaton, Walter Prichard. "A Forgotten American Poet." *Forum* 41 (January 1909): 62–70; considerably revised and included in Eaton's *Penguin Persons and Peppermints.* Boston: W. A. Wilde, 1922.

England, Eugene. "Beyond the Romantic Dilemma: A Study of the Poetry of Frederick Goddard Tuckerman." Ph.D. diss., Stanford Univ., 1974.

———. "The Forms of Loss in Tuckerman's Elegy." *Encyclia* 59 (1982): 35–44.

———. "Tennyson and Tuckerman: 'Two Friends . . . on Either Side the Atlantic.'" *New England Quarterly* 57, no. 2 (June 1984): 225–39.

———. "Tuckerman's Sonnet I: 10: The First Post-Symbolist Poem." *Southern Review,* n.s., 12 (Spring 1976): 323–47.

Evans, Oliver H. "The Sonnet in America." Ph.D. diss., Purdue Univ., 1972. The dissertation shows how Tuckerman's innovations in the sonnet form reflected unique personal vision and poetic skill, compared to the many other and more famous users of the sonnet in the nineteenth century.

Getz, John Raymond. "The Originality of Frederick Goddard Tuckerman." Ph.D. diss., Univ. of Pennsylvania, 1977. Getz focuses on Tuckerman's effective, "original" use of Wordsworth and Tennyson.

Golden, Samuel A. *Frederick Goddard Tuckerman: An American Sonneteer.* Univ. of Maine, Bulletin 54, no. 12 (April 1952). The material in this monograph was first developed for a master's thesis at the Univ. of Maine (1949); it was later revised and summarized for Golden's essay, "Frederick Goddard Tuckerman: A Neglected Poet," *New England Quarterly* 29 (September 1956): 381–93.

———. *Frederick Goddard Tuckerman.* New York: Twayne, 1966.

Groves, Jeffrey D. "Frederick Goddard Tuckerman in the Canon of American Literature." Ph.D. diss., Claremont Graduate School, 1987. Groves argues that Tuckerman, because he is as "useful to critics of a specific historical period" as his more famous contemporaries, should be (and is being) inserted into the American literature canon. He then demonstrates that usefulness with a critique of the poetry, focussed on the theme of grief, the Civil War poems, and "disrupting narratives" of linguistic richness and thematic complexity.

———. "A Letter from Frederick Goddard Tuckerman to James T. Fields." *The Huntington Library Quarterly* 52.1 (Summer 1989): 403–8.

Hagenbüchle, Roland. "Abstraction and Desire: Dissolving Contours in the Poetry of Frederick Goddard Tuckerman." In *American Poetry between Tradition and Modernism, 1865–1914,* edited by Roland Hagenbüchle, 70–86. Regensburg, W. Ger.: Pustet, 1984.

———. With Ludwig Deringer. "Amerikanische Lyrik des 19. Jahrhunderts." In *Die amerikanische Literatur bis zum Ende des 19. Jahrhunderts.* Edited by Helmbrecht Breinig, and Ulrich Halfmann. Tübingen, W. Ger.: Francke, 1985.

Kamei, Shunsuke. "Frederick Goddard Tuckerman no Shi." *Eigo Seinen* [The Rising Generation] (Tokyo), 116 (1970): 568–70.

Lynch, Thomas Patrick. "Quick Fire for Frost: A Study of the Poetry of Frederick Goddard Tuckerman." Ph.D. diss., Columbia Univ., 1969. Lynch concentrates on explication of poems and a telling critique of Momaday's edition.

———. "Still Needed: A Tuckerman Text." *Papers of the Bibliographical Society of America* 69 (1975): 255–65.

Marcus, Mordecai. "The Poetry of Frederick Goddard Tuckerman: A Reconsideration." *Discourse* 5 (Winter 1961–62): 69–82.

———. "The Text of Tuckerman's Poems." *Massachusetts Review* 7 (1966): 403–6.

Momaday, N. Scott. "An Edition of the Complete Poems of Frederick Goddard Tuckerman." Ph.D. diss., Stanford Univ., 1963. Critical introduction, pp. 1–58. This was published, with a shortened introduction and a foreword by Yvor Winters, by Oxford Univ. Press in 1965.

———. "The Heretical Cricket." *Southern Review,* n.s., 3 (Winter 1967): 43–50.

Mueller, Janet A. "Frederick Goddard Tuckerman: A Critical Study." Master's thesis, Stanford Univ., 1960.

Prince, Walter E. [Title unknown]. *Amherst Student,* Dec. 15, 1939. Reference is made in Golden, *Tuckerman* (1966), 153, to this general essay on Tuckerman, but the Amherst librarian has been unable to locate it in the given citation or elsewhere.

Solomon, Robert Joel. "The Sonnets of Frederick Goddard Tuckerman." Master's thesis, Univ. of North Carolina, 1974.

Weintz, Christian. "Frederick Goddard Tuckerman: The Wisdom of Perfected Grief." Ph.D. diss., Univ. of Minnesota, 1970.

Winters, Yvor. "A Discovery." *Hudson Review* 3 (Autumn 1950): 453–58.

———. "Critical Foreword" to *The Complete Poems of Frederick Goddard Tuckerman,* edited by N. Scott Momaday. Oxford: Oxford Univ. Press, 1965.

C. Commentary in works of literary history and criticism, etc. (chronologically arranged by first edition):

Allibone, S. Austin. *A Critical Dictionary of English Literature and British and American Authors.* Philadelphia: Lippincott, 1871.

Adams, Oscar Fay. *A Dictionary of American Authors.* Boston: Houghton Mifflin, 1884.

Appleton's Cyclopedia of American Biography. Edited by James Grant Wilson and John Fiske. Vol. 6. New York: D. Appleton, 1889.

Rutherford, Mildred. *American Authors: A Hand-Book of American Literature from Early Colonial to Living Writers.* Atlanta: Franklin Printing and Publishing, 1894. See "Addenda."

Emerson, Ralph Waldo. *The Journals of Ralph Waldo Emerson.* Edited by Edward Waldo Emerson and Waldo Emerson Forbes. 10 vols. Boston: Houghton Mifflin, 1909–14.

Herringshaw, Thomas William. *National Library of American Biography.* Chicago: American Publishers' Assoc., 1914.

Perry, Bliss. *The American Spirit in Literature.* Chronicles of America Series, vol. 34. New Haven, Conn.: Yale Univ. Press, 1918.

Dictionary of American Biography. Edited by Dumas Malone. New York: Charles Scribner's Sons, 1936.

North, William Robert. "Chinese Themes in American Verse." Ph.D. diss., Univ. of Pennsylvania, 1937.

Winters, Yvor. "Jones Very and R. W. Emerson: Aspects of New England Mysticism." Pp. 262–82 in Winters, *In Defense of Reason.* Denver: Alan Swallow, 1947. Published originally in Winters' *Maule's Curse* (1938).

American Authors: 1600–1900. Edited by Stanley J. Kunitz and Howard Haycroft. New York: H. W. Wilson, 1938.

Brooks, Van Wyck. *New England Summer, 1865–1915.* New York: E. P. Dutton, 1940.

Hart, James D. *The Oxford Companion to American Literature.* 4th ed. New York: Oxford Univ. Press, 1965.

Burke, W. J., and Will D. Howe. *American Authors and Books: 1640–1940.* New York: Gramercy Publishing, 1943.

Eidson, John Olin. *Tennyson in America: His Reputation and Influence from 1827 to 1858.* Athens: Univ. of Georgia Press, 1943.

Benét, William Rose. *The Reader's Encyclopedia.* 2d ed. New York: Thomas Y. Crowell, 1965.

Tennyson, Charles. *Alfred Tennyson.* London: Macmillan, 1949.

Concise Dictionary of American Literature. Edited by Robert Fulton Richards. New York: Philosophical Library, 1955.

Wilson, Edmund. *Patriotic Gore.* New York: Oxford Univ. Press, 1961.

Herzberg, Max J. *The Reader's Encyclopedia of American Literature.* New York: Thomas Y. Crowell, 1962.

McMichael, James. *The Style of the Short Poem.* Belmont, Calif.: Wadsworth, 1967.

Winters, Yvor. *Forms of Discovery.* Chicago: Alan Swallow, 1967.

Kramer, Aaron. *The Prophetic Tradition in American Poetry, 1835–1900.* Rutherford, N.J.: Fairleigh Dickinson Univ. Press, 1968.

Waggoner, Hyatt H. *American Poets, from the Puritans to the Present.* 1968. Reprint. Boston: Houghton Mifflin, 1984.

Fields, Kenneth. "Introduction" to *Quest for Reality: An Anthology of Short Poems in English.* Edited by Yvor Winters and Kenneth Fields. Chicago: Swallow Press, 1969.

Hubbell, Jay B. *Who are the Major American Writers?* Durham, N.C.: Duke Univ. Press, 1972.

Literary History of the United States. Edited by Robert E. Spiller et al. New York: Macmillan, 1973. No changes in the several other editions available.

Wilson, Edmund. *The Devils and Canon Barham.* New York: Farrar, Straus and Giroux, 1973.

Stauffer, Donald Barlow. *A Short History of American Poetry.* New York: E. P. Dutton, 1974.

Gelpi, Albert J. *The Tenth Muse.* Cambridge, Mass.: Harvard Univ. Press, 1975.

Callow, James T., and Robert J. Reilly. *Guide to American Literature from Its Beginnings through Walt Whitman.* New York: Barnes and Noble, 1976.

Grigorescu, Dan. *Dictionar cronologic literatura americana.* Bucharest: Editura stiintifica si enciclipedica, 1977.

Duffey, Bernard. *Poetry in America: Expression and Its Values in the Times of Bryant, Whitman, and Pound.* Durham, N.C.: Duke Univ. Press, 1978.

Webster, Grant. *The Republic of Letters: A History of Postwar American Literary Opinion.* Baltimore: Johns Hopkins Univ. Press, 1979.

Johnson, Robert K. "Tuckerman, Frederick Goddard." In

American Literature to 1900. New York: St. Martin's Press, 1980.

Stanford, Donald E. *Revolution and Convention in Modern Poetry.* Newark: Univ. of Delaware Press, 1983.

Stapleton, Michael. *The Cambridge Guide to English Literature.* Cambridge, Eng.: Cambridge Univ. Press, 1983.

Walker, Marshall. *History of American Literature.* Chicago: St. James Press, 1983.

Seed, David. "Alone with God and Nature: The Poetry of Jones Very and Frederick Goddard Tuckerman." In *Nineteenth-Century American Poetry,* edited by A. Robert Lee, 166–93. London: Vision Press, 1985.

Buell, Lawrence. *New England Literary Culture from Revolution through Renaissance.* Cambridge, Eng.: Cambridge Univ. Press, 1986.

V. BIOGRAPHICAL AND GENEALOGICAL SOURCES
   (arranged alphabetically):

Chamberlain, Allen. *Beacon Hill.* Boston: Houghton Mifflin, 1925. Cited in Golden, *Tuckerman* (1966).

Crawford, Mary Carline. "The Tuckerman Family." *Famous Families of Massachusetts.* Boston: Little, Brown and Co., 1930.

Cusing, Thomas P. Letter to Edward Tuckerman, Sr. July 31, 1841. MS. Am 1349.1 (1), Houghton.

Duyckinck, Evert A., and George L. Duyckinck. "Henry Theodore Tuckerman." In *Cyclopedia of American Literature.* Vol. 2. New York: Charles Scribner, 1855.

Farnum, Charles H. *History of the Descendants of John Whitman of Weymouth.* New Haven, Conn.: Privately printed, 1889. Cited in Golden, *Sonneteer* (p. 30).

Greenfield Gazette and Courier. May 5 and 9, 1873. Cited in Golden, *Tuckerman* (p. 157).

Hawthorne, Julian. *Nathaniel Hawthorne and His Wife.* 2 vols. Hamden, Conn.: Archon Books, 1968. This is a reprint of the 1884 edition by James R. Osgood and Co., Boston.

Hoge, James O., ed. *The Letters of Emily Lady Tennyson.* University Park: Pennsylvania State Univ. Press, 1974.

Hoge, James O., ed. *Lady Tennyson's Journal*. Charlottesville: Univ. Press of Virginia, 1981.

Kellog, Lucy Cutler. *History of Greenfield, 1900–1929*. Vol. 3. Greenfield, Mass.: T. Morey and Sons, 1931.

Lang, Cecil Y., and Edgar F. Shannon, Jr., eds. *The Letters of Alfred Lord Tennyson*. 2 vols. Oxford, Eng.: Clarendon Press, 1987.

Reid, Anna M. M. "Edward Tuckerman (1817–1886), Pioneer American Lichenologist: The Early Years." *Mycotaxon* 26 (July–September 1986): 3–16. (Pages 1–79 of this issue were reprinted for the New York State Museum as *History of North American Mycology*.)

Savage, James. *Genealogical Dictionary of the First Settlers of New England*. 4 vols. Boston: Little, Brown and Co., 1860–62.

Tennyson, Emily. Letter to Sophia May Tuckerman Eckley, June 18, 1873. MS. Am 1349.1 (7), Houghton.

[Tennyson, Hallam]. "Materials for a Life of A[lfred] T[ennyson]," 4 vols. (unpublished, [1895]), 2:152–53.

Thompson, Francis M. *History of Greenfield*. Vol. 2. Greenfield, Mass.: T. Morey and Sons, 1904.

Tuckerman, Bayard. *Notes on the Tuckerman Family of Massachusetts and Some Allied Families*. Boston: Riverside Press, 1914 (privately published).

Tuckerman, Charles Keating. *Personal Recollections of Notable People*. London: Richard Bentley and Son, 1895.

Tuckerman, Frederick. Handwritten genealogical journal written by Tuckerman's son. Presently in the possession of Hugh Clark, Amherst, Mass.

Tuckerman, Hannah. Letters to her parents while in Europe with Frederick, 1854–55. Presently in the possession of Hugh Clark, Amherst, Mass.

Vital Records of Greenfield, Massachusetts: To the Year 1850. Boston: New England Historic Genealogical Society, 1915.

Wordsworth, William. "Elegaic Stanzas," with a prose introduction; number 32 of "Memorials of a Tour on the Continent" (1820). In *Wordsworth's Complete Poetical Works*. New York: Houghton, Mifflin and Co., 1904.

Appendix II: Editing "The Cricket"

Tuckerman must have considered "The Cricket" his best poem; he made far more manuscript copies of it than any other work, apparently continuing to adjust small details for special effects he wished to achieve. Four of the manuscripts were available to Momaday; he described them in an appendix to his edition and also posited an order of their writing, which he enumerated "Crickets 1, 2, 3, 4." Momaday correctly deduced that the first edition—Cummington Press (1950)—was based on the somewhat inferior "Cricket 1" in the notebook Houghton MS. Am 1349 (3), but he was unable to account for the changes listed under "N. B." on the back page of that edition. The reason for the difficulty is that a photocopy of a *fifth* manuscript was made available to the Cummington editors after they went to press and was used as a basis for the added "N. B." In the edition done by the *Massachusetts Review* (1960), with an introductory note by Mordecai Marcus, the editors merely included the "N. B." changes in the Cummington text, so that they arrived at essentially the equivalent of that fifth manuscript. Golden, who had provided that copy to Cummington, pointed all this out in his book on Tuckerman in 1966 and asserted that "Cricket 5" was probably the poet's "final" and best copy; he had obtained a photocopy of "Cricket 5," when the original was at the home of Mrs. Margaret Clark in 1949, for his work on his master's thesis at the University of Maine, Orono (which kindly provided me with a copy). Apparently the original has been lost because no record of its disposition was left by Mrs. Clark, and I could not locate it at the Houghton Library or at the home of Hugh Clark in Amherst.

Careful examination of all these manuscripts has convinced me that beyond the quite obviously early "draft," "Cricket 1," the ordering of the remainder is far from certain. For instance, Momaday believed "Cricket 4" was later than "Cricket 3" (both are in Houghton MS. Am 1349-7) because "Cricket 3" is not punctuated at the ends of lines and part of it is copied in pencil; but it seems clear that Tuckerman was making a number of careful, complete copies on single large sheets ("Crickets 3, 4, 5") and that he merely saw that he was running out of room (and had left out a line) on the smaller paper of "Cricket 3" and quit—then later decided to crowd in the rest in pencil. "Cricket 2" (Houghton MS. Am 1349-4) actually appears, for some good reasons (e.g., it is the only one to introduce the improve ment—which Momaday in fact uses—of "laugh and blush" for "tittering blush" in line 60), to be the final copy *chronologically.* Tuckerman did not see the poem in print; we do not know which, if any, manuscript he preferred; and the differences in "Crickets 2, 3, 4, 5" are relatively minor (as Harry Duncan, editor of the Cummington Press says in a letter to me, "The remarkable fact about the versions of *The Cricket* is that they vary so little from the first draft to the final one, there being only the five verbal changes"). Therefore, we can most fruitfully opt for the best *combination.*

For a combined version, Momaday, an excellent poet himself, is probably the best guide. I have presumed to differ with him in only three cases: In line 68 I have used "shimmering," from "Crickets 2, 3, 5," instead of "glimmering," which appears only in "Crickets 1, 4" (Tuckerman, as I indicate in chapter 2, tended to overuse "glimmering" and then apparently repented, and that seems to be the case here). In line 85 "dorcynium" is a misspelling of "dorycnium" (Tuckerman probably read somewhere about this southern European plant with supposed magical qualities and slightly missed the spelling; had it been an American plant he would not have erred, and it is not likely a case of his deliberate slight modification of words for sound, a practice he seems to have reserved for people and place names). Momaday's comma at the end of line 21 is probably a typographical error, because it appears in none of the manuscripts and misleads the syntax. His dash at the end of line 129 seems to be a misreading of the cross of the "t" of "exist" in "Cricket 4" and should probably best be omitted to accord with all manuscripts except "Cricket 2," where there is a comma. In line 7 Momaday's assumption that "Cricket 4" is the latest manuscript copy leads to what seems a mistake, because the comma at the end, which appears only in "Crickets 1, 4," changes the sense in a way Tuckerman apparently recognized—and so removed it in the apparently succeeding manuscripts ("Crickets 3, 5, 2").

A careful collation convinces me that the probable order was *1, 4, 3, 5, 2* (it is also logical that the one careful ink version preserved in a notebook, "Cricket 2," would be Tuckerman's final choice); but that is not a very important matter, except to counter Momaday's overdependence on "Cricket 4" and Golden's on "Cricket 5" and to encourage us to be eclectic. Knowledge of the manuscript variants, beyond "Cricket 1," is useful to aid us in exercising good taste in selection, as Momaday has done, I believe, in almost all cases; as I show in my discussion of the poem, some of those variations help us see more clearly certain effects that Tuckerman was explicitly striving for in rhythm and connotation, but for which he went too far in certain cases (e.g., in "Cricket 2" he overdid the effect of "falling" with "faltering" in line 25, but he improved line 60 with "laugh and blush" for "tittering blush").

I came to the above conclusions in 1973. In 1975, T. Patrick Lynch, in an essay published in *Papers of the Biographical Society of America,* discussed "The Cricket" as part of a general critique of the Momaday edition. Based on his examination of changes that occur only in "Cricket 2," Lynch came to essentially the same conclusion I did—that "Cricket 2" is the final version—but he was not aware of "Cricket 5" and failed to see the evidence that "Crickets 3, 2, 5" were all fair copies made at about the same time. He does not seem to trust Momaday's ability to make good selections from those alternatives and thus proposes "Cricket 2" as the definitive manuscript base for any future edition, while I, for the reasons developed above, recommend the combination I have used in chapter 6.

General Bibliography

Abrams, M. H. *The Mirror and the Lamp: Romantic Theory and the Critical Tradition.* 1953. Reprint. New York: Norton, 1958.

————. *Natural Supernaturalism: Tradition and Revolution in Romantic Literature.* New York: Norton, 1971.

————. *A Glossary of Literary Terms.* 4th ed. New York: Holt, Rinehart and Winston, 1981.

Ahlstrom, Sydney E. *A Religious History of the American People.* New Haven, Conn.: Yale Univ. Press, 1972.

Astley, Russell. "Stations of the Breath: End Rhyme in the Verse of Dylan Thomas." *Publications of the Modern Language Association* 84 (October 1969): 1595–1605.

Ayer, A. J. *The Problem of Knowledge.* London: Macmillan, 1956.

Bartlett, Irving H. *The American Mind in the Mid-Nineteenth Century.* New York: Thomas Y. Crowell, 1967.

Bate, Walter Jackson. *John Keats.* 1963. Reprint. New York: Oxford Univ. Press, 1967.

Black, Caesar R., and Carlton F. Wells, eds. *The Recognition of Emily Dickinson: Selected Criticism since 1890.* 1964. Reprint. Ann Arbor: Univ. of Michigan Press, 1968.

Bloom, Harold. *A Map of Misreading.* New York: Oxford Univ. Press, 1975.

Bode, Carl. *An Anatomy of American Popular Culture, 1840–1860.* Berkeley and Los Angeles: Univ. of California Press, 1960.

Branch, E. Douglas. *The Sentimental Years: 1836–1865.* 1934. Reprint. New York: Hill and Wang, 1962.

Brooks, Van Wyck. *The Flowering of New England: 1815–1865.* Rev. ed. New York: E. P. Dutton, 1937.

Buell, Lawrence. *New England Literary Culture from Revolution through Renaissance.* Cambridge, Eng.: Cambridge Univ. Press, 1986.

Carafiol, Peter. *Transcendent Reason: James Marsh and the Forms of Romantic Thought.* Tallahassee: Univ. Presses of Florida, 1982.

Davie, Donald. *Articulate Energy: An Enquiry into the Syntax of English Poetry.* 1955. Reprint. New York: Harcourt, Brace, 1958.

————. *Purity of Diction in English Verse.* 1952. Reprint. New York: Schocken Books, 1967.

Dickinson, Emily. *The Complete Poems of Emily Dickinson.* Edited by Thomas H. Johnson. Boston: Little, Brown and Co., 1960.

Emerson, Ralph Waldo. *The Complete Writings of Ralph Waldo Emerson.* Edited by Edward Waldo Emerson. New York: W. H. Wise and Co., 1929.

————. *Emerson: Selected Prose and Poetry.* Edited by Reginald Cook. New York: Holt, Rinehart and Winston, 1950.

————. *Journals of Ralph Waldo Emerson.* Edited by Edward Waldo Emerson and Waldo Emerson Forbes. 10 vols. Boston: Houghton Mifflin, 1909–14.

Frye, Northrop. *A Study of English Romanticism.* New York: Random House, 1968.

————, ed. *Romanticism Reconsidered.* New York: Columbia Univ. Press, 1963.

Gelpi, Albert J. *Emily Dickinson: The Mind of the Poet.* Cambridge, Mass.: Harvard Univ. Press, 1966.

Golden, Samuel A. *Frederick Goddard Tuckerman: An American Sonneteer.* Orono: Univ. of Maine Press, 1952.

————. *Frederick Goddard Tuckerman.* New York: Twayne, 1966.

Gray, Asa. "Edward Tuckerman." *Proceedings of the American Academy of Arts and Sciences* 31 (1886): 539–47.

Gross, Harvey. *Sound and Form in Modern Poetry.* 1964. Reprint. Ann Arbor: Univ. of Michigan Press, 1968.

————, ed. *The Structure of Verse: Modern Essays on Prosody.* Greenwich, Conn.: Fawcett Publications, 1966.

Hagenbüchle, Roland, ed. *American Poetry between Tradition and Modernism, 1865–1914.* Regensburg, W. Ger.: Pustet, 1984.

Hallam, A. H. "On Some of the Characteristics of Modern Poetry, and on the Lyrical Poems of Alfred Tennyson." *The Englishman's Magazine* (August 1831): 616–28.

Happel, Stephen. *Coleridge's Religious Imagination.* Vol. 2. Salzburg: Univ. of Salzburg, 1983.

Harris, Daniel A. *Tennyson and Personification: The Rhetoric of "Tithonus."* Ann Arbor, Mich.: UMI Research Press, 1986.

Hartmann, Geoffrey, ed. *New Perspectives on Coleridge and Wordsworth.* New York: Columbia Univ. Press, 1972.

————. "Romanticism and 'Anti-self-consciousness,'" *Centennial Review of Arts and Sciences* 6 (1962): 553–65.

Higginson, Thomas W. "Cheerful Yesterdays." Part 4. *Atlantic Monthly* 79 (1897): 241–51.

Hooker, Richard. *Of the Laws of Ecclesiastical Polity.* 2 vols. 1907. Reprint. London: J. M. Dent and Sons, 1954.

Jorgensen, Bruce W. "The True Madmen of the Nineteenth Century." Ph.D. diss., Cornell Univ., 1977.

Kaye, Howard. "The Post-Symbolist Poetry of Yvor Winters." *Southern Review* 7 (Winter 1971): 176–97.

Kramer, Aaron. *The Prophetic Tradition in American Poetry, 1835–1900.* Cranbury, N.J.: Associated Univ. Presses, 1968.

Kronick, Joseph G. *American Poetics of History: From Emerson to the Moderns.* Baton Rouge: Louisiana State Univ. Press, 1984.

Lawrence, D. H. *Studies in Classic American Literature.* 1923. Reprint. New York: Viking Press, 1964.

Lee, A. Robert, ed. *Nineteenth-Century American Poetry.* London: Vision Press, 1985.

Lyons, Nathan, ed. *Jones Very: Selected Poems.* New Brunswick, N.J.: Rutgers Univ. Press, 1967.

MacEachen, Dougald B. "Tennyson and the Sonnet." *Victorian Newsletter* 14 (Fall 1958): 1–8.

Malone, Dumas, ed. *Dictionary of American Biography.* 10 vols. New York: Charles Scribner's Sons, 1928–37.

Marx, Leo. *The Pilot and the Passenger: Essays on Literature, Technology, and Culture in the United States.* New York: Oxford Univ. Press, 1988.

Matthiessen, F. O. *American Renaissance: Art and Expression in the Age of Emerson and Whitman.* 1941. Reprint. New York: Oxford Univ. Press, 1968.

McAdoo, H. R. *The Spirit of Anglicanism: A Survey of Anglican Theological Method in the Seventeenth Century.* New York: Charles Scribner's Sons, 1965.

McLuhan, H. M. "Tennyson and Picturesque Poetry." In *Critical Essays on the Poetry of Tennyson.* Edited by John Killham. London: Routledge and Kegan Paul, 1967, 67–85.

McMichael, James. "Rhetoric and the Skeptic's Void: A Study of the Influence of Nominalism on Some Aspects of Modern American Poetic Style." Ph.D. diss., Stanford Univ., 1966.

———. *The Style of the Short Poem.* Belmont, Calif.: Wadsworth Publishing, 1967.

Miller, Perry. *The Life of the Mind in America from the Revolution to the Civil War.* New York: Harcourt, Brace and World, 1965.

———. *Nature's Nation.* Cambridge, Mass.: Harvard Univ. Press, 1967.

Mondiano, Raimonda. *Coleridge and the Concept of Nature.* Tallahassee: Florida State Univ. Press, 1985.

Morison, Samuel Eliot. *Three Centuries of Harvard: 1636–1936.* Cambridge, Mass.: Harvard Univ. Press, 1946.

Oppolzer, Ritter von. *Canon der Finsternisse.* Vienna: n.p., 1887, 292 and plate 146.

Osgood, Samuel. *Student Life: Letters and Recollections for a Young Friend.* New York: James Miller, 1861.

Pinsky, Robert. *Landor's Poetry.* Chicago: Univ. of Chicago Press, 1968.

———. *The Situation of Poetry: Contemporary Poetry and Its Tradition.* Princeton, N.J.: Princeton Univ. Press, 1976.

Prince, F. T. *The Italian Element in Milton's Verse.* 1954. Reprint. Oxford, Eng.: Oxford Univ. Press, 1962.

Ricks, Christopher. *Tennyson.* New York: Macmillan, 1972.

———. "Tennyson's Methods of Composition." *Proceedings of the British Academy* 52 (1966): 209–30.

Rosen, Charles. "Isn't It Romantic?" *New York Review of Books* 20, no. 10 (June 14, 1973): 12–18.

Sewall, Richard B., ed. *Emily Dickinson: A Collection of Critical Essays.* Englewood Cliffs, N.J.: Prentice-Hall, 1963.

Smith, E. E. *The Two Voices: A Tennyson Study.* Lincoln: Univ. of Nebraska Press, 1964.

Stauffer, Donald Barlow. *A Short History of American Poetry.* New York: E. P. Dutton and Co., 1974.

Sucksmith, H. P. "Tennyson on Genius." *Renaissance and Medieval Studies* 2 (1967): 84–88.

Tennyson, Alfred, Lord. *The Poems of Tennyson: In Three Volumes.* Edited by Christopher Ricks. 2d ed., incorporating the Trinity College Manuscripts. Harlow, Eng.: Longman, 1987.

Thoreau, Henry David. *Walden and Civil Disobedience.* Edited by Owen Thomas. New York: W. W. Norton, 1966.

———. *A Week on the Concord and Merrimack Rivers.* Boston: Houghton Mifflin, 1893.

Very, Jones. *Jones Very: Selected Poems.* Edited by Nathan Lyons. New Brunswick, N.J.: Rutgers Univ. Press, 1967.

Waggoner, Hyatt H. *American Poets from the Puritans to the Present.* Rev. ed. 1968. Reprint. Boston: Houghton Mifflin, 1984.

Williams, A. T. P. *The Anglican Tradition in the Life of England.* London: Northumberland Press, 1947.

Wilson, Edmund. *Patriotic Gore.* New York: Oxford Univ. Press, 1962.

Winters, Yvor. *Collected Poems.* London: Routledge and Kegan Paul, 1960.

———. *Forms of Discovery: Critical and Historical Essays on the Forms of the Short Poem in English.* Denver: Alan Swallow, 1967.

———. *The Function of Criticism.* Denver: Alan Swallow, 1957.

———. *In Defense of Reason.* Denver: Alan Swallow, 1947.

———. "Poetic Styles, Old and New." In *Four Poets on Poetry.* Edited by Don Cameron Allen. Baltimore: Johns Hopkins Press, 1959, 44–75.

General Index

Page numbers in bold indicate illustrations.

Abrams, M. H., 4n, 15–16, 22; quoted, 145–46, 172, 191
Agassiz, Louis, 59, 60
Allegory, 5
Allusion, "transumptive," 93n
Analogy, 60
Anapest, 80, 200, 239
Anglican tradition, 16, 37–44, 47, 50, 60–61, 104, 128, 133, 141, 202, 265
Anti-Modernism, 3
Anti-Romanticism and anti-Romantics, 2. *See also* Tuckerman, Frederick Goddard, as anti-Romantic
Assonance, 171, 180
Astley, Russell, quoted, 180
Astronomy, 56, 68–69n; Tuckerman's journal of, 67–68, 70. *See also* Tuckerman, Frederick Goddard, interest of, in astronomy and meteorology

Bate, Walter Jackson, quoted, 214
Baudelaire, Charles Pierre, 134
Benét, William Rose, 242, 245
Bigelow, Jacob, 55, 57, 70; Tuckerman's copy of plant catalogue by, 69, 119. *See also Collection of Plants of Boston and Its Vicinity* (Bigelow); *Elements of Technology* (Bigelow) in Index of Poetry and Books
Bloom, Harold, quoted, 93–94

Boston, Massachusetts, 29–31, 38, 53, 63, 66, 69
Botany. *See* Tuckerman, Edward, Jr., botanical pursuits of; Tuckerman, Frederick Goddard, botanical interests of
Brooks, Van Wyck, quoted, 9–10, 31, 52, 74–75
Browning, Robert, 53, 96
Bryant, William Cullen, 228, 229, 230, 234, 258; quoted, 232–33
Buell, Lawrence, 224, 259–60
Bynner, Witter, 1n, 76, 77, 115n, 137, 224, 228, 231, 237–38, 239–41, 242, 244, 245; quoted, 1, 2, 42, 66, 169, 226, 247
Byron, George Gordon, Lord, 102, 109

Cady, Edwin H., quoted, 148–49n, 254–55, 263
Caesura, 160, 163; Tuckerman's use of, 200
Calvinism, 19, 37, 39, 40–42, 43, 259
Channing, E. T., 34–35, 38
Channing, William Ellery, 34, 38, 173, 225n; quoted, 97, 98–99, 228–29
Chant, 111, 112, 117, 164, 178
Christ. *See* Jesus Christ
Civil War, 58, 232, 269
Clark, Margaret (Mrs. Orton Loring) (granddaughter of

Index of Poetry and Books

Shorter works appear in roman type, while longer ones are set in italics. Page numbers in italic type indicate a quotation of any length from the work; page numbers in bold denote a holograph of the work; page numbers in roman signify discussion or some other mention of the work.